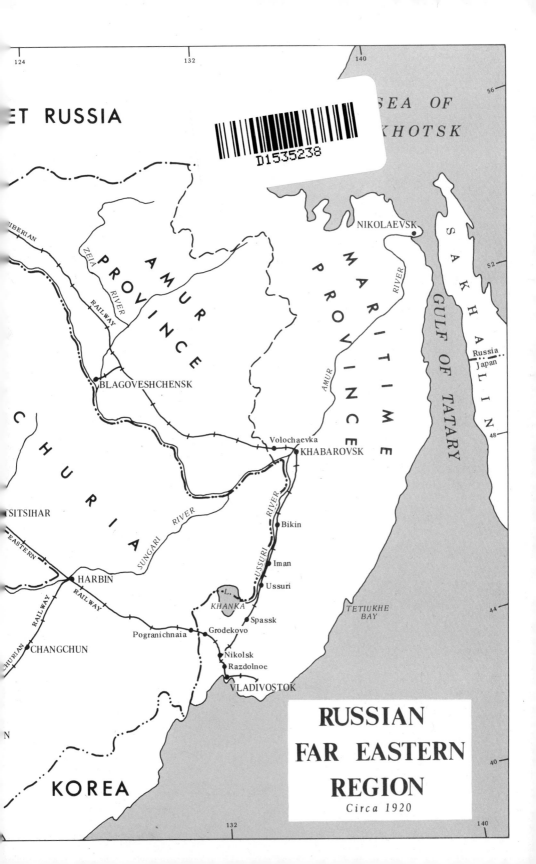

SEA OF OKHOTSK

ET RUSSIA

SIBERIAN

ZEIA RIVER

AMUR PROVINCE

RAILWAY

BLAGOVESHCHENSK

CHURIA

TSITSIHAR

AMUR RIVER

MARITIME PROVINCE

NIKOLAEVSK

SAKHALIN

Russia
Japan

GULF OF TATARY

Volochaevka

KHABAROVSK

SUNGARI RIVER

HARBIN

EASTERN

RAILWAY

RAILWAY

CHANGCHUN

KOREA

Pogranichnaia

USSURI RIVER

Bikin

Iman

Ussuri

L.
KHANKA

Spassk

Grodekovo

Nikolsk

Razdolnoe

VLADIVOSTOK

TETIUKHE
BAY

RUSSIAN FAR EASTERN REGION
Circa 1920

PUBLICATIONS ON RUSSIA AND EASTERN EUROPE
OF THE INSTITUTE FOR
COMPARATIVE AND FOREIGN AREA STUDIES
Number 6

This book is sponsored by the Russian and East European Program of the Institute for Comparative and Foreign Area Studies (formerly Far Eastern and Russian Institute), University of Washington, Seattle.

VLADIVOSTOK UNDER RED AND WHITE RULE

*Revolution and Counterrevolution
in the Russian Far East, 1920-1922*

CANFIELD F. SMITH

UNIVERSITY OF WASHINGTON PRESS
Seattle and London

*Publications on Russia and Eastern Europe of the Institute for Com-
parative and Foreign Area Studies is a continuation of the series
formerly entitled Far Eastern and Russian Institute Publications
on Russia and Eastern Europe.*

Library of Congress Cataloging in Publication Data

Smith, Canfield F   1936–
    Vladivostok under Red and White rule.

    (Publications on Russia and Eastern Europe of the
Institute for Comparative and Foreign Area Studies;
no. 6)
    Bibliography: p.
    Includes index.
    1. Vladivostok—History. 2. Soviet Far East—
History—Revolution, 1917–1921. I. Title. II. Series:
Washington (State). University. Institute for Compara-
tive and Foreign Area Studies. Publications on Russia
and Eastern Europe; no. 6.
DK265.8.V555S63   957'.7   75-17888
ISBN 0-295-95383-7

Acknowledgments

I MUST initially express my gratitude to my parents for the indirect way they have contributed to this book through their devotion, interest, and encouragement. My family has similarly supported me; and my wife, Georgene, spent countless hours typing and retyping this book from its roughest stage to the final copy, while my daughter Michele helped with the proofreading and indexing.

There are many people, named and nameless, who have been helpful in the various stages of this project and who, therefore, deserve recognition: at the University of Washington—Dr. Donald W. Treadgold for his stimulation in my undergraduate work and for his interest in this manuscript, Dr. John S. Reshetar, Jr., for his careful reading of the manuscript and his valuable criticism, and the staff of the publications group at the Institute for Comparative and Foreign Area Studies for their editorial ability, patience, and good humor, assets to any author; at the Hoover Institution—Mrs. Arline Paul for her friendship, encouragement, and assistance over the years and Mr. Charles G. Palm and Dr. Milorad M. Drachkovitch for their archival assistance and permission to use the photographs included in this book; at the Columbia University Archive of Russian and East European History and Culture—Mr. Lev F. Magerovsky for his generous assistance when I visited the archive; the staffs of the National Archives and

Library of Congress for their services; and Jeanette Warren for aiding me with the index. I would also like to pay tribute to the interlibrary loan system and staffs at libraries throughout the country whose assistance is so important to all scholars but who rarely get the credit they so richly deserve.

I wish to acknowledge the University of Virginia for its financial support when as a doctoral candidate I undertook the research for this book, the Alderman Library there for purchasing or otherwise making available research materials, and Drs. Norman A. Graebner and Enno E. Kraehe, who read the manuscript at the dissertation stage, for their criticism and encouragement.

Dr. Thomas T. Hammond, who patiently guided me through my doctoral work, deserves special mention. His stimulation and interest were important in the several stages of my graduate work at Virginia, and in his typically thorough and judicious manner, he read and reread my dissertation, offering valuable suggestions and encouragement. The best way I can show my gratitude to Professor Hammond is to attempt to emulate his scholarship.

CANFIELD F. SMITH

Contents

Illustrations

Introduction

LENIN'S HOSTILITY toward traditional values and institutions assumed international significance when he and his Party seized power in Russia in November 1917. An intense civil war followed, complicated by the intervention of various Allied Powers. The original aim of the Allies was to reopen the Eastern Front against the Germans, but by mid-1918 an increasingly important goal was the overthrow of Lenin's Communist government. After Admiral Aleksandr Vasilievich Kolchak, "Supreme Ruler of Russia," and the other major White leaders, generals Anton Ivanovich Denikin and N. N. Iudenich, had been defeated in late 1919, the new Soviet government still faced two threats in the west. Marshal Joseph Pilsudski, hoping to expand Poland's borders to their 1772 extent, launched an attack with French support in the spring of 1920. General Baron Peter N. Wrangel, who had taken command of Denikin's defeated army, began his offensive from the Crimea against the Reds while the latter were fighting the Poles. Thus Lenin's government was still struggling for its life in 1920 and did not possess the military strength to pursue Kolchak's defeated army eastward past Lake Baikal until after the defeat of the Polish forces and the Whites in the Crimean region.

Had the Red Army had the strength to pursue the beleaguered Kolchakist forces past Lake Baikal in early 1920, it would have faced several obstacles. Internally the Soviet government was threatened by economic breakdown and Lenin launched his New Economic Policy (NEP) early in 1920 to alleviate this crisis. The most serious external obstacles to the Red Army's advance into the Russian Far East were units of the Japanese army and the Whites they supported, most notably the Cossack leader, Ataman Semenov. Had the Japanese evacuated Russian territory early in 1920 when the American Expeditionary Force withdrew, the momentum of the Bolshevik victory would have helped the Communists extend their power to the Pacific Ocean, thereby ending the Russian civil war and Allied intervention in eastern Siberia, with the possible exception of minor pockets of White resistance. Such was not the case, however, and the struggle continued in the Russian Far East until late 1922.

Few writers have investigated the events in eastern Siberia* after the fall of Admiral Kolchak. Usually one finds a sentence or two stating that Soviet troops did not enter Vladivostok, the last important White holdout, until late 1922, but with no explanation as to what happened between 1920 and 1922. The single exception to this in English, other than very general works like E. H. Carr's A *History of Soviet Russia: The Bolshevik Revolution, 1917–1923*, is John A. White's impressive book, *The Siberian Intervention*. As the title suggests, the emphasis is upon the intervention, rather than the civil war; nevertheless, the subject matter is broader than the title indi-

---

*There is no satisfactory designation for the territory east of Lake Baikal. In tsarist days it was called the Far Eastern Region (krai) and consisted of four administrative provinces (oblasts)—Transbaikal, Amur, Maritime, and Kamchatka—and the Russian (northern) half of Sakhalin Island. Today the old Far Eastern Region is divided differently. The Transbaikal Province is a part of Eastern Siberia, while the Amur and Maritime provinces together form the Russian Far East. The focus of this study is Vladivostok and the Maritime Province, both in the Russian Far East, and so I have used this designation in the subtitle of this book. However, the stage for the larger events described here is eastern Siberia, or more specifically southeastern Siberia. I have, therefore, used "eastern Siberia" throughout most of this work to designate especially the more populous and politically and economically important areas that lie along the Trans-Siberian Railway east of Lake Baikal and along the Amur and Ussuri rivers. See end paper map and John A. White, *The Siberian Intervention*, pp. 21–25, 32–34.

cates. White gives a great deal of historical background on eastern Siberia and the civil war, and he describes in detail the intervention there up to the Japanese evacuation in October 1922. White also deals to some extent with the subject of this study and his book is an excellent point of departure, but his emphasis is different and more general. All other works in English concerning the Siberian intervention end with the American withdrawal in April 1920. The best of these is Betty Miller Unterberger's *America's Siberian Expedition, 1918–1920.*

Many articles and books on the Siberian intervention and civil war have been published in the Soviet Union since the Twentieth Congress of the Communist Party of the Soviet Union in 1956. Most of these emphasize the history and diplomatic use of the Far Eastern Republic, Japanese and American aggression, and the history and leading role of the Communist party in eastern Siberia. Among the best of the first category are L. M. Papin, *Krakh Kolchakovshchiny i obrazovanie Dalnevostochnoi respubliki* and M. A. Persits, *Dalnevostochnaia respublika i Kitai.* Among the best of the second category is E. I. Popova, *Politika SShA na Dalnem Vostoke, 1918–1922.* The most useful volume in the third category is Larisa I. Belikova, *Bolsheviki Primoria v gody grazhdanskoi voiny i inostrannoi interventsii.* Two more general books including these topics and others for 1918 to 1922 are F. N. Petrov et al., *Geroicheskie gody borby i pobed* and S. N. Shishkin, *Grazhdanskaia voina na Dalnem Vostoke, 1918–1922.* Almost no Soviet or Western work deals in detail with either the Communist-dominated or White governments in Vladivostok from 1920 to 1922. The best Soviet study on this has been done by P. S. Parfenov, a Communist participant in many of the events he described. His several works are listed in the bibliography under both primary and secondary sources. While Soviet scholars have given much attention, however selective, to the civil war in eastern Siberia from the fall of Kolchak to the Japanese withdrawal, Western scholars have virtually ignored this period. Yet, it was during this time that the civil war raged most fiercely there.

The civil war in eastern Siberia can be divided into two periods.

During the first, from 1917 to early 1920, European Russia and western Siberia received the full brunt of the fratricide and intervention; much less disruption and bloodshed occurred in eastern Siberia. Various power centers developed throughout Russia after the Bolshevik coup of November 7, 1917. However, as the situation in western Russia polarized between Red and White forces, eastern Siberia, less developed industrially and less influenced by bolshevism, came under the domination of White generals backed by various Allied governments and their armed forces. Japan was the Allied power most interested in the unsettled situation in Siberia; its influence had been on the rise in Asia during the previous decades, and the Russian civil war gave it the opportunity to exert its power there. The Japanese government hesitated to intervene at first but was encouraged to do so by its own military leaders and by Britain and France, who wanted Russia to remain in the war against Germany, and who subsequently hoped to remove the Bolsheviks from power.

A complicating factor was the troops of the Czechoslovak Legion along the Trans-Siberian Railway. These former prisoners of war were now moving eastward to Vladivostok and thence to Europe to the projected Czechoslovak state. The United States government reluctantly joined the Allied plans, ostensibly to help the Czechoslovaks leave Russia, but it also desired to keep an eye on Japanese activities. Accordingly, American troops joined the Japanese in the occupation of eastern Siberia in August 1918. This had the added effect of aiding Kolchak, established in power in Omsk as "Supreme Ruler" with the blessing of Britain and France in late 1918. The Japanese army, however, was not interested in aiding the formation of a unified Russian state and directed its efforts toward obstructing aid to Kolchak and lending assistance to Ataman Grigorii Mikhailovich Semenov, an unpopular Cossack leader whose center of power was in the Transbaikal region. Contrary to a previous Allied agreement providing for equal American and Japanese forces, the Japanese army dispatched ten times the number of troops (over seventy thousand) in the American Expeditionary Force. To thwart Japanese attempts to dominate the railway lines from Vladivostok to Omsk, the United States instigated the creation of the Inter-Allied Railway Commission. Although opposed by the Japanese, who hampered its activities, the commission was remarkably effective in keeping the railway lines open and in continuing to serve United States policy interests even after the American troops left Russia in April 1920.

White and Allied domination did not go unchallenged in this period. Especially after Kolchak was established in power, there was a spontaneous growth in partisan activity (which ultimately came under Bolshevik domination) in areas of Allied-White control. People in Siberia, in effect, had two choices: the Whites, who were popularly associated with the privileged classes, Cossack brutality and pillage, foreign intervention, and an unenlightened nationality policy; or the Bolshevik-dominated Soviet government, which, although disliked, was not despised as much as the Whites, and which did have more appealing slogans.

The failure of Admiral Kolchak to hold Omsk in late 1919 or to reestablish control in Tomsk or Irkutsk marked the conclusion of the first stage. The second stage, lasting from Kolchak's fall in December 1919 and January 1920 until late October 1922, is similar to the first in that, once again, there were various centers of power controlled, except for Semenov and the city of Chita, by Bolshevik-led partisans or other radical forces. Partisans forced General Rozanov out of Vladivostok in January 1920, and Communists helped establish an outwardly moderate zemstvo government. Similarly, radical forces pressured the Semenovites and other Whites out of Verkhneudinsk in the Transbaikal Province and established a zemstvo government there, which became the Far Eastern Republic in April 1920. In the Amur region, where the partisan movement was the strongest, the Japanese were convinced that they should leave Blagoveshchensk; and Communists there, led by Party member, M. A. Trilisser, created the most openly Bolshevik government in the Russian Far East, the only one of the three governments controlled by radicals that was soviet, rather than zemstvo, in form. Shortly after establishment of the Blagoveshchensk soviet government, revolutionaries forced White General Ivan Kalmykov to flee from Khabarovsk and then recognized the

newly established zemstvo government in Vladivostok. The Blagoveshchensk Communists looked to Vladivostok for leadership until
early April 1920, when they recognized the authority of Verkhneudinsk.
Other than Chita, the various centers of power were gradually unified
around two competing governments located in Vladivostok and Verkhneudinsk (later Chita, after Semenov was evicted from the Transbaikal
region).

Allied intervention played a part in this second stage of the civil
war, but the Japanese alone dominated the scene after April 1920. At
first the Japanese army occupied the Transbaikal, Amur, and Maritime
provinces, but as Japanese forces were gradually withdrawn from
these regions, Communist-led forces replaced them.

Vladivostok is the major focus of attention for a number of reasons: as a provincial capital it was the principal political and economic center in the Russian Far East; it was Russia's primary port on
the Pacific Ocean; and it was the eastern terminus of the Trans-
Siberian Railway. It was also the springboard for Allied intervention,
and it was where the major Allied governments retained diplomatic
representation in Russia. Finally, it was the seat of governments
competing with the Bolshevik-dominated Far Eastern Republic for
power over Russian territory east of Lake Baikal. It is the changes in
political power in Vladivostok from January 1920 to October 1922 with
which I am most concerned—the reasons for the initial successes of
these governments, as well as their political complexion, leading
personalities, basis of support, strengths, weaknesses, and reasons
for their failure are all important to an understanding of the period.

Japanese policies and actions cast a shadow over the political
and economic life of the territory they dominated, and no political force could make a move without first considering the potential
Japanese reaction. I hope to show how an important element of the
Japanese military command acted independently, often resulting in
a policy that was contradictory or unclear, even to the Japanese. The
effect on Vladivostok and its environs was uncertainty and an unsettled situation that was occasionally created deliberately by the
Japanese.

Another concern is how the various centers of power attempted to solve the "Siberian question" throughout this three-year period. In 1920 the Japanese sought to promote their own interests by exerting pressure alternately on Semenov (who was in Chita until October 1920), on the Far Eastern Republic, and on the Medvedev government in Vladivostok. Simultaneously these Siberian governments and two others, the radical government in Blagoveshchensk and a conservative government in Khabarovsk (which replaced the leftist-oriented government in April 1920), were conducting negotiations to further their respective interests. In 1921 and 1922 diplomatic efforts were made on a larger scale and took the form of international conferences: the Washington Conference on the Limitation of Armaments (November 12, 1921, to February 6, 1922), and the Dairen and Changchun conferences (August 26, 1921, to April 16, 1922, and September 4 to 26, 1922, respectively), the latter two involving Japan and the FER directly. These international conferences will be discussed only as they affected the political climate in Vladivostok. During the entire period there were various military efforts to settle the political question of who would ultimately control eastern Siberia. These military efforts, likewise, will be considered only as Vladivostok was directly concerned, such as General Rozanov's overthrow in January 1920, the White offensive during the winter of 1921 and 1922, and the final partisan–FER People's Revolutionary Army offensive, following the failure of the White offensive.

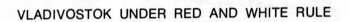

VLADIVOSTOK UNDER RED AND WHITE RULE

1

The Growth of Revolutionary Power
and the Overthrow of the Whites
January 31, 1920

BY 1920 the Maritime Province,[1] or Primorskaia oblast, had been under Russian control only about sixty years. In the late seventeenth century China and Russia negotiated their first treaty, the Treaty of Nerchinsk (1689), whereby Russia recognized Chinese sovereignty over what later became known as the Russian Far East. But China negotiated from a position of strength, and the result was an "equal" treaty by which China benefited more than Russia. Subsequently China weakened in both absolute and relative terms so that by the mid-nineteenth century the Western powers, including Russia, were well on their way toward transforming China into a semicolony. They eroded Chinese sovereignty and territory under a series of treaties known as the "unequal" treaties. Russia gained more territory than other European nations, acquiring most of the Amur and Maritime provinces by the treaties of Aigun (1858) and Peking (1860), clearing the legal path to Russian colonization in this area.

The first Russian settlers arrived at Vladivostok in 1860, thus for Eurasia it is a relatively young city, but a translation of its name, "Ruler of the East," indicates the role for which it was conceived.[2] Within twelve years of Vladivostok's establishment the Russian imperial government moved the main base of the Siberian Military Flotilla (Russia's Pacific fleet) from Nikolaevsk, located about eight hundred miles north on the mouth of the Amur River, to Vladivostok

3

and built strong shore fortifications there. Vladivostok became the eastern terminus for Russia's strategically important Trans-Siberian Railway, which was begun in the late nineteenth century. But Russia's thrust into Asia, accompanied by careless policies and reckless actions, annoyed Japan, which had its own plans for expansion in Asia. The result of this rivalry was the Russo-Japanese War (1904–5), during which Vladivostok was bombarded by a Japanese naval force (even though Vladivostok was not a focal point of that conflict). Contributing to Russia's defeat, as well as to the slower development of the Russian Far East, was the failure to complete the Trans-Siberian Railway; its eastern portion was not connected to its western line around the southern end of Lake Baikal until 1905, and the line through the Amur valley, completing an all-Russian route to Vladivostok, was not begun until 1908. The Russian government was concerned more with domestic matters as a consequence of the Russo-Japanese War and the 1905 revolution. Nevertheless, while the population in eastern Siberia remained relatively small, the population of Vladivostok grew from its meager beginnings in 1860 to 65,000 in 1914. Of this number about one-third were Chinese, many were Koreans, and the rest were largely immigrants from European Russia.

Although Vladivostok has an excellent natural harbor and was Russia's major Pacific port, by 1920 it was not yet developed commercially. Neither exports nor imports were substantial in volume because of the sparse population in eastern Siberia and along the Chinese Eastern Railway, the branch of the Trans-Siberian Railway crossing Manchuria. Most of the trade funneled through the newer Japanese port of Dairen to the south, which was well equipped for warehousing and loading goods, unlike Vladivostok, which also lacked maintenance workshops and water and coaling facilities. In spite of this, it was a city of opportunity that attracted men of commerce, both Russian and non-Russian. Before World War I Vladivostok was important as a governmental center in eastern Siberia, an administrative center for the Trans-Siberian Railway, a center of education with its Oriental Institute, the main base of Russia's Pacific fleet, and an important military outpost with a sizable army garrison based in the forts located on Russian Island and at Second River. Physically it is typical of port cities like Seattle and San Francisco and by 1914 Vladivostok was just beginning to spread out and extend over the hills that are characteristic of the Muravev-Amurskii Peninsula on which it is located. Vladivostok's major buildings, housing the offices of commercial firms or civil servants, were built of stone; lesser buildings were constructed of wood. Life was as good as in many European cities of equal size, and the cost of living was not high.

World War I caused Vladivostok to boom. Military goods were brought into the port, stockpiled, and sent across Siberia for the Allied eastern front, port and rail facilities were extended and improved, and railway cars purchased in America were assembled in Vladivostok. Many jobs were thus created by the war, while the war itself was fought elsewhere.

After the March 1917 Revolution life became less pleasant and conditions less stable as disorders and governmental changes occurred. Confidence and stability resumed for the short time that Admiral Kolchak was in power and the Allies were in Vladivostok, but when Kolchak's government crumbled in late 1919, uncertainty and disorder again prevailed and poverty set in. In 1917 there was a surplus of money, but a shortage of goods. By 1920 confidence in any Russian currency was lacking, and many refugees arriving in Vladivostok, as well as people living there, sold what they could at bargain prices in order to live or to leave. From 1917 on Vladivostok became more and more shabby, drab, and unhappy looking. Roads and buildings went unrepaired, wooden structures were vandalized by people searching for fuel, unemployment was rampant, and people were living and sleeping in abandoned buildings, in railroad cars, or wherever they could. What had been a very safe city now became one with a high rate of crime. Life itself was uncertain, and changes in government were not unexpected.

One such change occurred in July 1919 when Admiral Kolchak, then in Omsk, appointed General S. N. Rozanov as his representative in the Far East to establish military control.[3] Rozanov was typical of a group of White generals (including Ataman Semenov, I. P.

Kalmykov, and Pavel Pavlovich Ivanov-Rinov)[4] who were noted for their cruelty, self-interest, lack of scruples, unpopularity, and pro-Japanese sympathies. He retained his authority in Vladivostok only so long as Kolchak himself retained power, but Kolchak's fate was sealed by the disintegration of his armies and the inability of the French and British to help him. He finally came under the protection of the Czechs, whom he had alienated, and they turned him over to his opponents in Irkutsk on January 15, 1920. He was tried and executed in February 1920.[5]

Kolchak's defeat acted as a catalyst for the interventionist powers and revolutionary forces alike in eastern Siberia. The British and French no longer had any interest in remaining in Siberia and withdrew their missions. Early in January 1920 the United States government decided to evacuate the American Expeditionary Force.[6] The Czechs, who had grown as tired of the Russians as the Russians had of the Czechs, were interested in leaving as quickly as possible to return to their newly formed national state. Only the Japanese remained in eastern Siberia to protect what they considered their interests on the Asian continent and, perhaps, annex some territory. Had Japan withdrawn its armed forces when the United States did, the Communists would have had little difficulty in seizing power throughout eastern Siberia, for the Whites were demoralized and did not have sufficient strength or popular support to resist. The civil war and intervention would have ended in Siberia before it did in European Russia, where Lenin still had to deal with General Wrangel in the Crimea and the French-sponsored Polish invasion. Instead, the Japanese remained, giving a breathing space and some protection to the Whites, and the competition for the future of eastern Siberia intensified.

*   *   *   *   *

During January and February 1920 Communist-led revolutionary forces assumed control in most major cities in eastern Siberia—Irkutsk, Verkhneudinsk, Blagoveshchensk, and Khabarovsk. In Vladivostok General Rozanov's power was clearly slipping, and on January

31, 1920, in an easy, bloodless manner, he was overthrown. There were many factors favoring a coup, but it did not occur spontaneously —preparations had been made for several months by partisans and Bolshevik leaders.

The partisan movement had its roots in the social and economic development of the region with its resulting class conflicts,[7] but its real growth began in 1918 out of the resentments caused by Allied intervention and the accompanying White depredations. Touching the people in the villages hardest were the activities of White generals, many of whom were brutal in seeking recruits, ferreting out Communists, and administering cruel punishments, including death, for those who aided revolutionary forces or who illegally possessed weapons. Cossacks, already resented for their privileged position in Siberia, made up a large portion of these White forces. There was no way for peasants to protect themselves from these White activities except to organize partisan units and strike back. It was not, then, that the populace chose communism, but that there was no alternative for them in their search for self-protection. They organized themselves in an effort to get rid of the two oppressive groups—the Whites and the interventionists.

On June 29, 1918, the Czechs had overthrown the soviet government in Vladivostok and pressed to the north, occupying the railway line and major population points in conjunction with Japanese forces. Thus by the fall of 1918, revolutionary forces were pushed into the taiga north of the Amur River and into the forested hilly region typical of the Maritime region between Vladivostok and the Amur River.[8] These remote areas were the meeting ground of anti-White army regulars, partisans, and Bolshevik activists who fled from the cities after their Party organizations were crushed.

In the southern Maritime Province the main centers of revolutionary activity were in Anuchino, the Suchan mining region, and Olga.[9] Anuchino, located in a valley away from the Ussuri Railway line, had the advantage of being remote and difficult for an organized military unit to reach undetected. The Suchan mining region, important for coal and other resources, was connected by rail to the main railway line

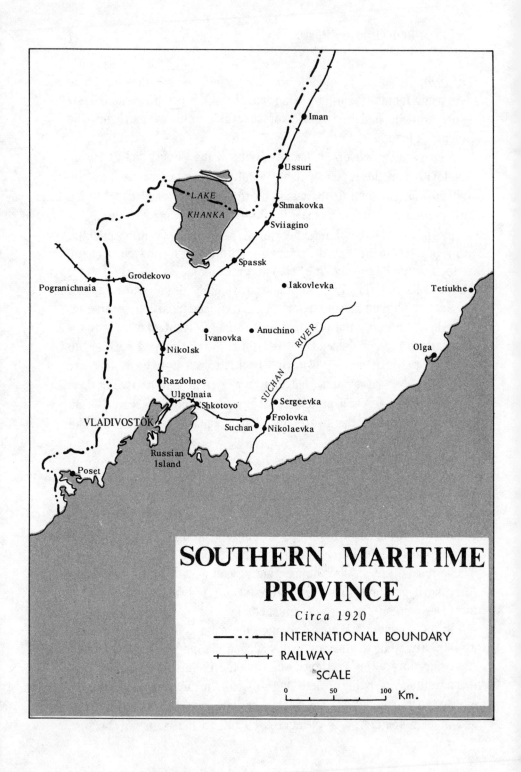

SOUTHERN MARITIME PROVINCE

Circa 1920

— — — INTERNATIONAL BOUNDARY

—+——+— RAILWAY

SCALE

0   50   100   Km.

leading to Vladivostok and was important to the partisans for the control of Vladivostok's coal supply. The Suchan miners were generally sympathetic to the partisans and provided them with mine explosives for destroying bridges, railway track, and other strategic targets. Olga, a port about two hundred miles north of Vladivostok, was used as a base because it was remote, but nonetheless had access to supplies brought in by boat.[10]

The work the Bolsheviks had done before mid-1918 to build their organization was destroyed throughout eastern Siberia by the Whites and interventionists, but the destruction of their links with each other and with Moscow was an even worse blow. The Czechs controlled the major means of communications, the Trans-Siberian Railway, from mid-1918 through 1919, and Semenov and his Cossack band, supported by the Japanese, controlled communications in the Transbaikal region from 1918 to late 1920. As a result of much planning and organizing, the Communists rebuilt their own organizations and gained a leading position over the partisan forces, but all of this was done with virtually no help from Moscow. Until late 1920 only an occasional agent, taking a circuitous route to avoid detection or traveling under the protection of a foreign flag, arrived in the Russian Far East to bring information and directives and to assist in the organizational process.[11]

The most important and largest Communist group in eastern Siberia was the Vladivostok Party organization whose leaders were generally very able young men and women in their 20s and 30s. After soviet power in Vladivostok was overthrown in June 1918, Communist leaders went underground and functioned unofficially as an obkom, or oblast committee, leading the Party faithful not only in Vladivostok, but throughout the Maritime Province, or oblast. In January 1919 these leaders formed the Maritime Oblast Committee (Obkom) under the chairmanship of I. G. Kushnarev and continued to carry on and expand their organizational activities.[12] Born in 1888, Kushnarev had been a Bolshevik since 1905, was active in Vladivostok Party work, and had held several responsible posts in eastern Siberia since the November Revolution. He was a trusted Party leader who was judicious and moderate in his approach to problems and in his actions. Another notable Obkom figure was S. G. Lazo, a talented though headstrong young Communist from the Amur region. He joined the Party after the revolution in 1918, when he was twenty-four years old, but his dedication and leadership ability were put to good use from 1918 until his untimely death in 1920. A. A. Shiriamov (1883–1955) was obviously one of the most important Obkom leaders. He was the oldest in age and in Party membership, having joined in 1900, and had served the Party in the Transbaikal region and then in the southern Maritime Province, both as a partisan leader and Obkom member. Later when he was a member of the Irkutsk Revolutionary Committee (Revkom), he helped the Bolsheviks establish their power in Irkutsk. He was also a member of the Dalburo and leader in the People's Revolutionary Army of the Far Eastern Republic. M. I. Gubelman (1885–1968), a Party member since 1902, was an important Vladivostok Communist and partisan organizer, but was second to Kushnarev, Lazo, and Shiriamov in leadership rank. Other Obkom members included A. A. Voronin (1881–1942), chairman for a time of the Vladivostok Gorkom (city committee); G. F. Raev (1885–1923), active in the Vladivostok Party, labor, and soviet activities; and Z. I. Sekretareva, active in Party affairs from 1917 and soon to be on the editorial staff of *Krasnoe znamia*, the Party organ published intermittently in Vladivostok since 1917 and distributed widely in the Russian Far East when possible.[13]

In the second half of April 1919 the Vladivostok Communist leaders, gaining confidence, wanted to expand their activities and jurisdiction over a larger area. They assembled the Third Far Eastern Krai Conference of the Russian Communist Party, and representatives from the underground Party organizations of Chita, Blagoveshchensk, Khabarovsk, Harbin, Iman, Spassk, Nikolsk, Vladivostok, and other centers attended. By having representatives from cities outside the Maritime Province, the Far Eastern Obkom (in reality the Vladivostok leaders) assumed new responsibilities and prestige as the Far Eastern Krai Committee (Kraikom). Thus virtually the same leaders headed the Far Eastern Kraikom, the Maritime Obkom (or Far Eastern Obkom, as it was sometimes called), and the Vladivostok Gorkom. The base of operations was in Vladivostok.[14]

In the fall of 1918, meanwhile, the partisans were secretly organizing in the villages throughout the Maritime Province. In December 1918 partisan leaders in the southern part of the province in the Suchan area held an organizational meeting at Frolovka, henceforth an important partisan center, and by February 1919 had made contact with the newly formed Maritime Party Obkom. They met again at Frolovka in March and elected the Provisional Military-Revolutionary Staff of Partisan Detachments of the Olga Uezd (district) to coordinate efforts for the establishment of local soviets.[15] Communist leaders were aware of this partisan activity and decided at the April krai conference to assert their leadership within the partisan movement, including broadening it and giving it unified leadership. Lazo, Gubelman, Raev, and other Bolshevik leaders went to areas with active partisan movements, and within a short period of time they had organized two conferences. The first of these, the First Congress of Insurgents of the Maritime Province, held from May 22 to 25 in Anuchino, elected the Oblast Revolutionary Committee (Obrevkom) of the Maritime Province, the highest organ of partisan power.[16] The second conference at Sergeevka (near partisan headquarters at Frolovka) was called by the Obrevkom from June 27 to July 3. This latter conference, the First Congress of Workers of the Olga Uezd, restored soviet power in the Olga Uezd since both interventionists and Whites had been driven from the area. It elected an Executive Committee (Ispolkom) of the Soviet of Workers, Peasants, and Partisan Detachments, headed by I. V. Slinkin, to direct the activities in the Olga Uezd and to maintain close relations with the Party Obkom. It also unanimously approved Sergei Lazo as commander in chief of the partisans in the Maritime Province, a proposal made by Communist leaders. Among the goals set at the congress were the further organization of the partisans, the disruption of enemy communications, and the disorganization of White forces through propaganda and through the organization of Communist cells within the White army units.[17]

Others were plotting against Kolchak and his subordinate in Vladivostok, General Rozanov, but it should not be assumed that these White leaders were completely without support. They were sufficiently strong to launch a counteroffensive in the southern Maritime region in July and August 1919, seriously crippling and demoralizing the partisans and the Bolshevik leadership.[18] In mid-November 1919 they crushed the Gaida uprising with Japanese assistance.[19]

Within two or three months, however, the Communists regained their strength and in November 1919 began planning an overturn in Vladivostok and other cities. The time was propitious: Kolchak's power was disintegrating, and there was widespread dissatisfaction with Rozanov's rule. Although authorities disagree, evidence suggests that credit for the plan should go to the Obkom leadership.[20] In November Lazo was called to Vladivostok and named leader of the military section of the Obkom,[21] a step taken by Party leaders who were laying the groundwork for a coup. Neither definite plans nor a specific date for the coup was made by the Bolsheviks until the second half of January, when events moved very rapidly, following Kolchak's fall and arrest, causing a very fluid situation in Vladivostok.

The Bolsheviks were not the only group interested in planning Siberia's future. In Irkutsk power was transferred to the Socialist–Revolutionary-dominated Political Center, which sent M. Ia. Lindberg to Vladivostok to work with other socialists to hasten a coup. He arrived under Czech protection on January 12, 1920, and participated in a meeting of various socialist groups, including the Bolsheviks. Lindberg proposed that power be seized under the banner of the Political Center. A major concern of all groups was what the response would be to the Allied powers who had military forces in Vladivostok at that time. They knew that the Japanese were closely tied to Rozanov, but the Americans and Czechs had no use for him, and Lindberg assured the assembled socialists that they could count on Czech and American support.[22] The Bolsheviks disapproved of this plan, ostensibly because they did not trust these assurances, but more probably because they wanted the initiative for any such move to be in their own hands and needed time to obtain Moscow's advice.[23]

The pace quickened. Partisan forces were on the move. A detachment led by G. M. Shevchenko surrounded Nikolsk, and fighting erupted.[24] The situation in Vladivostok during the last week of January was very tense.

At a Vladivostok Party conference on January 23 the vexing question of whether power should pass to soviets or zemstvos came into the open. Although zemstvos were not introduced in Siberia until 1917, they had been important organs of local government in European Russia long before the revolutions of 1917 and were, as a consequence, associated with the old regime or, at best, with the liberals or moderate socialists who constituted a major force in them. After the November Revolution the soviet wave swept Siberia, and these organs, representing more radical forces, either coexisted with the zemstvos or replaced them. The pendulum swung again in mid-1918 with the rising of the Czechs, who approved of the zemstvos and considered the soviets too radical. Power was ready to change hands again, and the problem reappeared.

The Bolsheviks in Vladivostok were in a precarious position, not only because of their numerical weakness, but also because of the presence of Allied military power. The majority of the delegates, including Lazo, favored power passing to soviets. Indeed, this had been the slogan of the Bolshevik leaders as they regained control over the partisan movement. Others, led by Kushnarev, were more cautious, recognizing the danger of trying to establish soviet power in the presence of the Allies, especially the Japanese.[25] The Americans had publicized their intention to evacuate by this time, and the Czechs were assembling in Vladivostok for their transfer to the Czechoslovak Republic. But until both left, they could prove to be an effective check to any action by the Japanese, with whom they had had previous differences of opinion and conflicts.

The decision was made at this January 23 conference to overthrow Rozanov's power and transfer power to a soviet. A Military-Revolutionary Staff (Voenrevshtab) was elected to accomplish the goal, with the energetic Lazo as its leader. The next day the Party Obkom confirmed the decision for an uprising, but with the change that power was to be passed to the Vladivostok Zemstvo Board headed by the Socialist Revolutionary, A. S. Medvedev, and not to the soviet, as the majority of Party leaders and members wanted.[26] The rationale was obvious—a way was needed to forestall possible interventionist action and the zemstvo was acceptable to the interventionists, while soviet power was not. It is not clear if this decision was made in Moscow. Obkom chairman Kushnarev had asked Moscow's advice on the question,[27] and the decision was in line with the thinking in Moscow, in view of Lenin's support of the formation of a buffer state in Transbaikalia as early as January 21, 1920,[28] but there is no evidence that Lenin's advice was transmitted to the Maritime Party leadership.

The Bolsheviks tried to convince the zemstvo leaders to assume leadership of the proposed zemstvo government. P. M. Nikiforov, a leading Communist, asserted that these negotiations were prolonged by the reluctance of the zemstvo leaders to assume power without a broad base of support.[29] Just six months prior to this Medvedev had sent a delegation representing the Zemstvo Board to the First Congress of Workers of the Olga Uezd requesting the congress to coordinate its activities with the Socialist Revolutionaries (SRs) for the purpose of establishing the zemstvo in power in the Maritime Province.[30] In the January negotiations the zemstvo leaders probably were reluctant to accept the conditions of the Bolsheviks, which amounted to complete dictation of policy.

While the Bolsheviks were negotiating with the zemstvo leaders, they were also issuing directives preparatory to the coup. On January 25 the Communist Voenrevshtab appealed to the soldiers and officers of the Vladivostok garrison to recognize the Zemstvo Board as the legitimate government. The soldiers were also asked to organize a committee in each unit and arrest any officer not obeying its orders, to establish close contact with other units, and not to act without the approval of the Voenrevshtab.[31] One unit, the Egerskii Battalion, responding to an unpopular order from Rozanov, acted hastily and mutinied, but Rozanov was able to have the unit disarmed and removed from the scene.[32] The Bolsheviks then decided to mask the actions of the Voenrevshtab by organizing a coalition to direct the coup. In this way they could accomplish the same purpose they had in mind when they called for a zemstvo instead of a soviet government: by giving the appearance of a broader base for their actions they could hasten the erosion of Rozanov's support and check potential interventionist interference. The new organization, termed the United Operative Staff, consisted of representatives of the Zemstvo Board and various political parties—Bolshevik, SR, and others, but it was led by the Bolshevik Lazo.[33] Voenrevshtab leaders still formulated directives, but they now issued them through the United Operative Staff. These directives stressed recognition of the Zemstvo Board as the new government, forbade hasty, reckless activities that might arouse the interventionist forces, and insisted that no actions be taken without the approval of the United Operative Staff.[34]

Communist accounts of the next few days, up to the actual overturn, suggest that events went according to plans worked out by the Bolshevik leaders. However, their accounts have gaps and leave some questions unanswered, for example, how negotiations were conducted between the Bolsheviks and the Zemstvo Board in Vladivostok and the exact relationship between the Bolshevik leadership and the partisan forces led by Gavril Shevchenko and others.

The partisans seemed to have acted somewhat independently. Nikiforov has noted that the Party leaders in Vladivostok sent a directive notifying the partisans of the formation of the Voenrevshtab to coordinate activities, but he also said the directive did not arrive.[35] The partisans, having surrounded Nikolsk a few days earlier, entered the city on January 26 and seized power after the Kolchakist garrison there mutinied.[36] The Japanese under these circumstances declared their neutrality.[37] It was necessary for the revolutionary forces to control stations along the railroad leading to Vladivostok to assure that aid sent from Semenov to Rozanov could not get through.[38] The seizure of Nikolsk and other points along the railroad within a short period of time was, therefore, probably part of a broader plan worked out by the Bolshevik leadership.[39]

By January 28 the situation was extremely serious for Rozanov. Most Maritime towns were in revolutionary hands. The soldiers at the

Vladivostok fortress under Bolshevik influence no longer obeyed the orders of their superiors.[40] Not even the last-minute effort of Rozanov to win popular support by declaring an amnesty for political prisoners, or to exert his authority by arresting the zemstvo leaders and establishing a tight censorship, could stem the tide.

The overturn was set for January 31. On January 28 or 29 a delegation from Nikolsk carried an ultimatum to Rozanov to abdicate by 9:00 A.M. on January 31 or the city could be taken by force.[41] The plans included seizure of communications, a general strike by the trade unions, and a march on Vladivostok by both partisans under Shevchenko and armed troops from Ugolnaia. On the morning of January 31 revolutionary forces entered the city. Rozanov had been refused asylum by the Americans,[42] but the Japanese saved him by clothing him in a long Japanese officer's cape and military cap and hustling him to Japanese headquarters.[43] Despite their declared neutrality, the Japanese gave this last assistance to Rozanov and to other Whites who wished to leave Vladivostok because of the uncertainty of their future under a revolutionary government. They were put aboard the steamer *Orel* and taken to Japan.[44]

The January 31 coup was, by all accounts, bloodless and accomplished with facility for several reasons. General Rozanov was not popular, and his military support evaporated after Kolchak's fall, evident from the number of desertions from his ranks in December and throughout January.[45] Unlike the revolutionaries' careful design, he had no plans for defending his authority. A close observer, Colonel K. N. Khartling, who was attached to the Training Instructor School on Russian Island, maintained that the only real plans made by Rozanov and those close to him were for their own evacuation from the city. A number of officers attempted to organize some resistance to the revolutionary forces, which they knew were planning a seizure of power, but they were arrested, along with Khartling, before they could offer any resistance.[46] Communist sources claim that General Oi, commander in chief of the Japanese Expeditionary Force, promised to aid Rozanov in suppressing the revolution, but then did not because of American protest and the suddenness of the coup.[47] When he could not count on their assistance, Rozanov's only recourse was to seek safety with the Japanese. The apathy of many citizens of Vladivostok helped the coup; they certainly were not interested in perpetuating Rozanov's power and were not necessarily enthusiastic about another power being imposed from the outside. Bolshevik planning and organization, coupled with partisan power, tipped the balance, causing Rozanov's fall and the establishment of the new government. This was Vladivostok's sixth or seventh government (depending on how one figured) since 1917.

2

The Provisional Zemstvo Government
and the Japanese Offensive
February-April 1920

THE GOVERNMENT that assumed power on January 31, 1920, was not its own master. In effect, there was a dual authority comparable to the situation in St. Petersburg in March 1917. The recognized government was the Provisional Zemstvo Government of the Maritime Province, and the power behind this government was the Communist party and its supporters. One liberal Russian, arriving on the scene in March 1920 commented that a most unusual situation existed in Vladivostok—the Socialist Revolutionaries, unlike those in Irkutsk, acted as a screen for the Communists, who acted like moderates and supported a moderate government. The presence of the Japanese, of course, explained the unusual harmony between the two groups.[1]

The zemstvo government, lacking any sort of legislative organ, was an executive body headed nominally by the Zemstvo Board chaired by A. S. Medvedev.[2] One astute observer characterized this government, which claimed jurisdiction over an area larger than Japan, as a "tragedy of power." It included two teachers, one distinguished doctor, and one intelligent land surveyor —all valuable zemstvo workers, but inexperienced for this larger leadership role.[3] There were many departments under this executive power, but the most important, the economic and military, were staffed by Communists. This was in accord with Communist plans as outlined in a speech by P. M. Nikiforov at a mass meeting immediately after the January 31

18

overturn: for tactical considerations the Communists would participate only in the economic and military spheres.[4] The Communists understood the realities of power.

The most important civilian department was the Financial-Economic Council headed by P. M. Nikiforov, a prominent eastern Communist who was among the more than 500 prisoners released from jail by the new authorities.[5] Other important Communists headed various divisions within this council, for example, Vasilii Grigorevich Antonov—Supply Committee, and I. G. Kushnarev—Transport Committee.[6]

Military control was essential. This was accomplished through the Military Council nominally headed by M. Ia. Lindberg, but in actuality Sergei Lazo was in charge. Accounts of the nature and make-up of this council are vague and conflicting. Evidently the Voenreshtab of the Obkom transformed itself into the Military Council[7] and allowed the participation of some SRs. General Vasilii Georgevich Boldyrev, an astute and reliable observer, has indicated that it was the center of competition between Socialist Revolutionaries and Communists, but the Communists made the major decisions and used the council to establish Communist cells and political commissars in all units.[8]

The armed forces, consisting primarily of Red Army personnel, former Kolchakists, and other White troops, were nominally led by Colonel Arkadii Anatolevich Krakovetskii,[9] an SR undoubtedly selected because he was mild-mannered, pliable, and, therefore, a good front man for the Communists. There was a great deal of distrust within the armed forces, not unlike what Trotsky experienced in creating the Red Army. Those loyal to the revolution were uncertain of the loyalty of the former White soldiers, particularly the officers, hence the necessity of placing plenipotentiaries, or political commissars in all units.[10] The term *commissar* was avoided because it might arouse the interventionists.

Maritime leaders recognized a need for reorganizing the armed forces. A commission headed by General Boldyrev undertook this task, but the plan it adopted was developed by Lazo and approved by the Party.[11] All forces east of Lake Baikal would be included in nine or ten divisions and two brigades under three separate armies: the

Amur, the Transbaikal, and the Far Eastern. The Far Eastern Army would consist of four of the divisions and the two brigades.[12] Before the reorganization could be effected, however, it was cancelled by Party leaders on orders from Moscow, which did not want to arouse Japanese suspicions or anxieties.[13] Instead, the Communists accelerated an auxiliary plan that had been in progress since the January 31 overturn, the preparation for an eventual conflict with the Japanese. Japan's overwhelming superiority meant that the Russians would stand no chance in open field warfare, so preparations were laid for a second partisan war. Partisan forces were reorganized and strengthened, and supplies were taken to remote mountain areas.[14] The large gold reserves in Vladivostok were moved to Blagoveshchensk for safekeeping after the Japanese forces occupying the Amur region had withdrawn and the area was safely under the control of the local Bolshevik-directed soviet. The most noticeable military reform was that ranks and other symbols of traditional authority were zealously and publicly abolished.[15]

The new government was substantially more popular than Rozanov's regime had been. Communist writers, of course, attest to this, but so do some non-Communists, such as General Boldyrev.[16] More political activity was allowed. This particularly benefited the Communists, who were now allowed to function legally. They held their first city conference on February 3 and resumed publishing their official organ, *Krasnoe znamia*, on February 7. There was some political retribution in the form of arrests and seizures, and one writer complained of other abuses by Chekists in the name of the new regime.[17]

The Medvedev government followed basically moderate policies in order not to arouse the fears of the interventionists. It planned no large-scale confiscation of property, though some was confiscated. The Zolotoi Rog Theater with all of its equipment, for example, was turned over to Proletkult, an organization created to agitate and propagandize among the workers.[18] Trade and commerce remained as they were—some carried on through cooperatives, but most was in private hands, domestic and foreign, especially American and Japanese. The new government also allowed foreign banks to operate. These policies were not considered permanent by the Communists but, rather, policies that could change depending on how the political winds blew.[19]

The most uncertain factor in Far Eastern politics was Japan. Britain and France had lost interest in Siberia with the fall of Kolchak, and the departure of American and Czechoslovak troops was imminent. Japanese forces, however, remained, while civilian and military policymakers vacillated and struggled, trying to decide which policy to follow.[20] Meanwhile, there was a growing radicalization of Bolsheviks, partisans, and workers who wanted to follow the examples of Irkutsk and Blagoveshchensk, where soviet rule had been established. Once again the issue of moderate zemstvo rule versus soviet rule became a paramount issue within Party ranks. In mid-February Obkom chairman Kushnarev was delegated to go to Moscow to report on the Maritime situation, to seek guidance on Communist policy in the Maritime Province, and to ask the Soviet leaders to send a representative to Vladivostok to direct internal policy,[21] a journey deemed necessary because communications between Soviet Russia and the Maritime Province still were hampered by Semenov's control of Transbaikalia. There was some wireless contact with Irkutsk, as Lazo mentioned in a wire to Blagoveshchensk, but it was circuitous (via Okhotsk) and apparently not reliable, judging from comments made now and then by various Party leaders about poor or no links with Moscow.[22] Travel through the Transbaikal region was difficult without Semenov's approval unless one traveled under Czech protection, as Kushnarev did. Indeed, it was because of this problem that Kushnarev reported in person to Moscow and that he sought a Soviet plenipotentiary to come to the Maritime Province to serve as Moscow's voice there.

While Kushnarev, the leading voice for the retention of zemstvo rule, was away from Vladivostok, Communists favoring sovietization pressed their point of view. They included most of the young leaders like Lazo and Gubelman, the majority of partisan commanders, and P. V. Utkin, editor of *Krasnoe znamia* and acting Obkom chairman in Kushnarev's absence.[23]

Ataman Grigorii Mikhailovich Semenov
Courtesy of the Hoover Institution, the Edison Collection

General Sergei Nikolaevich Rozanov
Courtesy of the Hoover Institution, the Edison Collection

The campaign for sovietization of the Maritime Province began in the latter half of February. An article appeared in *Krasnoe znamia* on February 25 deriding the SRs for their belief that the zemstvo government was an ideal, not a tactical measure leading to ultimate unification with Soviet Russia. The article then continued in praise of soviet power.[24] By March 2 the Obkom decided to press officially for sovietization. An Obkom memo signed by Utkin informed the Medvedev government that the masses were demanding soviet power. The government was told to work for the election of soviets and, once the process was completed, to pass its power to these organs at an oblast congress of workers.[25] Support for this position was promoted by Party activists in various mass organizations in early March.[26]

On March 16 at Nikolsk, Vladivostok Bolsheviks convened the Fourth Far Eastern Krai Conference of the Communist party. Although representatives from outside the Maritime Province attended, notably from Blagoveshchensk, most of the delegates came from centers in the province, such as Nikolsk, Spassk, Khabarovsk, Iman, Razdolnoe, Shkotovo, and, of course, Vladivostok. In reality, therefore, this was an oblast conference whose impact was largely limited to the Maritime Province, and more especially to the southern part of it.[27]

The conference was called primarily to deal with the problem of sovietization, for which pressure was growing within the Party and which was favored by the conference delegates. Opposing sovietization was V. D. Vilenskii, who had arrived on March 14 under Czech protection as Moscow's plenipotentiary representative in the Far East,[28] and whose importance showed Lenin's interest in eastern Siberia. Vilenskii was born in Siberia and joined the revolutionary movement there in 1903. Although a Menshevik from 1912 to 1917, he was sensitive to Russian events and joined the Bolsheviks after the November Revolution. His Siberian background blended well with his interest and ability in foreign relations so that for several years after November 1917 he was one of Soviet Russia's leading experts on the Far East.[29] Vilenskii spoke to the conference in very moderate terms, explaining that Soviet Russia did not have the strength to send the Red Army beyond Lake Baikal. Therefore, Moscow supported the formation of a buffer republic as a diplomatic tool to force the Japanese out of Russian territory in a peaceful manner.[30] Opposing this point of view were Lazo, Gubelman, Utkin, and other young radicals. In his speech Lazo said that he did not prefer a buffer state, but that if Moscow insisted upon it, it must be soviet in form.[31] This point of view prevailed, was embodied in the resolutions passed by the conference, and was justified in a telegram to the Central Committee in Moscow.[32]

The election of a new Krai Committee was another important item on the agenda. Elected as full members were P. M. Nikiforov (chairman), I. G. Kushnarev, Sergei Lazo, Ia. F. Iakovlev, N. V. Kholodov, Vsevolod Mikhailovich Sibirtsev (secretary), and four candidate members—including P. V. Utkin and Moisei Gubelman.[33] (Of those named only two, or possibly three, favored a continuation of the zemstvo government.) The most important members, Nikiforov, Kushnarev, and Lazo, formed a Politburo and continued to dominate Communist affairs through the Vladivostok Gorkom, Maritime Obkom, and Far Eastern Kraikom.[34]

On March 28, 1920, Kushnarev finally returned from Moscow with instructions that sovietization should cease and a buffer state be formed.[35] A new organ of power, the Far Eastern Bureau of the Russian Communist Party (RCP[b]), or the Dalburo,[36] was created to consolidate Soviet power in the territory east of Lake Baikal (just as the Sibburo or Siberian Bureau of the Central Committee RCP[b] had been created earlier to consolidate Soviet power in western Siberia) and to direct the establishment of a buffer republic. On instructions from the Central Committee of the RCP(b) the Dalburo was created on March 3, 1920, by and subordinated to the Sibburo in a special resolution.[37] Communist leaders in Vladivostok undoubtedly learned of the Dalburo's existence and membership from Vilenskii, but they had to wait for Kushnarev's return to learn of its details.

It is both indicative of the political situation in eastern Siberia and portentous of subsequent events that the membership of the Dalburo was divided into two groups. At this time there were two Communist-dominated governments competing for power in the Russian

Far Eastern Region—the Provisional Zemstvo Government in Vladivostok and the Provisional Zemstvo Government of Pribaikalia. Communists also controlled Blagoveshchensk in the Amur Province, but they did not compete for regional power. They were somewhat under the influence of the Maritime Bolsheviks because of the latters' prestige and active leadership, but in May the Blagoveshchensk leaders gave their support to the Verkhneudinsk government in the Transbaikal Province (which includes Pribaikalia).

The dilemma Communists faced was how to remove the "Chita stopper," as Semenov's power base in the Transbaikal region was called. They hoped that Semenov and his Japanese protectors could be forced out peacefully, but until that happened, the Russian Far Eastern region could not be unified. The Dalburo was formed to deal with this problem, and the tactic employed was to form a buffer state with moderate political institutions and policies that would not alarm the Japanese.

The idea of a buffer did not originate with Lenin or, apparently, even with the Bolsheviks, but Lenin saw its wisdom.[38] However, he did not specify where its capital would be nor did he give any other details except that the Bolsheviks must control it[39] and that it must be "under a democratic flag."[40] Vladivostok had certain advantages as an important city with able Communist leaders. Its main disadvantage was its distance from Irkutsk, important because it was in Soviet-controlled territory and was the headquarters for the Sibburo.

The government of Verkhneudinsk was dominated by an extraorninary figure. Aleksandr Mikhailovich Krasnoshchekov was born near Kiev in 1880, but was deported to Siberia, as many people were, because of his revolutionary activities. He was arrested again in 1905, but escaped and ended up in the United States, where he eventually settled in Chicago, studied law, and became an attorney. When the revolution broke out in Russia in 1917, it attracted numerous revolutionary exiles and many, including Krasnoshchekov, returned to Russia via Siberia and again became involved in revolutionary work. Krasnoshchekov was the most prominent of these returned émigrés in Siberia, serving as a member of the Nikolsk city council

in 1917 and after the November Revolution as the president of the Far
Eastern Council of People's Commissars, a responsible post indeed.
When the Allied intervention began in mid-1918, Krasnoshchekov was
forced to flee, an experience that made him realize that wishful thinking and radical actions did not always produce the desired results.
He became convinced that the only way to ease the foreigners out and
to unify Siberia with Soviet Russia was through the use of a democratic buffer state. Persuading the Soviet leaders of this, he began
his experiment in Verkhneudinsk, arriving there as the partisan forces
were driving out the Semenovites and other Whites.[41] By March 1920,
however, the Verkhneudinsk government was still in its formative
stage and had no advantage as a capital for the buffer state except
its location near Soviet territory, which made it easier to defend and
control. The situation in eastern Siberia was still fluid and Lenin had
not given his approval to either Vladivostok or Verkhneudinsk as the
capital of a single buffer state; rather, both governments had received
Lenin's blessing as regional governments.[42]

It is not surprising that the Dalburo was divided into two sections—Verkhneudinsk (represented by A. M. Krasnoshchekov, A. A.
Shiriamov, and N. K. Goncharov)[43] and Vladivostok (represented by
Maritime Politburo members Kushnarev, Nikiforov, and Lazo).[44] This
division reflected the situation in the Russian Far Eastern region,
but it also contributed to the rivalry between the two centers. There
is no evidence that the six Dalburo members met as a unit during the
first few months of the Dalburo's existence,[45] nor, with their different
perspectives and interests, did they follow identical policies. Rather,
each group did what it could to develop its own base of power as the
capital of the proposed buffer state.

When Kushnarev returned to Vladivostok in late March, he brought
directives from Moscow designed to strengthen and enlarge the Provisional Zemstvo Government in Vladivostok and enhance Communist
control of it. Sovietization was to cease, as was military reorganization, as previously stated; and the zemstvo government was to be
enlarged from an oblast to a krai government, including not only the
Maritime Province, but now also the Amur region, Sakhalin Island,

Kamchatka Peninsula, and the Railway Zone in Manchuria.[46] Two representatives each from workers' congresses of the Amur and Maritime regions and one each from Sakhalin and Kamchatka were to be added to the government,[47] thereby increasing Communist representation in the executive branch of the zemstvo government.

On March 29 the Maritime Communist leaders began following Moscow's directives. They annulled the decision of the Nikolsk conference calling for sovietization, and they ordered the Medvedev government to remain in power and broaden its scope by adding the representatives. The next day the government issued such a declaration.[48]

On April 1 the First Congress of Workers of the Maritime Province met at Nikolsk. This body, chaired by Utkin of the Krai Committee and including leading Communists such as Kushnarev among its other officers, was originally scheduled to vote power to the newly created soviet organs. The six-hundred-odd delegates, mostly partisans having arrived with that in mind, were determined to do so. By now, however, Party discipline had been enforced on such recalcitrant Party leaders as Lazo, who had a great deal of support among the partisans because of his role in planning for the January and February overturns. When he spoke in favor of the Dalburo position calling for the formation of a buffer state and a retreat from sovietization, he brought many of the delegates over to his point of view, and the congress passed a resolution embodying the Party's position. It also resolved to support enlarging the government in line with Kushnarev's directives and elected Nikiforov and Kushnarev to represent the Maritime Province in the reorganized Provisional Zemstvo Government;[49] these actions, however, subsequently became a dead letter. Medvedev assured the congress that his government was subordinate to the directives of the Communists.[50]

The Japanese, interested in all political activities in eastern Siberia, had Japanese press and military representatives among the observers at this congress.[51] It must have given some satisfaction to the military observers when, during the course of the proceedings, a wire was received from Petr Semenovich Parfenov, a political commissar in Krakovetskii's staff, stating that Japanese General Oi had presented the Maritime government with an ultimatum. This evoked a protest from the congress, and Vilenskii, Medvedev, Lazo, and others hurried to Vladivostok.[52] Before describing the negotiations between the Japanese and the Medvedev government resulting from the ultimatum, it is necessary to examine the negotiations in progress between the Medvedev government and General Voitsekhovskii, commander of the Kappelites in Chita.

The Kappelites

When Admiral Kolchak's government fell late in 1919, his forces retreated across Central Asia and Siberia to escape the advancing Red Army. Communist propaganda would have one believe that these defeated armies consisted of men who favored a return of the tsar and opposed the working class; while this may be true in some cases, it certainly did not apply to the Kappelites. They were units consisting largely of workers from the Urals who had been under the inspired leadership of General Vladimir Oskarovich Kappel until his untimely death by frostbite on December 11, 1919. The journey of these several thousand troops from western Siberia to Lake Baikal has gone down in history as the "Icy March." Numerous accounts are left of the suffering endured by these men, many with their families, in their struggle against weather, disease, Red Army troops, and partisans.[53] Their arrival in Verkhneudinsk in February 1920 was one of relief for them, for they now had a chance to rest on territory occupied by Semenov and the Japanese. The reception was apparently amicable and within a short time the two White armies—the Kappelites, now led by General Voitsekhovskii, and the Semenovites—moved on to Chita, which was Semenov's headquarters until he was chased out in late October of that year.

Ataman Grigorii Mikhailovich Semenov (1890–1946) was a young Cossack leader who served as an officer in the tsarist forces during World War I. His prominence in eastern Siberia derived from his geographical and ethnic origins: he was native to Transbaikalia and, as evidenced by his facial features, was part Buriat Mongol. The Provisional Government believed that Semenov could serve the anti-German effort and sent him to raise a Buriat Mongol unit. His headquarters were in Harbin, but after the fall of the Provisional Government in November 1917 he directed his energies against the Bolsheviks by invading the Transbaikal region in January 1918 and destroying Soviet power there. By May 1918 Soviet forces had driven Semenov back into Manchuria, but when the Czechs seized the Trans-Siberian Railway during the summer of 1918, Semenov once again was able to move into Transbaikalia. In theory he was a part of the general effort to unseat the Bolsheviks, or so the British and French hoped; the Japanese had their own interests and supported Semenov's machinations, which included hampering the flow of munitions to whomever he disliked, such as Admiral Kolchak himself.[54]

The Kappelites were obviously presented with a dilemma that necessitated much soul-searching. They were now in Semenov's home territory, but they knew that he was a vassal of the Japanese, who were occupying Russian territory for more than altruistic reasons. Moreover, the Kappelites were bitter because Semenov had not supplied Kolchak with men and supplies and had retarded the movement of materiel from Vladivostok to the front. They also did not like being associated with a cutthroat like Semenov, but realized that at this point they had little choice. After consulting with the older officers, Kappelite commander General Voitsekhovskii subordinated his army to Semenov's over-all command; in exchange, Voitsekhovskii became one of the three corps commanders. This marriage of necessity, however, did not survive.[55]

On February 28 Voitsekhovskii sent a telegram to General Boldyrev via General Dmitrii Leonidovich Horvath, the Russian power in Harbin and the Railway Zone at the time, stating that 30,000 troops, consisting mostly of workers and peasants, would support any democratic government firmly opposed to communism and Soviet power.[56] Because the Kappelites were physically and militarily weak, they obviously could not return west to Soviet-held territory, nor could they push their way through the Transbaikal and Amur regions because of partisan strength there. A better choice was to cross Manchuria on the Chinese Eastern Railway, but they had to overcome several obstacles. Besides the approval of the Inter-Allied Railway Commission, which administered the Railway Zone, they needed the permission of the Chinese government, which had taken advantage of the chaos caused by the Russian civil war to exert its authority in Manchuria; Japanese acquiescence, since Japanese military forces operated freely from the Transbaikal region to the Maritime Province; and the cooperation of the railway workers, because the Bolsheviks had substantial influence among them. A great deal of skill and care would have to be used to reach the Maritime Province, over a thousand miles away, and then the Kappelites would have to obtain permission to enter the province.

The Communists were aware of the telegram Boldyrev received and were concerned about his answer. In his reply to Voitsekhovskii, Boldyrev stressed that what Russia needed above all was an end to civil strife to protect its national interests; therefore, the Maritime government could not participate in an armed struggle against Soviet Russia.[57] Lazo and Nikiforov, who had called on Boldyrev on March 4 to learn of his attitude and answer, were satisfied and the message was cleared with Medvedev the next day and sent through the British mission.[58] These preliminary feelers and the Kappelites' feeling of desperation in their association with Semenov resulted in negotiations between Voitsekhovskii's representative, Colonel Petrov, and representatives of the Medvedev government. At first Voitsekhovskii's conditions were the following: (1) he would recognize the authority of the zemstvo government provided that he be named commander in chief of all the forces of the Far East; (2) the army must retain officers' ranks and shoulder straps; (3) Semenov must be removed from Russian territory, even arrested if possible; and (4) he approved making peace with Soviet Russia if it recognized an independent buffer state, which could be created in the Russian Far East.[59]

The removal of Semenov was a major goal of all who desired unity in eastern Siberia, but the Communists did not have full trust in Voitsekhovskii. Finally an agreement was reached that would have had Voitsekhovskii agree to recognize the zemstvo government, approve some other non-Communist as commander in chief (the Kraikom favored Boldyrev for tactical reasons, while Voitsekhovskii favored either Generals Diterikhs or Pepeliaev),[60] arrest Semenov, and accept a political commissar (Utkin) in Chita to assure that the agreement would be fulfilled. But before Voitsekhovskii's approval could be obtained,[61] the Japanese began their offensive in the Maritime Province.

The Rise of Japanese Power

The phenomenal rise of Japanese power in Asia before World War I is well known. Japan had successfully challenged China in 1894–95 and Russia in 1904–5, thus heightening Japan's confidence and prestige and whetting the appetite of Japanese expansionists within military, business, and political circles. The expansion of a more powerful state at the expense of less developed states, and even of other powers in which decay had set in, was an old game in Europe. There was a scramble for colonies and spheres of influence in Africa and Asia in the last two decades of the nineteenth century, and partition into spheres of influence of the home and colonial territories of the defeated powers became a principal war aim of both sides in the course of World War I. Japan was one of the nations most determined to benefit from the war and events in Russia in 1917 and 1918 gave it an opportunity to broaden its designs on the Asian continent to include not only China (especially Manchuria), Korea, and Mongolia, but also Siberia as far as Lake Baikal or even the Ural Mountains.[62]

Although the Japanese government opposed Japan's becoming militarily involved in Siberia, her military leaders favored intervention and applied continuous pressure upon the civilian leaders. Britain and France wanted to bolster their Russian ally with military units as early as July 1917,[63] but could not spare the manpower themselves, so it was natural that they should think of American and Japanese armed forces serving the Allied cause. The collapse of Russia's Provisional Government, as well as the armistice and subsequent Brest-Litovsk treaty between the new Soviet government and imperial Germany in March 1918, only made the situation more desperate for the Allies. Germany was now freed of its Eastern Front and could concentrate its energies on fighting the Allies on the Western Front.

In spite of this Allied need, President Woodrow Wilson remained opposed to any United States involvement in Russian affairs, and he opposed unilateral action by the Japanese. In general the Japanese government did not want to intervene without the approval of the United States, so that Wilson's attitudes and policies were critical in initiating an Allied policy of intervention.[64]

In March 1918 Wilson approved sending American troops to Murmansk and Archangel to prevent the ports and supplies from falling into German hands.[65] This decisive move now involved American forces on Russian soil and the same justification could be used for a similar move into Vladivostok. As a result of the Bolshevik victory in November 1917 and the signing of the Treaty of Brest-Litovsk, however, bolshevism was seen by more Japanese leaders as a potential threat to Japan. When anti-Communist elements were gathering to begin action against the Soviet government, Japanese leaders became more receptive to intervention, but still hesitated to act without American agreement or support. A great deal of pressure was brought to bear upon Wilson, but not until the revolt of the Czechs did his resistance break and then he appealed directly to the Japanese for a joint intervention.[66] At Wilson's insistence, American and Japanese forces were to be limited to about seven thousand each, but within weeks Japan had sent several times that number until over seventy thousand Japanese soldiers were on Russian soil.

The Czechoslovaks seized most of the Trans-Siberian Railway during the summer of 1918 and seemed to take care of themselves adequately without outside help. In hindsight, it seems ludicrous that they should ever have been used as an excuse for Allied intervention in Siberia. There were other reasons why the Japanese, in particular, were in Siberia, and they became more evident as time passed. The British and French lost interest in the Siberian intervention when Kolchak fell, and the United States became increasingly uneasy and hard pressed to justify its Siberian policy. Thus, the United States notified Japan in January 1920 of its decision to withdraw its expeditionary force, which it accomplished by April 1920.

Japan obviously could not remain in Siberia under the guise of aiding the Czechs, who were withdrawing from the region. Japan, therefore, had to reexamine its own policy, make some determinations regarding immediate and long-range goals, and articulate its new policy to answer its critics abroad and at home. This reexamination of policy would have been facilitated if there were unity of purpose among Japan's military and civilian leaders and its people, but Japan was divided. The Siberian policy was increasingly questioned in the press and the Japanese Diet—an embarrassment to the military leaders who favored expansion in Siberia, but whose actions so far had brought no concrete return for the huge cost involved. As the Siberian policy became more unpopular at home, military leaders sought a way to turn an unprofitable, unpopular venture into one that would reap rewards for Japan and save face for the military. Often in the next two and one-half years this would take the form of machinations and actions designed to present a *fait accompli* to civilian leaders and to delay Japanese evacuation from the Russian Far East.

The rumor mill was fed in the first three months of 1920 in Siberia by various policy statements of Japanese representatives—official and unofficial, civilian and military. The Japanese government was led by Premier Hara Takahashi, a political moderate who opposed Siberian intervention from its inception. Since becoming premier in September 1918, Hara had favored a withdrawal of Japanese forces. He had won support as early as December 1918 from War Minister General Tanaka Giichi and from the Diplomatic Advisory Council, a body of top military and diplomatic leaders.[67] Chief of Staff Uehara Yusaku and the majority of military leaders in Japan and abroad opposed Hara's policy, however, resulting in delay and compromise because of Hara's fear of alienating the military and upsetting Japan's body politic.[68] The premier had difficulty controlling the military, justifying its actions, and giving a clear statement of Japanese policy, for example, when replying to an interpellation in the House of Representatives in early February.[69] General Oi, commander in chief of the Japanese Expeditionary Force, was quoted on one occasion as saying that Siberia was part of the larger Asian picture,[70] and on another that the Japanese "can not let bolshevism penetrate to the Far East."[71]

The January 1920 announcement of America's plan to evacuate Siberia prompted Hara to move in the same direction to avoid excessive criticism at home and alleviate the suspicions of other nations, particularly the United States. The same month Premier Hara and War Minister Tanaka agreed to withdraw from Siberia at an "appropriate" time but decided to occupy Vladivostok and the Railway Zone indefinitely to protect Japanese interests in northeast Asia.[72] This decision was conveyed unofficially to Japanese military commanders in Vladivostok so that they could make the necessary preparations, but it did not become official policy until it was acted upon by the Japanese cabinet in late February or March.[73]

The plan was a product of the compromise Hara felt compelled to make with the military leadership. It called for the evacuation of the Amur region, which was carried out immediately, and the Transbaikal region, accomplished in the fall after the Czechs had passed through. Japanese forces would be stationed in northern Manchuria to prevent Bolshevik troops from entering the Railway Zone and would remain in Vladivostok and Nikolsk to protect Japanese interests in Korea.[74] Thus, the plan was to consolidate Japanese power in the Maritime Province and presage Japanese plans for Vladivostok, not to provide for the evacuation of Japanese troops from all of eastern Siberia.

The Medvedev government was naturally uneasy with the Japanese pronouncement. In a note to the Japanese Diplomatic Mission on March 2, it accused the Japanese of violating Russian sovereignty, creating problems with their presence, and committing atrocities. It demanded that the Japanese complete the evacuation of the Amur region and immediately begin their evacuation of the Russian Far East, assuring the Japanese that the Provisional Zemstvo Government would look after the safety and protection of all.[75]

The Japanese did not respond until the end of March, but a March 15 interview by General Takayanagi, chief of staff of the Japanese

Expeditionary Force in Siberia, was ominous. He stated that aid to
the Czechs and protection of the railways were means, not aims. He
would not say what Japan's aims were except that they had been
worked out by the government independently of the Allies and that
they coincided with the aims of the Japanese army.[76]

Simultaneously, an event was occurring north of Vladivostok that
would be used by Japan as a justification for a more militant policy
in the immediate future, and it would cloud Soviet-Japanese relations
until a treaty was signed in 1925. This was the Nikolaevsk incident,
in reality a series of incidents from March to May 1920. Nikolaevsk
is a city near the mouth of the Amur River important for its flourish-
ing fishing industry and proximity to commerce on the Amur. The
Japanese, with their large economic interests in Siberia and in the
waters between Japan and the Asian coast, considered their army's
presence in Nikolaevsk desirable. Japanese troops had occupied the
city and had worked in cooperation with the White detachments there
since the spring of 1918. In addition to a small garrison of about three
hundred troops, there were a few hundred Japanese civilians residing
in Nikolaevsk, most of whom were involved with various commercial
enterprises. In prerevolutionary times the mixing of populations—
Russian, Chinese, Japanese, and others—was natural and peaceful,
though, perhaps, not without jealousies and other human frailties.
The Japanese inhabitants, whether merchants or servants in a Russian household, suffered more than most in eastern Siberia during the
intervention. Because of their race, they were associated with Japanese policy, and ultimately were either massacred, as were many of
those living in Nikolaevsk, or forced to leave everything behind and
emigrate to Japan.

Nikolaevsk was the goal of a revolutionary group, led by Iakov
Triapitsyn, a spirited partisan leader, heading down the Amur River
early in November 1919. An indecisive armed struggle to seize Nikolaevsk ensued, followed by a truce on February 28. Partisans, Whites,
and Japanese managed to coexist for almost two weeks. However, the
Japanese and Whites broke the truce, attacked the partisans by surprise on the morning of March 12, but were eventually defeated by

them. Over one hundred Japanese were killed, and Japanese leaders viewed this as only the first step in the annihilation of the Japanese population in Nikolaevsk; the final step came in May when several hundred Japanese lost their lives.[77] Japanese military leaders in both instances, but particularly after the second, tried to reap as much propaganda value as possible to prolong their stay in the Russian Far East and to justify the expense of their interventionist policy.

Soviet representative Vilenskii arrived in Vladivostok in mid-March 1920 carrying Soviet Foreign Minister Georgii V. Chicherin's February 24 peace offer to the Japanese. The Soviet leaders were aware of unrest in Japan due to economic distress and to the growing opposition to the Siberian intervention; with the other Allies either withdrawn or making plans to withdraw, they pressed for Japanese withdrawal. Soviet Russia did not have the military strength to force Japan out, but it possessed in Siberia a fertile area for economic exploitation; thus Chicherin: (1) assured Japan that Russia would not interfere in Japan's internal affairs;[78] (2) recognized the "special economic and commercial interests of Japan in the Far East, which surpass in several respects those interests of other countries"; (3) offered to conclude an economic agreement beneficial to Japan; and (4) indicated the Soviet desire to enter into peace negotiations with Japan leading to the reestablishment of normal relations.[79]

By the end of March Japan's policy toward Siberia was clarified in a series of meetings of Japan's leading civilian and military leaders, including Prince Yamagata Aritomo, a venerated Genro,[80] and the emperor himself. The General Staff's policy prevailed, and in a brief statement issued on March 31, 1920, Japan officially declared its intention to retain troops in the Russian Far East. It noted that the original reason for Japanese intervention was to assist the Czech troops, but that other concerns forced Japan to cancel its decision to evacuate. These included Japan's proximity to the region in question, its concern for the safety and lives of its citizens residing in Siberia, and the danger to the peace of Korea and Manchuria. As soon as the situation was "normal," the Japanese would withdraw "as early as possible."[81]

Two days later, on April 2, General Takayanagi handed an ultimatum to the Medvedev government. He stated that he had been authorized by his government to conduct negotiations with the Medvedev government with the aim of assuring that conflict would be avoided while Japanese troops remained in Siberia. The Japanese demanded of the Medvedev government:

1. To take care of our troops, providing them with quarters, food, means of transportation, mail privileges, etc.
2. To obey all the regulations contained in the agreement concluded between our Government and our command on the one hand and the Russian authorities on the other hand, on the basis of the agreement concluded between the Allied powers or the Allied command, no matter when these regulations were instituted.
3. Not to arrest without our knowledge or restrict the liberty of persons who actively aided our military operations.
4. To cease all the activities of secret organizations and groups menacing the safety of our troops and the public peace in Korea and Manchuria.
5. Not to publish articles and provocative attacks against our troops and our Government.
6. To exert all efforts in order to insure the safety of life, property, and other rights of our subjects in the region, including the Koreans.[82]

Most of the important Bolsheviks were at the First Congress of Workers of the Maritime Province at Nikolsk, but, upon being wired about the ultimatum, they hurriedly returned to Vladivostok.

A Russo-Japanese Conciliatory Commission was formed to negotiate the Japanese demands. The Russian delegation included General Boldyrev; P. A. Tseitlin, an important Communist and also head of the political department of the Maritime Military Council; Colonel Popov, the only Russian fluent in Japanese; Moisei Gubelman; and others. The Japanese delegation included General Takayanagi, considered a Russophobe; Colonel Isome; Professor Higuchi, long a student of Russia and fluent in Russian; and others.[83] The commission met for two days, most of which was spent arguing over the second demand of the Japanese ultimatum. The Russians, recognizing their own weakness and Japan's designs, hoped to smooth the situation over or at least buy time by acceding to the Japanese demands. After some rather interesting verbal duels involving Takayanagi, Isome, and Tseitlin (at one point Tseitlin was asked whether he adhered to the "Lenin system" or the "normal system," to which he replied that he adhered to both), agreement was finally reached on the afternoon of April 4,[84] and would be signed the next day. The Japanese demands were accepted almost *in toto*. Minor changes in wording were made and the controversial second demand was worded in the following manner:

2. To consider as effective all those decisions concerning military affairs exclusively which were entered into by the Japanese Government or the Japanese command on the one hand and the Russian authorities on the other hand, on the basis of the agreement between the Allied powers or the Allied command. If these decisions should be found to be not in accordance with the interests of Russia or the Russian Army, the Russian military authorities will make a proposal to reconsider such.[85]

Although it had long been expected that the Japanese were preparing some action, there was widespread relief that this crisis was over and that the agreement was about to be concluded with General Voitsekhovskii. Parfenov noted that

we informed our garrison of the agreement reached, recalled the state of seige, and permitted the unit commanders to allow their men short leaves from the barracks. The commanders in their turn were over-zealous; as a result, in a short while half our garrison was on leave for twenty-four hours, this being on Saturday. Clearly, this was just what the Japanese tried to bring about.[86]

The Japanese were not waiting precisely for this to happen. The offensive throughout the Maritime Province did occur several hours later, but the ultimatum and negotiations had been a ruse; the offensive had been planned for some time, and this relaxation merely made their task easier.

The Japanese Offensive of April 4–5

No available documentation gives a precise date when the Japanese began planning the April 4–5 offensive. A report of a commission formed by the Maritime government to investigate these events contended that the offensive was in preparation by the Japanese military leaders with the concurrence of the Japanese government from the second half of February. As substantiation, they pointed out that the Japanese were: (1) evacuating the Amur region, but building up their forces in the Maritime Province; (2) transporting troops from Japan to the Maritime Province; (3) seizing most of the important points of the Vladivostok fortress district; and (4) fortifying strategic locations, such as hills, roads, and barracks.[87]

These measures, however, indicated only that the Japanese were implementing the general policy Hara and Tanaka had decided upon in January, to remain in the Vladivostok area. Evidence suggests that there was still uncertainty among Japanese leaders and that a more definite policy was set only in late March during a series of meetings of high officials, which included Matsudaira Tsuneo, the head of Japan's diplomatic mission in Vladivostok. Matsudaira arrived in Tokyo on March 18, reportedly to participate in discussions concerning the transfer of power to soviets in the Maritime region.[88] This does not mean, however, that the military command did not make its own plans in anticipation of an approval of its policy or in an attempt to force events to create policy. According to his memoirs, General Nishikawa reported to his staff that no offensive action could be taken in early March because of the unsettled conditions of the Japanese troops just withdrawn from the Amur region; also, by the end of March the Japanese staff was making plans to disarm Bolshevik forces in order to assure pacification of the territory. A part of these plans included the negotiations of April 3 and 4, which were to break down and thereby provide a reason for disarming the Russians.[89] In March several Russian conservatives and moderates, including General Boldyrev, were approached by the Japanese to head a new government.[90]

The real preparations for the April offensive, however, began only a few days before the attack. On March 20, there was lively Japanese activity in Nikolsk, which included unloading military supplies, digging trenches, and patrolling the town.[91] General William S. Graves, commander of the American Expeditionary Force, noted in Vladivostok's environs two days before he left on April 1 the digging of trenches and filling of sandbags.[92] Communications by wire and road came under Japanese scrutiny and control. More ominous were the overt acts of the Japanese visible to the civilians as well as to the military within Vladivostok, for example, the requisitioning of buildings or parts of buildings for setting up machine guns facing key locations, including the zemstvo building, and the posting of Japanese guards outside them.[93] The city was tense, thus when agreement was reached within the Russo-Japanese Conciliatory Commission on April 4, there was a great feeling of relief.

The offensive began Saturday night. The officer on watch aboard the U.S.S. *Albany* reported seeing two flashes of light at 10:12 P.M., which signaled its beginning.[94] Bursts of gunfire followed; then, after two hours of silence, heavy firing began at about 12:30 to 12:40 A.M. and continued throughout the night.[95] A Red Cross representative on the scene said the firing was a demonstration of Japanese gunnery. There was little return fire in Vladivostok; rather, Japanese troops seemed to be firing at random to surprise and intimidate the Russian population. Few lives were lost in Vladivostok itself and most damage was superficial.[96]

The seizure of the Maritime Province was efficient and well-coordinated. By mid-morning of Palm Sunday, April 5, Vladivostok, Olga, Nikolsk, Khabarovsk, Shkotovo, Spassk, and other points were either under Japanese attack or control. Resistance was offered in several of the northern towns, notably Khabarovsk, and Russian losses ran quite high,[97] but in Vladivostok the operation was almost without opposition. By the early hours of April 5, all major governmental institutions and means of communications had been seized, all Russian forces remaining in the city had been disarmed, and many Russians, including government and Party leaders, had been arrested.

When the Japanese began their action against Vladivostok, the Communists convened a joint meeting of the Dalburo and Military Council. P. M. Nikiforov, I.G. Kushnarev, S. G. Lazo, V. M. Sibirtsev, A. N. Lutskii, and P. A. Tseitlin decided that no resistance should be offered because of the overwhelming Japanese military superiority; rather, all armed forces that could should avoid arrest and leave Vladivostok for the hills with their weapons.[98] They also agreed that the Party should go underground. Nikiforov, Kushnarev, and Tseitlin then left the staff and advised the others to follow them, but Lazo and other members of the Military Council remained to dispose of secret records. Nikiforov tried to persuade them to leave, knowing that their important Party and military positions endangered their lives, and even tried to impose Party discipline. Finally, he sent the militia to get his comrades, but by that time Japanese forces had surrounded the building. Military Council members Lazo, Sibirtsev, and Lutskii were arrested and never seen again; later it was learned that they had been burned alive in a locomotive boiler.[99] Other leaders did not suffer the same fate because they wisely sought safety in the Czechoslovak headquarters. These included Nikiforov, Kushnarev, Vilenskii, Zemstvo Board members S. I. Afanasev and P. Popov, Commander of the Armed Forces Krakovetskii, his political assistant Parfenov, the chief of the militia, and many others. Medvedev was with Czech High Commissioner Dr. Girsa.[100]

The Korean section of Vladivostok was particularly hard hit. Although they resided on Russian territory, the Japanese considered Koreans as Japanese citizens, or at least Japanese wards because Korea at the time was dominated by Japan. For four hours Japanese troops laid seige to the Korean section, engaging in wholesale beatings and slaughter, pillaging, and even setting fire to the school. The Japanese subsequently returned and again harassed the population. In all, about three hundred Koreans were killed and about one hundred arrested. This conduct had two purposes—to intimidate the Korean population and to attempt to uncover members of a Korean nationalist organization.[101] The Japanese had been disturbed by young Korean revolutionaries causing unrest in Korea.

The timing of the offensive was masterful. The possibility of forceful opposition was nullified by the Czechoslovak and American withdrawals and by confusion and dissension within the ranks of the Maritime armed forces. The investigating commission reported that first, there was friction between the regulars and the partisans; second, the Russians had no plan for meeting a potential threat; and third, there was a division of opinion and authority between the command of the military forces under Colonel Krakovetskii and the Military Council and its political representatives. During the April 4–5 events all three were giving orders, which only added to the confusion.[102] The attack came on Palm Sunday when Russians would be less vigilant, especially so in Vladivostok where an agreement with the Japanese was to be concluded. When the attack began, Medvedev, Krakovetskii, and other leaders thought it was a local incident, but its continuation and Japanese refusal to be contacted revealed the seriousness of the situation. It was then that the government and Party leaders made other plans, not for defense, but to avoid conflict and to secure their personal safety.[103]

Vladivostok lay helpless and affronted by Japanese indignities— the hoisting of Japanese flags above all buildings, ill treatment of Vladivostok citizens and leaders, and the like. General Oi placed the blame for the offensive on the Russians, stating that they had fired the first shots and had refused to obey Japanese orders to cease fire,[104] a charge that was echoed by Minister of War General Tanaka four days later,[105] but which convinced no one. The investigative reports by the Maritime government's commission and by Dr. Girsa both placed the blame squarely on the Japanese.[106]

The attack brought forth protests from both the Provisional Zemstvo Government[107] and the Vladivostok city duma,[108] but the protests were ignored. By Monday, April 6, government members were allowed to resume their posts, but their sphere of activity was limited, and the prestige of both the government and the Communist party was damaged.[109] Remarkably, in spite of Japanese attempts to form a new government, almost no members separated from the zemstvo government, and no "old regimists" stepped forward to work with the Japanese.[110] The principal exception was Colonel Krakovetskii, who left Vladivostok and was replaced on April 7 by General Boldyrev as commander of the now emasculated military forces. Boldyrev, the pragmatic, patriotic, and honest moderate, was chosen because of the trust both the Japanese and the Communist leaders had in him.[111]

One of the most important reasons for the Japanese offensive of April 4–5 was the army's desire to remain in the Russian Far East to reap some benefit for itself and Japan and thus save face; the Japanese army had no previous experience in returning empty-handed. Economic gain was also a motivation. Japan acquired control over the economic activities of the Maritime Province, especially in fishing, mining, and lumbering, by keeping the Russian Far East in a continuous state of chaos until the end of 1922, and redirected a great deal of trade to Japanese-controlled Dairen, Vladivostok's major competitor. There was a fear of the spread of bolshevism to Japan and more immediately to Korea and Manchuria. Nascent Communist movements and nationalist unrest did plague the Japanese, particularly in Korea, prompting them to work for the formation of a buffer state in eastern Siberia, and the imprudence of some Communists in pressing rapidly for sovietization in the Maritime Province was alarming. Acts such as the theft in February of ten French tanks left under Japanese protection,[112] the March events in Nikolaevsk, and the calling of a congress to end the zemstvo government and to establish a soviet government gave fuel to the arguments of the army leaders. The Japanese felt that sovietization might be accompanied by a unification of eastern Siberia; the negotiations between the Maritime government and White General Voitsekhovskii pointed in this direction. All of this was undone by the April 4–5 offensive, but there were other repercussions as well. The Japanese succeeded in disarming the Russian forces and flotilla. They also seized the military stores stockpiled in Vladivostok and sixteen carloads of silver ready to be shipped north.[113] These actions remained a subject of discussion until the Japanese left.

The regulation of the Russian military potential was another major goal of the offensive and was discussed for two weeks by a

renewed Russo-Japanese Conciliatory Commission. An agreement
between the Maritime government and the Japanese command was
signed on April 29, 1920, and supplemented by another on June 15,
1920.[114] The former established a demilitarized zone along the rail
lines of the Maritime Province, prohibiting all armed forces except
Japanese within thirty kilometers (about 18½ miles) of the railway
lines without permission of the Japanese command.[115] The latter
limited the Maritime government to a militia of 4,250 men, two-thirds
of whom to be armed with sabers and revolvers, while only one-third
to be allowed to carry rifles.[116] This poorly armed militia was the
only official Russian armed force to protect the whole area from
Vladivostok to the region north of Khabarovsk. On August 3, 1920,
the disarmed status of the Siberian flotilla was formalized.[117] It is
easy to understand why these agreements came to be popularly termed
the "Far Eastern Brest–Litovsk." [118] Japan controlled the military
force (with the exception of the partisans), major communications,
and the entire coastline of the Maritime Province.

The Japanese offensive dealt a blow to the Communist organization in the Maritime Province. In the brief time between January 31
and April 4 the Party had been able to operate in the open, but now
the Japanese had succeeded in arresting or murdering some of the
Party's most able leaders, in disarming most of the armed forces
loyal to the Party, and in disrupting communications between Vladivostok Communists and their comrades in other cities.[119] As a result,
the Communists decided to create a Revolutionary Staff (Revshtab) to
continue the struggle with the Japanese. The Revshtab, which included Nikiforov, Kushnarev, and Gubelman,[120] had two tasks: to
reorganize the shattered military forces, with particular attention
being given to restoring order within the partisan organization and to
strengthen the Party organization in Vladivostok.[121]

The Japanese offensive renewed White confidence, and many
Whites, freed from prison and under the protection of the Japanese,
were able to participate openly in political activities without fear of
arrest by the leftist-controlled police or militia.[122] The Communists

clearly had their work cut out for them in meeting the conservative challenge.

*   *   *   *   *

As one might expect, with Russian sensitivities so blatantly violated, bitterness toward the Japanese was strong, and Russians tended to set aside their differences to work together to provide a national front against the Japanese. This took three concrete forms: the broadening of the Maritime government to include bourgeois elements; the establishment of a legislative branch, the Popular Assembly; and the attempt by the various governments in eastern Siberia to unify and form a moderate buffer state—a prerequisite for Japanese withdrawal. It is significant that with the Japanese occupying the Maritime Province, the focal point of this buffer state shifted from Vladivostok because it was feared Japan would use it as a pawn, to Verkneudinsk, which had proclaimed itself the capital of the Far Eastern Republic on April 6, immediately following the Japanese seizure of the Maritime Province.

3

The Provisional Zemstvo Government's Role in the Unification of Eastern Siberia
April-December 1920

The FAILURE of the Japanese to form a government after the April 4-5 offensive made the question of unifying eastern Siberia more urgent. Most Russians desired unification to rid themselves of the Japanese and to restore normalcy, but they disagreed about the conditions of such a unification. The Japanese, also desiring a solution, found their situation was even more complicated than that of the Russians.

Domestic pressures in Japan demanded a resolution of the Siberian question. Opinions expressed in the Japanese press favored evacuation, but military and political leaders were more interested in what benefit might be derived from the venture, which had been so costly, both in money and prestige, to the nation and to its military establishment. The government and the military had their differences, but they concerned means more than ends.

The Japanese wanted a buffer state that would stretch from the Pacific Ocean to Lake Baikal. It would have to be non-Communist and have its capital in Vladivostok, both conditions favoring Japanese influence on its government. Whether the government would be democratic was of lesser importance. The Japanese placed their hopes variously with Cossack atamans, such as Semenov, with Russian old-regimists like General Horvath, and with moderates like General Boldyrev. It was important that Communists have little, if any voice in the buffer state, and the moderate and conservative elements should direct the state to Japan's political and economic benefit.

To try to achieve an acceptable solution or simply to bide time while the problem resolved itself, the Japanese negotiated with all parties including representatives of Soviet Russia, the Far Eastern Republic (FER), the Maritime government, Semenov, and conservatives in Harbin. They also put pressure on Vladivostok leaders to lessen Communist control over the Maritime Province by broadening the base of government.

That Maritime Communists were in a difficult position was not fully appreciated by Communist leaders in Verkhneudinsk and Moscow. The Japanese could not form a puppet regime, but they did succeed in demolishing the Communist-led military forces in Vladivostok and other cities, giving a considerable setback to the Communist organization there, depriving it of some of its able leaders, and driving the Communists underground. The April 29 agreement left the Maritime leaders powerless, but at least it temporarily stabilized the political situation in the province. This and Japan's failure to follow up the April 4–5 offensive with further military or political action encouraged the Communists to operate more openly. On May 14, 1920, they abolished the Revolutionary Staff and functioned openly through their Politburo, headed by Nikiforov.[1]

The question of the creation of a buffer state had become the dominant issue in Vladivostok. On May 11, 1920, General Oi issued a statement that was both hopeful and portentous for the Siberians. He repeated that the Japanese had no territorial ambitions in Siberia, as both Matsudaira, chief of the Japanese Diplomatic Mission in Siberia, and Viscount Uchida Yasuya, Japanese foreign minister, had stated.[2] All three men justified Japan's actions on the basis of Russian provocations and Japanese self-defense. (Matsudaira's claim that Japan acted with the approval of the Allies, however, had elicited a denial by the United States on May 7.)[3] The three leaders reiterated Japan's intention to withdraw its troops, but whereas Matsudaira and Uchida linked Japanese withdrawal to the Czechs', General Oi added a new reason for Japanese presence in the Russian Far East—Japan's interests in Manchuria and Korea.

The transport of the Czecho-Slovaks is now rapidly drawing to an end. The Japanese troops, therefore, take pleasure in declaring that they will be quite ready to withdraw when the Far Eastern conditions in Russia settle down, when Manchuria and Korea are freed from any menace, and the Japanese residents' lives and property are thus rendered entirely safe.[4]

Oi expressed his hope that a buffer state would be formed that would bring tranquillity to eastern Siberia under a government satisfactory to the people and that would also reestablish mutually beneficial Russian-Japanese economic relations.[5]

This prompted cooperation among the various socialist groups in the Maritime Province that were meeting to establish a common program. On May 14 an interparty conference of socialists called for the unification of the eastern Siberian oblasts. According to the resolution, the new state, which would include the Maritime, Amur, and Transbaikal provinces, Kamchatka Peninsula, and Sakhalin Island, must have a popular and socialist base, be approved by all oblasts as well as by Soviet Russia, and have an autonomous domestic life. The declaration was signed by the organizations representing the Communists, SRs, Left SRs, SR-Maximalists, Anarchist-Communists, and Mensheviks.[6] No capital was specified, but Vladivostok was the preferred site.[7]

There already was a self-proclaimed buffer state in existence. The Provisional Zemstvo Government of the Pribaikal region declared itself the Far Eastern Republic on April 6, the day after the Japanese offensive in the Maritime Province, claiming jurisdiction over the same areas as those in the declaration of the Vladivostok socialist conference, with the addition of the Railway Zone in Manchuria.[8] On May 14, 1920, Chicherin sent a telegram informing Krasnoshchekov that the Soviet government recognized the FER's jurisdiction over the entire area east of Lake Baikal and the Railway Zone, on the terms in the FER declaration of April 6.[9] More specifically, the Sibburo of of the Central Committee RCP(b) on May 23, 1920, in its "Theses

Concerning the Work of the Dalburo RCP(b)" affirmed Verkhneudinsk as the center of the Far Eastern Republic with Vladivostok as one of its departments. There is no evidence, however, that such a precise directive reached the Maritime Communists until midsummer. Furthermore, Soviet representative Vilenskii consistently spoke for making Vladivostok the capital, supporting the Maritime Communist leaders. As late as August 16, the Sibburo received a letter from Vilenskii to this effect,[10] and he was recalled for continuing to press what was considered by that time an erroneous policy.

No matter what the pretensions to power or the desires of the political leaders in Vladivostok or Verkhneudinsk, Semenov and several thousand White troops, supported by the Japanese Fifth Division, still remained in Chita. They controlled both rail and telegraph, and if they prohibited travel across Manchuria or Transbaikalia, it was necessary to take a longer route via China and Mongolia. Soviet representative V. I. Khotimskii, traveling from Verkhneudinsk to Vladivostok in August and September,[11] and a delegation from the Amur region, traveling to Verkhneudinsk at about the same time,[12] had to take the longer route, both journeys exceeding a month.

Vladivostok Communists and socialists hoped that by presenting a united front, and by carrying out the April 29 agreement, eastern Siberia might be unified and the Japanese eased out. To gain cooperation of partisan leaders in the Maritime Province and Communists controlling the Amur in Blagoveshchensk, a mission (headed by P. V. Utkin and assisted by Colonel P. A. Lutskov and Japanese Captain Nakasima) was sent to various centers of tension along the Ussuri Railway and to Blagoveshchensk to convince partisans to honor the April 29 agreement and withdraw behind the thirty-verst zone. It also sought cooperation with and recognition of the Maritime government by Blagoveshchensk, then under the authority of the able Communists S. M. Seryshev, P. P. Postyshev, and A. K. Flegontov,[13] who would not recognize the Medvedev government. They considered the April 29 agreement a disgrace[14] and the Vladivostok leaders as prisoners of the Japanese. On May 21 Krasnoshchekov sent a telegram to Blagoveshchensk claiming jurisdiction over the entire Russian Far Eastern

Region, prompting the leaders there into action. Communist and public organizations held meetings, which resulted in the recognition of Verkhneudinsk as the center of the Far Eastern Republic and a rejection of Vladivostok's claim.[15]

The Coalition Cabinet

Meanwhile, Maritime Communist leaders in Vladivostok pressed for the formation of a coalition cabinet and elections for a representative body.[16] On May 29, 1920, the new cabinet, the Council of Department Heads, held its first session. Nikiforov served as chairman and also headed the Department of Labor, and Communists controlled other key departments, such as Communications, State Control, and Foreign Affairs. Non-Communists actually held the majority of cabinet positions but were not an organized opposition.[17] Because of the Communists' superior organization and determination, the new coalition government was directed and led by the Maritime Party leaders. The goals of the council, which included unification of the Russian Far East, the creation of an anti-Japanese front, and unification with Soviet Russia,[18] reflected more the will of the Communists than that of the other parties of the coalition, who favored removal of the Japanese, but had reservations about uniting with Soviet Russia.

One of the first moves of the new government was to tackle the problem of financial reform. Vladivostok, particularly, faced continued financial crisis from 1920 to 1922 because of the civil war and Allied intervention.[19] It suffered a loss of revenue from timber, fisheries, and other industries in Japanese-occupied areas of the Maritime Province.[20] Operation of the Ussuri Railway drained its resources because, although the Vladivostok government was obliged to pay its workers (when it could), the Japanese and other Allies did not choose to pay the cost of transporting their armed forces. Allied indebtedness to the Ussuri line alone amounted by September 1921 to 1,644,852.56 gold rubles, of which the Czechs owed 891,847.14 and the Japanese 482,119.52.[21] In addition, the disruptions had decreased international trade in Vladivostok, and Japanese desires to stimulate trade at Dairen and their importation of supplies for their forces resulted in more loss of revenue. Unemployment increased as many refugees, pouring into the Maritime Province, especially from late 1919 throughout 1920, ended up in Vladivostok. The last great influx occurred in the winter of 1920–21 when the Semenovites and Kappelites were driven from the Transbaikal region and when conservative rule was overthrown in Khabarovsk. The government by necessity was forced to provide relief and, if possible, jobs to dampen this potentially dangerous refugee element.

Financial stability in the Maritime Province received another blow in early May when the Soviet government decided to repudiate all Siberian currency except that still in use in Soviet-controlled Russia, namely, some notes issued by the tsarist regime and the Provisional Government. Furthermore, the Far Eastern Republic intended to exchange the currency in circulation for its own paper money, popularly known as "buferki."[22] All this shook the confidence in other Russian paper money still in circulation, with the result that businessmen preferred to use foreign paper or metal currency when it was available. By far the most common currency in May 1920 was the Japanese yen, and its use was encouraged covertly and overtly by the Japanese to help strengthen their hold on the Maritime Province.[23]

Prompted by the FER plan, Vladivostok authorities resolved to issue new paper money of a high quality,[24] and did so on June 5, 1920. People in Vladivostok were given ten days, and those outside the city were given twenty days, to exchange unauthorized bills for the new money at a rate of 1/200. The object was to stop the influx of valueless currency, notably Kolchak notes, from the west and to have a new currency that would be strictly accounted for.[25] This reform was promulgated by the coalition cabinet, and approved by Vilenskii and by the Soviet government in Moscow.[26] There was widespread opposition, however, in the business and foreign community, primarily over the question of backing for the new currency. Finance Department head S. A. Andreev assured the Consular Corps that there were sufficient gold reserves in Blagoveshchensk,[27] where they had been taken for safekeeping just prior to the Japanese offensive. Blagoveshchensk, however, did not recognize the Maritime government, and later it was learned that the gold was being spent freely.[28] Confidence was lacking in the new currency from the beginning.[29] Japan was also determined to defeat the currency reform for political reasons and led the opposition for the next month and a half, including a boycott of the new currency.[30] It became as valueless as the old, and the Council of Department Heads was discredited, resulting in the formation of a new coalition cabinet in early July 1920.[31]

Pressure for change was building. The failure of financial reform strengthened the opposition in the Popular Assembly. There was some scandal associated with the Justice Department and some governmental committees. Most important, perhaps, was pressure exerted by the Japanese. According to Soviet historian Papin, Japanese diplomat Matsudaira informed a group of Popular Assembly representatives, who had called on him regarding Japan's desire for a buffer state centered in Vladivostok, that if the Maritime government would include bourgeois members in its council and negotiate with Semenov, the Japanese would withdraw from the Transbaikal region.[32] Nikiforov indicated that the trading classes, motivated by economic considerations, made the first move in mid-June.[33] A delegation of the Exchange Committee consisting of B. Iu. Briner, E. I. Sinkevich, and I. I. Tsimmerman, concerned about the financial crisis, called upon Nikiforov, as chairman of the Council of Department Heads, to discuss a cooperative struggle against Japanese intervention. This led to a heated discussion among the top Maritime Communists, and they then referred the question to leading Party activists.[34] By a vote of thirty-six to thirty-five a majority opposed the decision of the Maritime Politburo to broaden the coalition cabinet to include bourgeois members. Those who opposed the move unanimously supported the Maritime Politburo's decision if the members of the Politburo would assume the responsibility for their own actions before the Central Committee in Moscow.[35]

The next day the Maritime government asked the *tsenzoviki*, or "qualified bourgeoisie," to join the cabinet, precipitating a debate in nonsocialist circles. The more conservative of the nonsocialists refused to enter the cabinet, believing that further inept rule by the socialists and the resulting chaos would hasten the decline of socialism.[36] The more moderate nonsocialists of the Trade-Industry group, however, were delighted with the opportunity to share executive power, just as they now had a voice in legislative matters. They had various motives, not the least of which was patriotism. There was an upsurge of a feeling of unity among both socialists and nonsocialists, which caused them to try to work together to solve domestic problems, unify the diverse regions in eastern Siberia, and thus to present a united front against the Japanese.[37] This was evident in the rallying of most Russians around government efforts to defeat the Japanese-led boycott of the new currency.[38] Cooperation by the nonsocialists might also extend their own influence to further the non-Communist cause and even undermine the Communist-dominated FER. This attitude was expressed by the prominent bourgeois Vladimir P. Anichkov, an employee of the Russo-Asiatic Bank in Harbin: he wanted the bank to expand its activities throughout eastern Siberia and into the FER.[39]

The coalition cabinet formed in early July was much more moderate than the cabinet it replaced. A Menshevik, M. S. Binasik, was the new chairman, and Communists headed only two departments, Labor (Nikiforov) and Communications (Kushnarev); nonsocialists now headed five departments.[40] By October, however, the coalition had broken up over several issues, and in the end, rather than serve the interests of the nonsocialists, it helped the Communist-directed government gain the cooperation of an important segment of the nonsocialist population. There were strong indications of an attempted coup by the right wing in late May 1920,[41] but there were no further moves in this direction until later in the year, perhaps in part due to the tacit cooperation of the socialists and the Trade-Industry group.

The Popular Assembly

Another pressing matter for the first coalition government was to prepare for the elections to the Popular Assembly. The elections held on June 15 reflected not only the political atmosphere in the Maritime Province, but also the predominance of the left-wing socialists in the government and electoral commission and even, perhaps, irregularities that occurred during the elections. No parties to the right of the

Cadets, who were moderate liberals, were allowed representation. N. A. Andrushkevich, the monarchist editor of the conservative newspaper, *Slovo*, and a competent observer, was critical of the method of election whereby organizations such as trade unions were guaranteed a certain representation. He also noted that children were observed voting and that many people were voting more than once.[42] A total of 28,853 votes were cast and 130 delegates elected. Their political distribution consisted of: 75 peasants, the majority Communist-sympathizers; 26 Communists and union members controlled by the Communists; 9 SRs; 4 Mensheviks; 2 Popular Socialists; 9 Trade-Industry members; 4 Cadets; and 1 nonparty member.[43] The nonsocialist elements were weak in numbers, but they were a valuable intellectual force and included parliamentarians who were skilled in debate.[44]

The first Popular Assembly session opened in Vladivostok on June 20, 1920, with 109 elected members present.[45] In subsequent sessions other delegates were present, but the Popular Assembly represented only the Maritime Province, Sakhalin Island, and the Kamchatka Peninsula. Even within the Maritime Province, no delegates were ever elected from Khabarovsk. This city had been controlled by conservatives since early April when the Japanese army seized control from radical forces, and the conservative leader, K. T. Likhoidov, refused to recognize the Provisional Zemstvo Government in Vladivostok. In spite of this, a delegate representing the peasant and socialist groups, including the Communists, read a joint declaration stating their hope that the Popular Assembly would be the nucleus for the unification of all the oblasts in the Russian Far East until a constituent assembly could be called to create a state structure for the Far Eastern oblasts.[46] This was, of course, in direct competition with the Verkhneudinsk government.

The first few Popular Assembly sessions were devoted to speeches by government representatives regarding the state of the Maritime Province and the direction it should take. M. S. Binasik, representing the socialists and Peasant Group, offered a resolution consisting of guidelines for future actions of the assembly: the cessation of the civil conflict in Siberia; the formation of an independent Far Eastern

Republic with close political and economic ties with Soviet Russia; the establishment of democratic political forms and bourgeois-capitalist economic forms; class harmony; and peaceful relations with all neighboring peoples.[47] This resolution was passed by the assembly.

Efforts toward Reconciliation

The most important move the Popular Assembly made concerned the establishment of a commission to take practical measures to bring about a reconciliation of the eastern Siberian oblasts. Japan continued its pressure for the establishment of a buffer state, and the Verkhneudinsk leaders discussed this question with the Japanese between May 25 and July 15 when they negotiated the Treaty of Gongota. This treaty, signed on July 15, 1920, by General Takayanagi and V. S. Shatov, concerned the political situation in Transbaikalia.[48] Its main intent and effect was to stop hostilities between the two parties and to establish a neutral zone between the People's Revolutionary Army (PRA) and the Far Eastern Republic and Semenov's forces in Chita. This would allow the Japanese to withdraw their forces from this territory in line with a decision made by the Japanese government in June.[49] The treaty also stated Japan's opinion that the Verkhneudinsk government was not the sole government in the Russian Far East, but merely one of several;[50] nevertheless, it was a significant boost for the political pretensions of the FER. A note, signed two days later by Takayanagi and Shatov, dealt more narrowly with the subject of a buffer state. Both sides agreed to the necessity of an independent non-Communist buffer republic to be formed by a conference of representatives of the Russian Far East. It was also indicated that the Japanese forces, although committed to withdrawal by their government's official statement on July 3,[51] might be evacuated more quickly if the Russians could hasten the formation of an acceptable buffer state.[52]

The Maritime political leaders took the initiative in calling a conference of representatives of the various centers of power to bring about their unification. On June 23 Nikiforov proposed to the Council of Department Heads that a parliamentary delegation be sent to the

Amur and Transbaikal regions to gain support for a conference of oblast representatives in Vladivostok, thus paving the way for a constituent assembly.[53] On July 3 this proposal was accepted by the assembly, and a commission representing all factions was elected.[54] When the commission reported back at the seventh session on July 17, invitations had already been dispatched to Blagoveshchensk, Chita, and Verkhneudinsk to send delegations to the proposed conference. A delegation from the Amur region was already on its way. Chita replied that it would welcome a conference, but wanted it held in Harbin. No reply was received from the FER.[55] The commission proposed to select a parliamentary delegation to go to Verkhneudinsk. It was obvious in the debate that followed that the most difficult task would be to reconcile Chita and Verkhneudinsk. Deputy Korovin-Karpov, a Siberian SR, said his party would have nothing to do with Semenov.[56] Cadet L. A. Krol, on the other hand, said that Semenov was no different from Krasnoshchekov and that negotiations would have to be carried on with both.[57] The assembly resolved to dispatch a parliamentary delegation to the Transbaikal region, but it did not select the delegates until the next session on July 21.[58]

The conference of oblast governments sponsored by the Maritime government was doomed from the beginning. Krasnoshchekov ignored the invitation and the Amur delegation refused to participate in any negotiations with Semenov's representatives.[59] K. T. Likhoidov led a delegation from Khabarovsk, but the Vladivostok and Amur delegations refused to negotiate with it because they considered the Likhoidov government a tool of the Japanese, so Likhoidov and his party returned home. The Amur delegation remained for some time in Vladivostok, apparently attempting to influence Communists there to recognize Verkhneudinsk, but, at the same time, the Japanese were attempting to influence that delegation to change its attitude regarding Semenov and Chita.[60] On July 28 Semenov's delegation arrived, led by his foreign minister, S. A. Taskin, and including generals Khreshchatitskii and M. Afanasev and several other members.[61] The Vladivostok delegation was politically mixed and consisted of Nikiforov (Communist), Vinogradov and Tsimmerman (*tsenzoviki*), and Binasik (Menshevik).[62]

Semenov's demands were much greater than his position in the Transbaikal region warranted, but apparently Matsudaira and Oi were working behind the scenes to force an agreement favorable to both Semenov and the Japanese.[63] Semenov's demand for the recognition of his supremacy in the Russian Far East on the basis of Kolchak's having named him his successor was totally unacceptable. His delegation then tried to have him named commander in chief of the armed forces of the new buffer state and leader of the Cossacks.[64] Points more readily acceptable to both sides concerned the state that would emerge, for example, that it would be independent and bourgeois democratic in form.[65] The negotiations lasted through most of August, but yielded no positive results. Meanwhile, Semenov's position had weakened in the Transbaikal region because the Japanese were evacuating their forces, completing the process by mid- to late August.[66] Also, General Khreshchatitskii and Nikiforov were conspiring to have Semenov removed from eastern Siberia,[67] and Vladivostok's parliamentary delegation in Verkhneudinsk were engaged in complex and significant talks.

The parliamentary delegation authorized by the Popular Assembly was a mixed group consisting of two Communists, I.G. Kushnarev and B. A. Pokhvalinskii; one Menshevik, A. I. Kabtsan (chairman); two peasant representatives, V. P. Aboimov and M. I. Pliukhin; and two *tsenzoviki*, S. P. Rudnev and I. I. Eremeev.[68] The delegation left Vladivostok on July 29, stopped in Harbin for private conversations with various leaders there, and went on to Chita. There the delegation met with Semenov, who later met privately with the Communist delegates. Semenov, aware of his weakening position in Chita, seemed eager to come to an understanding with the Communists and assured Kushnarev that he had no binding commitments with the Japanese (although he admitted receiving one million yen from them), that he wished to bring an end to civil strife, and that he would cooperate fully with the government that emerged from these conferences.[69] No agreement could be reached, however, until after the delegates had returned from their talks with the FER leaders in Verkhneudinsk.

From Chita the delegation passed on to Gongota, a station on the Trans-Siberian Railway a short distance west of Chita that marked the end of the territory under the influence of Semenov and the Japanese. Negotiations were in progress there between Japanese Colonel Isome and a military mission from Verkhneudinsk;[70] these concerned larger Siberian questions and not local political or military problems.[71] For four unpleasant days the Vladivostok delegation was detained at Gongota while FER representatives pressured them to exclude Semenov from any unity conference and to convene the constituent assembly in Verkhneudinsk.[72] The delegation resisted until B. Z. Shumiatskii, an important Communist and a leader in both the FER and the Communist International, arrived. Under his persuasion, a majority of the delegation finally accepted the declaration. Kabtsan refused to agree to it, and Rudnev and Eremeev were not even allowed to see the document until later. The two *tsenzoviki*, feeling it was pointless to go on, threatened to return to Chita, but Kushnarev convinced them to continue to Verkhneudinsk.[73]

The nine days spent at Verkhneudinsk were even more uncomfortable than those spent at Gongota. Relations between the Communists from the two cities were strained during the meetings. Kushnarev explained that the delegation had no power to make policies or sign declarations and that any action it took must be approved by the Popular Assembly.[74] Boris Shumiatskii spoke on the role of the Far Eastern Republic, how it was, in effect, an instrument of Soviet policy, and how all efforts must be spent to remove the "Chita stopper" and unify the Russian Far East around Verkhneudinsk.[75] Finally, an agreement was signed that was similar to the one signed at Gongota, but softer in tone. The *tsenzoviki* would agree neither to the exclusion of Semenov nor to close economic and political ties with Soviet Russia, but they did agree to a unity conference in a location free from foreign influence, that is, in Chita or Verkhneudinsk.[76]

The delegation returned to Chita on August 25. By this time the Japanese forces had withdrawn from the Transbaikal region, and

Semenov had moved his government to Dauria, nearer to the Manchurian border. The next day Semenov talked with the delegation, but this time Rudnev had his own plan for an agreement. Semenov would relinquish his authority to a popularly elected assembly in Chita and Transbaikalia, placing Chita under the authority of the Popular Assembly in Vladivostok, but he would remain Field Ataman of the Cossack troops and would be the commander in chief of forces in the Transbaikal region.[77] Rudnev hoped that in this way Verkhneudinsk and Blagoveshchensk would be balanced by a Chita-Vladivostok alliance at the proposed unity conference. The agreement was signed, but this time Kushnarev would have nothing to do with the decision of the delegation majority.[78]

In the end the Popular Assembly rejected both agreements. News of the first reached Vladivostok almost immediately after it was signed, resulting in protests from the Japanese and demands within the Popular Assembly for the recall of the delegation.[79] On August 17 the Council of Department Heads repudiated the commission for exceeding its authority.[80] There was a similar storm of protest in the Popular Assembly when it learned of the agreement with Semenov, and this agreement, too, was repudiated.[81] After the return of the parliamentary delegation on August 28, the Popular Assembly debated the question of unity and the delegation's role in it. The assembly resolved that: (1) the declaration issued at Gongota had lost its significance; (2) the protocol signed by Semenov and the delegation was unacceptable; (3) the agreement signed at Verkhneudinsk was accepted as a basis for unification of the Russian Far East.[82]

It had taken several months for Soviet and FER leaders to bring the Maritime Communists around to their way of thinking. The more moderate Communists like Nikiforov and Kushnarev preferred Vladivostok as the capital, as did the Soviet plenipotentiary, Vilenskii. In part, this stemmed from personal differences with Krasnoshchekov and other Verkhneudinsk leaders, evident especially through July 1920. This rivalry proved to be the chief weakness of the Dalburo as it was originally organized in March 1920, and at a Maritime oblast Communist conference on July 10 it emerged clearly. Shumiatskii, who

was sent to the conference by the Verkhneudinsk branch of the Dalburo, demanded an end to the coalition government, an immediate
recognition of Verkhneudinsk, and dissolution of the Vladivostok
government. He then demanded the expulsion of the Maritime leaders
from the Party for insubordination to Verkhneudinsk. Nikiforov commented that Shumiatskii forgot that there were three Dalburo members
in Vladivostok possessing the same authority as those in Verkhneudinsk.[83] There was also Japanese pressure to have the capital in
Vladivostok, to which leaders there were very sensitive. Matsudaira
at one time informed Medvedev that the Japanese could not guarantee
the safety of a delegation traveling to Verkhneudinsk, but could to
Vladivostok.[84]

The change in the attitude of the Maritime Communist leaders
toward the location of the center for the buffer state came in July and
August following a realistic appraisal of the Maritime Province's
political position relative to Verkhneudinsk's and in response to
pressure from the Sibburo, Verkhneudinsk leaders, and Lenin himself,
once he had come to a firm decision. Lenin's directive was issued as
a resolution of the Central Committee of the RCP(b) of August 13,
1920. It stated that the buffer state must be bourgeois-democratic in
form (a mere formality since it was to be led by Communists), and
that its capital must be at Chita and not at Vladivostok.[85] It is interesting to note that Semenov was not yet out of Chita at this time, but
the Japanese forces propping up Semenov were withdrawing.

In order to effect the provisions of the Verkhneudinsk-Vladivostok
agreement, a governmental delegation consisting of P. M. Nikiforov
(chairman, Communist), A. I. Kabtsan (Menshevik), and E. A. Trupp
(SR) was dispatched to Verkhneudinsk in mid-September.[86] The moderate nonsocialists refused to participate in this enterprise.[87] Matsudaira warned the delegation that he would not guarantee its safety
through Semenov's territory. Nikiforov replied that Semenov was a
Japanese responsibility and that the delegation would not reverse its
decision to proceed to Verkhneudinsk through Manchuria and the
Transbaikal region.[88] At Manchuria Station, the last station on the

Chinese side of the railroad before entering Russian territory, the delegation was detained for four days on Semenov's orders.[89]

Semenov's activity from June until October was vigorous, multi-directional, and increasingly desperate. The Kappelite leaders had decided in the middle of the summer that they could no longer work with the Cossack chief and that their only course was to leave the Transbaikal region and go to the Maritime Province. General Diterikhs was sent to Vladivostok in mid-August to negotiate the Kappelites' entry.[90] Semenov, determined to remain in the Transbaikal region, tried to hinder Diterikhs's talks with the Maritime leadership and in other ways sabotage the Kappelites' withdrawal. He also tried to convince the Japanese to delay their evacuation; negotiated with conservatives in Vladivostok and with Communists from both Vladivostok and Verkhneudinsk to allow him to remain in Chita as commander in chief of forces there; created popular organs of government in Chita with which he could make an arrangement to stay as military leader; and, finally, when all these moves failed, he recognized General Baron Peter Wrangel as the only Russian power in the Russian Far East.[91] This last act demonstrated the desperation of the White cause. In late October and November Wrangel was offering the last armed resistance to the Soviet government in western Russia. The Soviets had just concluded hostilities with the Poles in mid-October and now could direct all their force against Wrangel. By mid-November Wrangel's Volunteers, as the Whites on the southern Russian front were called, along with their families, were being evacuated from the Crimea.[92]

When the Vladivostok deputation arrived at Manchuria Station, Semenov sent General Khreshchatitskii to negotiate on his behalf, but Nikiforov refused. After four days the Vladivostok delegation was allowed to proceed to Dauria where Semenov himself attempted to negotiate with Nikiforov, and again Nikiforov refused. After two more days the delegation was allowed to go to Chita, which was under Kappelite control.[93] There General Voitsekhovskii, the leader of the Kappelites, approached Nikiforov regarding the placing of his forces under the zemstvo government in Vladivostok. Nikiforov promised to convey his proposal to the government in Verkhneudinsk.[94] This probably displeased Voitsekhovskii because he preferred the Vladivostok government to the one in Verkhneudinsk, although either was preferable to Semenov's.[95] After receiving permission by direct wire from Verkhneudinsk, Nikiforov and his group proceeded there.[96]

This preliminary conference was a very short meeting of four delegations, one each from Vladivostok, Verkhneudinsk, the Amur region, and Chita. They decided that a conference would be held in Verkhneudinsk or Chita that would include, as well as these four regions, delegations representing the eastern Transbaikal region and Sakhalin. The government formed at this time would then call a constituent assembly to draw up the constitution for the future Far Eastern Republic.[97] Until then, however, the declaration of independence of the existing Far Eastern Republic issued on April 6, 1920, would be considered the fundamental law.[98] At the close of the Verkhneudinsk conference the Amur delegation and Nikiforov remained in Verkhneudinsk, while Trupp and Kabtsan returned to Vladivostok to report to their respective parties.[99]

The most important event in Vladivostok in the first half of October was the failure of the coalition cabinet; its foundations had never been firm, and it became increasingly weakened by attacks from right and left.[100] General conditions in Vladivostok made orderly government difficult at best. The financial reform attempted during the summer had failed and Vladivostok was continuously gripped by a financial crisis, with accompanying labor unrest and other related problems.[101] Banditry was on the rise, causing concern and anxiety, and leaders and other citizens were often attacked.[102] The Japanese were an unsettling element, not only because of their presence, but also because it was felt that often they were behind the lawlessness and "incidents."[103] There was constant disagreement over policy between the bourgeois and socialist cabinet members, as described previously.[104] The bourgeois members grew more frustrated at their inability to influence government policy,[105] and the Communists became more determined not to allow the bourgeois members to hinder progress toward unification or in other ways to block government policy.[106] As early as September 7, 1920, Maritime Communist leaders considered ending the coalition with the *tsenzoviki*;[107] Verkhneudinsk and Moscow had been pressuring Party leaders in Vladivostok for some time to end the coalition and dissolve the government in favor of Verkhneudinsk.

The issue that finally ended bourgeois participation concerned foreign affairs. Dissatisfaction in this realm had long lain under the surface. On September 24 several conservative members of the Popular Assembly addressed an open letter to the head of the Department of Foreign Affairs requesting clarification of a statement made in *Krasnoe znamia* that the Far Eastern Republic could speak for the Vladivostok government in its negotiations with Japan.[108] The last straw, however, concerned the government's approval of FER policy with regard to the Iurin mission in China.[109]

Ignatius L. Iurin, a close associate of Krasnoshchekov and later FER foreign minister, led a delegation to Peking for the FER (backed by Soviet Russia) to establish political and economic relations with China. Stalling the negotiations, China demanded that representatives be sent from the other centers in the Russian Far East to show broad support for the mission. The Medvedev government sent A. F. Agarev, an engineer and a Menshevik, whose qualifications included revolutionary activity in his student days and emigration to the Far East before the revolution.[110] Russian moderates and conservatives opposed the Iurin mission, which they saw as a threat to their interests in China—representation in Peking by tsarist Ambassador Prince Nikolai Alekseevich Kudashev and the question of Russian extraterritorial privileges in the Railway Zone in Manchuria.[111] Not only did the moderates and conservatives oppose FER policy, they also disliked the arbitrary manner in which Vladivostok's policy was being made and executed, without debate in the Popular Assembly; accordingly, on October 13, the bourgeois members left the coalition.[112] As might be expected, the rightist press (*Slovo* and *Vladivo-Nippo*) blamed the Communists and their supporters for the demise of the coalition, while the leftist press (*Krasnoe znamia* and *Dalnevostochnoe*

LEADERS OF BOLSHEVIK, KRASNOSCHOKOFF (R) & MOUHIN (L)

過激派主領 カラスニシチョーコフ（右）ムーヒン（左）

Aleksandr Mikhailovich Krasnoshchekov, right, with Mouhin,
another Bolshevik in the FER region
Courtesy of the Hoover Institution, the Shapiro Lavrova Collection

obozrenie, the Maritime government organ dominated by leftists) blamed the bourgeois members.[113] The real cause, of course, was the impossibility of reconciling two antagonistic points of view.

The Chita Conference

Meanwhile events were moving rapidly in Transbaikalia. Neither Krasnoshchekov nor G. Kh. Eikhe, commander in chief of the FER People's Revolutionary Army, would negotiate with the Kappelites in China because both believed that they would soon drive the Whites into Manchuria. Commenting upon this attitude, Nikiforov noted that this would only create future problems within the Maritime Province, as, indeed, it did.[114] Partisan forces occupied Chita on October 22, 1920, removing the final obstacle to convening the proposed unity conference there.

On October 28 representatives from the various oblasts assembled in Chita to begin their work. The only representative from Vladivostok was Nikiforov, who had remained behind when Trupp and Kabtsan had returned to Vladivostok. By this time a delegation was formed in Vladivostok consisting of Trupp and Binasik from the Council of Department Heads and Kabstan and Rumiantsev from the Popular Assembly.[115] G. K. Rumiantsev was the leader of the Peasant Group and was included because of the strength of his party in the Popular Assembly.

Before the delegation departed from Vladivostok on October 29, Maritime leaders received the "Declaration of the Conference of the United Provinces of the East," published in Chita that day. It proclaimed the creation of a new Far Eastern Republic, differing from the earlier FER in that representatives from all provinces of eastern Siberia, not just the Transbaikal region, were involved in its creation. The declaration detailed the type of government to be established and the disposition of the various governments and armed forces located throughout eastern Siberia. The text of the declaration was accompanied by a statement from Nikiforov to the effect that Vladivostok was being presented with a *fait accompli*, and that the Vladivostok delegation should sign the declaration by telegraph.[116] This caused a furor in Vladivostok because it had been the position of leaders there that there would be no unification of the Far Eastern oblasts without the participation of delegations from all oblast governments, including the Maritime government. The delegation issued its own declaration that Nikiforov had exceeded the wishes of the Vladivostok government and then left for Chita the same day.[117]

On November 5 the Council of Department Heads, chaired by Boldyrev in the absence of Chairman Binasik, asserted that Chita's declaration was premature and nonbinding in the Maritime Province until a joint agreement could be reached.[118] This brought an immediate response from Krasnoshchekov and Nikiforov, who asked the Maritime leaders why they were sabotaging the laws of the united government. They responded by repeating the Vladivostok position. They could not recognize the Chita government until their delegation had reached Chita and come to an agreement; the political situation in the Maritime Province excluded any other course of action.[119]

The Vladivostok delegation arrived in Chita on November 7. The next day it proposed that a preparliament be created as a temporary higher organ of government until a constituent assembly could meet and that the zemstvo boards be retained as local organs of government. Neither proposal was acceptable to the Communists, who fully controlled the Chita proceedings.[120] The conference elected a new provisional government on November 10, 1920, with Krasnoshchekov as president and Nikiforov as premier, and adjourned. Before the political leaders in Vladivostok were ready to accept the unification of eastern Siberia on Chita's terms, the newly elected FER government under Krasnoshchekov's leadership assumed that it was the legal government of the entire region and sent numerous decrees to the Maritime Province to hasten the centralization of the state. Chita also issued orders to Communist and public organizations and to governmental departments to recognize the new state, causing consternation among government employees as they did not know whom to obey. Administrative chaos resulted.[121] On November 11 Chita dispatched a telegram to "The President of the Popular Assembly and Medvedev," apparently already treating Medvedev as a private citizen and not as the head of the Maritime government. It proposed to the

Popular Assembly that it dismiss the Council of Department Heads and elect some assembly members to the Zemstvo Board in order to expand and strengthen it as the local government.[122] The leaders in Chita could act in such an arbitrary manner in the territory they controlled, but they could not impose their will similarly on Vladivostok with its responsible government and with the presence of the Japanese army.[123]

The next day General Oi summoned Medvedev as the head of the government, Boldyrev as acting chairman of the cabinet, and representatives of all factions of the Popular Assembly to his headquarters to inform them of the Japanese position. The delegates were kept waiting for an inordinate amount of time, and when Oi received them, he read his statement in Japanese—both actions an affront to their sensitivities. Oi reminded the Russians that wherever Japanese troops were located communism would not be tolerated and that the April 29 agreement and others would remain in force, concluding with the warning: "The Japanese command, therefore, cannot allow any third person without the knowledge of the Japanese command to dare upset the existing political order and tranquillity in the krai."[124]

The Council of Department Heads now had to make its position on the unification known to the Popular Assembly. Boldyrev was chosen to speak before the assembly on November 18. Following a heated debate, the assembly adopted a resolution that accepted the Chita declaration of October 29 as a basis for unification, but indicated it would recognize the Chita government only after further negotiations. The conditions for negotiating included preserving the assembly as a responsible legislative body for the Maritime Province and preserving a local executive organ responsible to the assembly, while passing responsibilities to the central government in the areas of the military, finance, and foreign affairs. The assembly strongly recommended that the new state should permit the participation of all democratic parties as a guarantee that democratic principles would be adhered to. Finally, the resolution declared that no action would be taken regarding recognition until the government heard from Chita or until its delegation returned from Chita.[125]

Ironically, had Krasnoshchekov been more moderate and followed
a more gradual approach, allowing the decisions to be made after the
Vladivostok delegation arrived in Chita, he probably could have succeeded in effecting his plans with much less opposition. His methods,
however, created strong opposition not only from the Japanese and
nonsocialist elements, as one would expect, but also from the Socialist Bloc. The exception to this was the Maritime Communist party. By
this time it had been brought completely under the direction and discipline of the Dalburo, now united into one group and centered in
Chita. The Maritime Obkom was chaired by V. I. Khotimskii, who had
been sent earlier by the Dalburo to direct the Maritime organization,
and who was pressuring the Medvedev government to recognize Chita
as the central government.[126] But the Japanese supported Vladivostok.
Their attitude may be seen in many statements, including General
Oi's on November 11, and in a note from General Takayanagi to Krasnoshchekov, which criticized the shabby treatment accorded the
Vladivostok delegation, the undemocratic Communist nature of the
Far Eastern Republic, and illegal FER military activities.[127] The
Japanese, however, made no overt moves to alter the course of events;
rather, they followed a wait-and-see posture, applying pressure as
they could. The situation was still in flux, and the Japanese themselves felt domestic pressures against further military embroilment.
Furthermore, it was reported that Krasnoshchekov had received positive instructions from Moscow (about which, presumably, the Japanese
knew) to begin a general offensive against the Japanese should they
hinder the formation of the buffer state or make excessive demands
upon Chita.[128]

The Vladivostok press during November was largely critical of
the results of the Chita unity conference and the arbitrary manner in
which Krasnoshchekov ran the conference and the government after
its formation. The exception to this was the extreme leftist press—
Krasnoe znamia and *Dalnevostochnoe obozrenie*. The rightist press—
the Japanese-subsidized *Vladivo-Nippo* and *Slovo*—roundly denounced
any thought of cooperating with Krasnoshchekov or Chita. The more
moderate press, both socialist (*Volia*, SR) and nonsocialist (*Vecher*

and *Golos rodiny*, both liberal), were more rationally critical of the methods employed by Chita and generally supported the position of the Maritime government, that is, nonrecognition of Chita until the issue was debated by the members of the Maritime Popular Assembly.

On November 27 the Vladivostok delegation returned from Chita, complaining of their ill treatment and of their inability to communicate freely with Vladivostok.[129] This inflamed the debate that had been progressing during their absence, both within party caucuses and later in the Popular Assembly. The nonsocialist factions, including the moderate Progressive Democrats and the conservative Trade-Industry group, opposed the recognition of Chita even before the Vladivostok delegation returned. They considered Krasnoshchekov a mere tool of Soviet Russia and said that there was no possibility for democracy in the future state, pointing out that the first act of the new government was the undemocratic treatment of the Vladivostok delegation. Both nonsocialist groups stated they would support the zemstvo government only if it did not recognize Chita.[130]

The position of the Communists was for full and immediate recognition of the Chita government with no autonomy for Vladivostok.[131] The Peasant Group at first had been opposed to Rumiantsev's joining the Chita government,[132] but on his return to Vladivostok Rumiantsev convinced them to vote for the recognition of the Chita government and for the dissolution of the Popular Assembly.[133] The SRs and Mensheviks reluctantly approved the recognition of Chita, although neither had any faith in Krasnoshchekov nor in his pledge that the republic would be democratic. Both, however, recognized the new state for what it was, a *fait accompli*, and placed their hope in the future constituent assembly.[134] A strong motivating force for this distasteful decision was the genuine fear of civil war. After Semenov had been forced out of the Transbaikal region, he had proceeded to the Maritime Province under Japanese protection, met with his supporters at Grodekovo, where they were gathering, and conferred with General Oi in Vladivostok.[135] Semenov later admitted that he was planning to seize power in Vladivostok.[136] There was no question when it came to a choice between Semenov, for whom moderates and leftists alike had no regard or respect, and Krasnoshchekov, whose government might conceivably be influenced. It was felt that a leftist united front would restrain forceful action by Semenov and his supporters.

While the Popular Assembly debated, the Japanese again tried to influence the decision. On December 1, 1920, they sent two notes to Vladivostok leaders warning them of the consequences of Vladivostok's recognition of Chita.[137] On December 2 the Japanese sent an eight-point questionnaire to Tseitlin, chairman of the Russo-Japanese Conciliatory Commission, inquiring whether the proposed state would be democratic and independent in foreign policy. They implied that the answers to these questions would be influenced by the continued presence of Japanese forces in the Maritime Province.[138] On December 5 the Popular Assembly, not heeding the Japanese warnings, passed a resolution introduced by A. I. Kabtsan for the Socialist Bloc by a vote of 79 to 33. It contained the following points:

1. Recognition of the government elected at Chita on November 9 as the central government of the Russian Far East with full legislative and executive power until the convocation of a constituent assembly;

2. Approval of the October 28 declaration published by the Chita conference;

3. Approval of the law regarding the constituent assembly, which was passed by the Chita conference;[139]

4. Retention of the Popular Assembly as the leading organ of power in the oblast until the convening of a constituent assembly.[140]

Several proposed amendments were defeated, including one introduced by the SR B. Ia. Gurevich, who noted the inconsistency of the first and fourth points and who favored more autonomy for Vladivostok than was implied in the resolution.[141] What passed was, in effect, a resolution embodying the principle of a "buffer within a buffer," an autonomous Maritime Province within a centralized buffer state whose capital was now in Chita.

A bill embodying the "buffer within a buffer" principle was introduced in the Popular Assembly. After a debate, recognition of Chita was made official by the passage of the bill on December 11, 1920.[142] A new Council of Department Heads, responsible to the Popular Assembly, was approved. The new cabinet reflected the real power within the assembly; the chairman was Vasilii G. Antonov (Communist), editor of *Krasnoe znamia*, and its other members were either Communists or Peasants who cooperated with the Communists.[143]

On December 12 the Maritime Zemstvo Board resigned its authority in favor of the central government in Chita,[144] and a few days later the Popular Assembly adjourned.[145] Meanwhile, governmental departments were gradually being liquidated and their affairs were being transferred to Chita.[146] Although an orderly transfer of power was taking place, the future of the newly unified buffer state was cloudy. The nonsocialists resolved that they would not obey Communist-tainted orders and would take all measures to keep Vladivostok from becoming Communist.[147] Liberal leader L. A. Krol derisively described the Antonov cabinet as the directors of a funeral procession.[148] The balance of power was shifting in the Maritime region. While most important Communists were now going to the Transbaikal region to work with the new government, thousands of White troops, defeated in Transbaikalia, were pouring into the Maritime Province and tensions between Communists and non-Communists heightened. These forces formed a basis of support that Whites, with tacit Japanese approval and aid, would use to bring their own designs to fruition, the creation of a non-Communist base of power in the Maritime Province.

4

The Establishment of a White Government
in Vladivostok
May 26, 1921

THE MOOD in Vladivostok in the first half of 1921 was increasingly restive. The slight spirit of unity that had existed in the summer and fall of 1920 had now vanished. There was dissatisfaction among moderates and conservatives because the newly created Far Eastern Republic was (and probably would continue to be) Communist dominated, and the entry of the Kappelites and Semenovites into the Maritime Province was causing political, economic, and social disruption.

The White troops in and around Chita in the late summer and fall faced a serious dilemma. The Semenovites knew that they could not hold the Transbaikal region against partisan and Far Eastern Republic (FER) forces without the aid of either the Japanese, who had declared in June their intention to leave, or of the Kappelites, who would no longer cooperate or coexist with Semenov.

There was only one direction—east—that these White forces could move. First, however, arrangements would have to be made with the Japanese, the Chinese, and, most important, with the authorities in the Maritime Province about where they would settle. What would the future hold for these Whites who had fought the Communists the thousands of miles from the Urals? How long would it be before Soviet power extended to the Pacific Ocean? What possibility would there be of emigrating when the only wealth most of the refugees possessed was what they were carrying? Whatever property they had owned was left behind, had become valueless with the changes in government, had dissipated because of inflation, or had been used to buy what food they could find. The anxiety, desperation, and depression these people experienced is difficult to imagine.

An earlier settlement between the Kappelite leaders and the Maritime zemstvo government to enable the White soldiers and their families to stay in the Maritime Province was cut short by the Japanese offensive.[1] In August General Diterikhs was in Vladivostok, trying again to reach an agreement with the government,[2] and General Voitsekhovskii made a similar attempt with Nikiforov when the latter passed through Chita in the course of the intergovernmental negotiations then in progress.[3] Krasnoshchekov and his military commander, Eikhe, seemed interested only in a military victory, not in what lay beyond. By his own admission Eikhe underestimated both the numbers of Whites involved and the intensity of their animosity towards the Communists.[4]

Before any decision was reached, the Whites were ejected from Chita and then from Transbaikalia entirely. The first echelons of Whites crossed into Manchuria in late November,[5] forcing some action to be taken regarding their disposition. The Chinese reluctantly allowed the Whites to enter Manchuria, but only after they were assured that the Russians would not detrain until they reached the Maritime Province.[6] The Chinese were reasserting their authority and sovereignty in the Railway Zone, and they did not wish to see the Russian population grow or the zone become involved in the Russian civil war, as Mongolia had. In addition, economic conditions in Manchuria were in disarray; there were already too many unemployed persons without adding further to the difficulties.[7]

The Japanese played a curious role in the movement of the Whites. They were obligated to Semenov because of their close relationship with him over the previous two or three years and, therefore, transferred him, his staff, and his loyal troops to Grodekovo,[8] a town less than ten miles inside the Russian border in the Maritime Province. They also assisted in the transfer of the Kappelites by pressuring the Maritime government to accept them as refugee Russian citizens rather

than as a defeated army.[9] The Japanese publicly favored a disarmed
status, thus upholding the April 29, 1920, agreement by allowing only
a small armed militia within the thirty-verst zone over which the Japanese acted as guardians of the peace. They sympathized with the
White cause, and yet a fully armed White army could upset Japanese
plans to have the Whites dependent upon the Japanese for supplies,
especially weapons. As a result, the Japanese ostensibly enforced
the disarmed status, yet some White units were able to carry con-
cealed arms into the Maritime region.[10]

Communist leaders of the FER and Vladivostok differed on the
extent to which the Whites were a threat and on how to deal with them.
The Dalburo, underestimating their number and viewing them as a defeated army, initially opposed negotiations.[11] By November 30, however, FER Deputy Foreign Minister I. S. Kozhevnikov, who was in
Vladivostok, realizing how many people were involved in the White
exodus, created a special commission to deal with the problem, but
nothing came of this effort.[12]

Meanwhile the Whites were being pressed by partisan and FER
forces and were concentrating on the Russian side of the Russo-
Chinese border. On November 24 they crossed into Manchuria[13] and
settled around Manchuli (or Manchuria) Station for several days while
they waited for permission and assistance in proceeding eastward.
This sparked a debate within the Maritime Council of Department
Heads on November 26. The majority of members voted to have the
director of Foreign Affairs protest to the Japanese and Chinese authorities for allowing this movement and to inquire about the aims of
the Whites.[14] Boldyrev and three other members expressed the minority
view that it was impossible to refuse Russian citizens access to
Russian soil.[15] The Japanese responded to this council action with
two communications to Boldyrev: the first, on November 26, denied
Japanese assistance to the Kappelites in Manchuria; and the second,
on November 28, added that the only way the Whites could enter the
Maritime Province was with the help of the Chinese and the Maritime
government. The Japanese command, contradicting General Takayanagi's public statement, admitted assisting Semenov in reaching

Grodekovo on November 27,[16] where he remained for several days before going on to Vladivostok. Later he claimed that he had intended to overthrow the government in Vladivostok and would have done so had the Kappelite leaders not refused to subordinate themselves to him.[17] Semenov's presence in Vladivostok caused a great deal of indignation and brought protests from the Popular Assembly and the Consular Corps. On December 5 Semenov left Vladivostok for Port Arthur, where he plotted until the following May.[18]

On November 29 the first echelon of Kappelites set out from Manchuli for Pogranichnaia, the last Chinese station before entering the Maritime Province.[19] During December these unfortunate soldiers and their families, numbering between twenty five and thirty thousand,[20] were living in railway cars and camps all along the Chinese Eastern Railway. The Chinese took measures to prevent their detraining in unauthorized areas, as when they passed through Harbin, but this was not always successful.[21] Upon arriving at Pogranichnaia, the refugees requested permission to enter the Maritime Province.

Divided over whether or not to allow the Kappelites to proceed, the Maritime government took no action, which antagonized both the local population and the many Kappelites who had illegally slipped across the border. On December 2, 1920, General Boldyrev, acting on his own responsibility as head of the military, gave tacit approval to the refugees' entering the province by arranging accommodations for the care of the sick and wounded. He was sympathetic to the plight of the refugees, and had concluded that the government must act to relieve the situation.[22]

Boldyrev's action raised a furor within the government, resulting in his resignation from the council,[23] but it also thrust the issue into the open and forced the Communists to reassess their own position. Most of the parties, except for the Peasant Group and the Communists, favored allowing the Whites to enter the Maritime Province. But realizing that the refugees would enter the province anyway, the Peasant Group proposed, with the Communists' support, the formation of a commission "to work out the conditions and take the necessary measures for moving and quartering the . . . [White] units as unarmed people, followed by the wounded, the infirm, women, and children."²⁴ During the debate that followed, the nonsocialist bloc protested by walking out of the session, and the SRs refused to have their members participate in the commission. When the commission was finally elected on December 8, the Communists held three of the seven positions, including the chairman, Petr Parfenov, and the Peasant Group also held three.²⁵

The commission met on December 8 with Colonel Lovtsevich, who claimed not to represent an army, but people of a former army. He spoke eloquently about how the civil war was over and about the exhaustion of the members of the former army. He assured the commission that the refugees would not be used against the government by the Maritime bourgeoisie, by Semenov, or by the Japanese.²⁶ Meanwhile, the Communist Party Obkom instructed the commission to resist the White entry into the Maritime Province, except for single individuals, the sick, and refugees, and to attempt to effect a dispersal of the Whites to areas where Japanese troops were not located.²⁷ These instructions were already a dead letter because the White troops were congregating in Pogranichnaia, while the Japanese were aiding the Semenovites in Grodekovo. In addition, the authorities in Vladivostok and Chita were not taking practical measures to deal with the situation.

The commission finally passed a resolution embodying the principles under which it would operate. Besides allowing the hospital and refugee cars to enter, the following was resolved:

1. To inform Chita about the situation and ask its assistance;

2. To ask the Vladivostok government to publish acts with regard to fulfilling the proposals of the commission by all its means and institutions;

3. To clarify the question of quartering the refugees;

4. To name itself the "Parliamentary Commission on the Movement, Reevacuation, and Demobilization of the Former Kappelite and Semenovite Armies";

5. To ask the government for funds;

6. To name a representative to go to Pogranichnaia to handle the receiving and control of the echelons; and

7. To appeal to the soldiers and officers of the White army in the name of the commission.[28]

Parfenov then informed Eikhe about the commission's action. Eikhe expressed his concern that there were so many Whites involved[29] and that White officers had made some rather bellicose statements. Kappelite Commander General G. A. Verzhbitskii, upon arriving with his staff in Harbin, had talked militantly and frankly about "impending battles in new conditions."[30] Eikhe and Krasnoshchekov immediately published a full amnesty for all White troops, calling upon them to end the fratricide and either join the FER People's Revolutionary Army or return to civilian life.[31] This, of course, did not arrange for the disposition of the White refugees.

The commission spent the next three weeks traveling to stations along the railway line between Vladivostok and Harbin in an attempt to make arrangements with the various parties involved—the chiefs of the garrisons in Nikolsk, Spassk, and other centers where the White forces would be settled; the Chinese authorities at Pogranichnaia, Harbin, and Peking; the Inter-Allied Railway Commission, which controlled movement along the Chinese Eastern Railway; and the White commanders. However, the commission's basic strategy was to retard the movement of the Whites eastward into the Maritime Province and to encourage their return westward to the Transbaikal region and Soviet Russia itself. The lack of funds and facilities to house and care for so many refugees account only in part for this strategy. More important was the Communists' desire to prevent a build-up of an anti-Communist military force in the Maritime Province, but even as the commission was involved with this effort, its work was being undermined.

The momentum of the White movement eastward made the flow almost irreversible. The refugees' plight was desperate, but they also hated communism and had a deep distrust of Soviet Russia and the FER, so resisted Communist persuasion to return. The Chinese, desiring to clear the Railway Zone of refugees, thwarted the commission's strategy by hastening the movement eastward.[32] Furthermore, hundreds of Kappelites were crossing the border on foot and horseback, carrying what provisions they could with them.[33] As might be expected, conflicts broke out when they got to Grodekovo, where the Semenovites were settling.[34] This enmity was one of the constant hindrances to White unity from early 1920 to the end of White activities in eastern Siberia in late 1922.

Ironically, Communists' activities in Vladivostok also undermined the work of the Parfenov commission. Maritime Obkom Chairman Khotimskii and FER Deputy Foreign Minister Kozhevnikov, on their way to Chita from Vladivostok, informed Parfenov of the arrangement that Tseitlin had made with the Japanese to quarter the Kappelites at Nikolsk and Razdolnoe. Tseitlin then informed Parfenov that the Maritime government would admit the Whites as an organized body if disarmed and subordinate to the government and if Verzhbitskii would order his army not to engage in politics. Verzhbitskii agreed, and the nonsocialist moderates and SRs gave their guarantee that the agreement would not be broken. The commission acquiesced, and after a few minor difficulties the way was open for the eastward movement of the Whites.[35] The transfer of the refugees was largely completed in January.[36]

The White refugees were settled in three major centers—Grodekovo, Razdolnoe, and Nikolsk—and to a lesser extent in several other locations—Poltavka, Spassk, and Poset. They were organized into three corps: the first consisted of Semenovites, while the second and third were Kappelites. The First Corps posed the gravest threat because of its ties with the Japanese and because, as Cossacks, they had a potential source of strength among the native Cossack population along the Ussuri River. Grodekovo had been a center of support for Semenov for several months and the arrival of his staff and army in November, numbering perhaps five thousand,[37] consolidated his power. Although Semenov was forced to reside outside of the Maritime Province, he maintained his influence in Grodekovo through General Savelev, whom he had appointed commander in chief in November.[38] The conditions under which the Semenov army lived were not good; hundreds lived in boxcars, barracks, or other poor housing, but it was better in Grodekovo than in other centers. Semenov had obtained all the gold the Kappelites brought with them when they entered the Transbaikal region, which he had turned over to the Japanese for safekeeping when he evacuated Transbaikalia.[39] It was well known that the Japanese provided Semenov with financial support. Grodekovo was supposed to be under the administrative and military control of Vladivostok through its representatives and a militia, but, in fact, was more influenced by the armed force of Semenovites. Illegally wearing their faded uniforms and drilling in a military fashion, they were openly hostile to both Vladivostok and Chita.[40] The Maritime government sought permission to disarm the Semenovites, but were blocked by the Japanese.[41] As General Savelev admitted in an interview, the relationship between his army and the Japanese was very close—they were his protectors. He did not act unless he had notified the Japanese of his intended actions; otherwise, they got very suspicious.[42]

The Kappelite forces, numbering about ten thousand, made up the Second and Third Corps located in Nikolsk and Razdolnoe respectively.[43] They, too, were crowded into boxcars and old barracks, but their plight was worse then the Semenovites'. They refused to subordinate themselves to General Savelev, as Semenov had ordered in late November;[44] so if any support was received from Semenov, it was minimal. In an April interview Kappelite Colonel Savechuk stated that his men had received no pay since December. They were especially bitter over the stealing of their gold by Semenov and felt he should return or at least share it.[45] Since the Kappelites refused to subordinate themselves to Semenov, they were denied Japanese financial assistance[46] and lived on what provisions they carried with them or could acquire from sympathetic citizens in the Maritime Province.[47] Relief work in Vladivostok was carried on during the first few months of 1921 by moderates and conservatives to collect funds for the support of these refugees, as well as to create closer ties between the two.[48]

The White refugees thus settled in various locations around the Maritime Province, and many took up trades or engaged in agriculture; but they retained their basic military organization, as well as their devotion to the anti-Communist cause. (Before the March Revolution, Russians in exile cheered revolutionary acts and other incidents that might either contribute to the overthrow of the tsarist government or bring about substantial reform. When the tsar abdicated, many of these exiles returned to Russia to help remold their country according to their own beliefs.) Anti-Communists were encouraged by any adversity Lenin's government faced, and events in 1921 were heartening. Economic breakdown, famine, political repression, and general despair in Soviet Russia sparked widespread peasant rebellion in late 1920 and 1921 and an uprising at the Kronstadt naval base in Petrograd, once a Bolshevik stronghold, in March 1921. When this news reached the Russian Far East, there was a wave of agitation and enthusiasm among the refugees and nonsocialists in Vladivostok.[49] This was only one factor among many that helped to weaken the Antonov government in Vladivostok.

The Antonov Government

Vasilii Grigorevich Antonov, a former teacher, had been a Bolshevik since 1906 and was a trusted member of the Party. He did not have the same stature within the Party as Nikiforov, Kushnarev, or Tseitlin, but neither was he a nonentity. Chairman of the Maritime Popular Assembly elected in mid-1920 and a Dalburo member for a short time in 1920, he was now head of the caretaker government in Vladivostok for the Communists. As an individual he held the respect even of moderates,[50] but his government, although well-meaning, was increasingly unpopular, especially with the rightists and Kappelites. Its influence was weakened because it was without strength to enforce its assumed authority. Most leading Party members had gone to Chita and were concentrating their attention and energies on the government there. Regular communications between the two cities were lacking;[51] only occasional decrees arrived from Chita, which Antonov could not easily enforce.[52] The militia was neither large enough nor sufficiently armed to do the government much good, and the partisan forces, which were not permitted to operate within the thirty-verst zone, were inactive at this time because Communists controlled all the major cities of eastern Siberia. Thus the government was powerless against White activities like those in Grodekovo, as well as the increasing lawlessness in the Maritime Province caused largely by *khunkhuz* bands.

The khunkhuzes were groups of Chinese bandits that roamed the rural areas, looting, kidnapping people and holding them for ransom, and even occasionally entering Vladivostok in their depredations. Not a new phenomenon, they had terrorized residents and travelers along the Trans-Siberian Railway for a number of years.[53] It was generally felt, with supportive evidence, that they were often organized by the Japanese military command to stir up trouble, giving the Japanese a reason to remain longer in the Maritime Province.[54] Whatever the cause, they were becoming more active in the spring and provided another reason for unrest.[55]

The financial situation in Vladivostok was desperate. The currency had depreciated to the point where it was valueless, causing more unemployment and further depressing business. Trade was often carried on either on a barter basis or with the small amount of silver still in circulation, although much silver was being hoarded; the most widely used and stable currency was still the Japanese yen.[56] The government was living far beyond its means. Considered a temporary government, its tax base was small and its influence did not extend beyond the southern Maritime Province, and yet it had a structure of sufficient size to administer a much larger area. Many people were living off the government by drawing on government rations and supplies, such as fuel for cooking and heating.[57] Moreover, the government was often unable to meet its payrolls,[58] adding to the economic distress and social unrest. It was charged with secretly supplying money to Russian, Korean, and Chinese partisans,[59] and it was accused of bribery and extortion.[60] These latter charges had sufficient basis, in fact, for the Popular Assembly to approve the appointment of a "super-inspector" to deal with corruption.[61]

There were other reasons for the lack of funds. Revenue was being

lost because of the diversion of trade from Vladivostok to Dairen.
This can be attributed in part to the political and economic instability
of Vladivostok, which created higher risks and costs for the shippers,
but it was also to the advantage of the Japanese to divert trade to
Dairen. There were only strong suspicions about their support of the
khunkhuzes, who disrupted traffic along the rail lines, but the Japanese also simply held up railway cars on various pretexts, causing
delay and uncertainty for shippers.[62] The government's financial
picture would have been brighter had it been paid by the various
Allied governments, especially the Japanese, for transporting troops
and for customs duties. Antonov claimed the Japanese owed his government 15,000,000 yen.[63]

The government had few alternatives in dealing with the financial
crisis. It could issue no more paper money, and the unemployed or
irregularly paid workers could pay no more taxes. Some new taxes and
higher license fees affecting business primarily were levied,[64] but
this in the long run could be a counterproductive measure. The most
obvious short term method of obtaining funds was the sale of goods
stockpiled in Vladivostok. The sale of arms was precluded because
they were controlled by the Japanese, but there were other valuable
stocks such as rails, farm equipment, and medical supplies.[65] Early
in March the Council of Department Heads appointed a commission
consisting of Antonov and several of the department heads to supervise the disposition of the goods.[66] The sale and export of certain
goods had been prohibited earlier, so the commission proposed the
repeal or alteration of this limitation to allow the commodities in
question to be sold either at home or abroad.[67] This issue created a
furor in the press and within the Popular Assembly. Antonov declared
that the goods belonged to the Far Eastern Republic, the government
superior to his own, but he admitted that he had been ordered by
Chita to sell the material. The opposition contended that FER jurisdiction was limited, and the government was not obliged to follow
Chita's orders,[68] insisting that the government unload goods that had
already been illegally loaded on ships bound for Europe.[69] On March
19 the assembly voted against the government by 58 to 10, whereupon

the Antonov cabinet resigned. The assembly accepted Antonov's resignation but voted a few days later to restore him and most of his cabinet to their former positions. This curious action, led by the Peasants, may be explained by the feeling that there were no other suitable candidates and Antonov, now somewhat chastened, enjoyed the confidence of the Communists and the Peasants.[70] The sale issue was still not resolved; in April and May the press reported goods being sold and shipped, and the debate in the press continued.[71]

An epidemic of pulmonary plague, which spread to the Maritime region from China in March and peaked in April had a further depressing effect, as well as diplomatic repercussions. Most fatalities, which ran into the hundreds, were among Chinese. The government closed Vladivostok to Chinese laborers from Chefoo (on the Shantung Peninsula) due to arrive to work as they did each spring. The Chinese government protested the closure, denying that the epidemic had begun in Chefoo, as the Russians contended.[72] Whether the plague did originate in or spread from Chefoo or Manchuria is uncertain, but the arrival of 10,000 Chinese would most certainly have caused adverse economic effects. It was to the benefit of the government to provide employment for the restless unemployed, who were already so numerous there.

The Nonsocialists

While the Communists were focusing their attention and energies on Chita, non-Communists were trying to decide whether to work with the Communists, while retaining an autonomous status in the Maritime region, or, in the case of the rightists, to overthrow the leftist Antonov government in Vladivostok. The most active political forces in Vladivostok were the Communists and the right wing of the nonsocialist bloc in the Popular Assembly. They represented the extremes of the political spectrum and had the most to lose, economically and politically, if the other gained power. Caught in the middle were the Mensheviks and SRs, who were torn between cooperating with and opposing the Communists. Philosophically they had much in common with the Communists, and certainly they found common ground in opposing

Japanese intervention, but they opposed the Communists' methods
and resented Krasnoshchekov's high-handed manner of dealing with
the Maritime government. The SRs and Mensheviks believed in popular
sovereignty and wanted an independent buffer in the Russian Far
East, although they generally favored close ties with Soviet Russia.
They hoped to guide this buffer state along a democratic path and,
therefore, many SRs and Mensheviks worked with the Chita and Vladivostok governments. This is why Binasik (Menshevik), Trupp (SR),
and others had remained in Chita after the unity conference in November.

The moderate nonsocialists, such as Cadets L. A. Krol, M. M.
Pavlovskii (editor of *Vecher*), and Kurtev (editor of *Golos rodiny*),
and Vasilii Boldyrev, had political views similar to the SRs and
Mensheviks and, therefore, faced a similar dilemma. Philosophically,
they differed from the socialists, especially the Communists, but
they shared with the Mensheviks and SRs a belief in democratic
methods and a hatred for the Japanese intervention. They were, however, less patient with the FER and the Communist-dominated government in Vladivostok so that their attempts at cooperation, most
notably in the fall of 1920 with their participation in the coalition
government and the unity negotiations, were not long-lasting. They
hoped, unrealistically, to create a democratic buffer state in the
Maritime Province, even though the Communists were determined to
prevent this. Being moderate in their views and political habits, they
talked more than they acted. They vacillated between cooperation
with the rightists, whom they disliked less than the Communists, and
cooperation with the Antonov government, which they thought might
be influenced along more democratic and independent lines.

The right wing of the nonsocialists, to whom the term "nonsocialist" was most generally applied, was hostile to the socialists of all
parties. Politically they ranged from dedicated monarchists to conservative republicans, and they had nothing philosophically in common
with the socialists. They were not as committed to democratic methods as the other nonsocialists and moderate socialists, as their subsequent actions indicated. Like the Communists, they believed the

goal justified the means. They could plan a coup with no regrets, and they could take a much more favorable view toward the Japanese because, as long as the Japanese were present, they could enjoy political and economic rights.

The rightists were not all pro-Japanese. N. A. Andrushkevich (editor of *Slovo*) knew the Japanese were double-dealing and looking out for their own interests, but he preferred the Japanese presence to Red rule. It was only after the Japanese offensive in April that his newspaper and *Vecher* could be published.[73] Vladimir P. Anichkov, important in financial circles, compared the Japanese occupation with the Tatar yoke. Nevertheless, he felt that living with the Japanese in Russia was preferable to living in Japan and noted how much freer he felt after the Japanese offensive.[74] The conservative nonsocialists' solution to their plight ranged from waiting until bolshevism died from within to more aggressive designs, even to collaboration with the Japanese.

Into this political milieu came the Kappelites and Semenovites. Semenov had little support in Vladivostok, although some rightists would have cooperated with him because of their mutual hatred for socialism and communism. He did have considerable support among Cossacks in Grodekovo and along the Ussuri River, among political leaders in Harbin, and within the Japanese command; however, he was forced to reside outside the Maritime Province and could not participate directly in the political activity of Vladivostok, a decided disadvantage. Semenov also had a bad reputation with the general public and with the Kappelites because of his style of rule, his close association with the Japanese, and his own and Cossack ambitions, which took precedence over national goals. If the Kappelites could have forgotten their personal differences with the Semenovites, they would still have had difficulty in cooperating, for example, in an offensive against the FER. Should such an offensive be successful and should Soviet Russia be crumbling from within (always a White hope), they were convinced that Semenov and his followers would not march past Lake Baikal. The Kappelites were prepared, if the opportunity arose, to march past the Urals.[75]

The confidence of the Whites had been dealt a heavy blow by the overthrow of Rozanov on January 31, 1920, but with the Japanese offensive it quickly returned. By April former officers of Semenov, Rozanov, and Kalmykov were in Vladivostok wearing insignia and decorations outlawed by the zemstvo government.[76]

A rightist coup was averted in May only by prompt governmental and Dalburo action and Japanese warnings against such machinations.[77] In June Whites were causing trouble in railway stations north of Vladivostok within the thirty-verst zone in which the Japanese were supposed to be keeping order. A band of men led by the Cossack Bochkarev disarmed the militia and murdered, raped, or beat several Russians at the Spassk and Ussuri stations. Shortly after this, the important Communist and zemstvo government representative, P. V. Utkin, was murdered by a Cossack officer, who went unpunished and settled in Grodekovo.[78] In the second half of July large public masses were held in honor of Nicholas II in Nikolsk and Vladivostok.[79] Tension mounted in August as another coup was feared.[80]

There was no end to the rumors and apparent intrigues among various groups of Whites throughout 1920 and into 1921. It is difficult to tell how much the Japanese were behind these intrigues. The summer and fall of 1920 were very active politically in eastern Siberia and in Vladivostok; plans had to be tentative because conditions changed frequently. Chita's success in unifying the provinces east of Lake Baikal stimulated political activity among all nonsocialists. By this time it was easy to perceive the political complexion of the new buffer state, and the inclusion of the Maritime Province in this Communist-dominated state greatly agitated the conservatives.

There were two trends to this political activity on the right. First, the nonsocialists were preparing for the elections to the FER Constituent Assembly that would be held throughout the Russian Far East in January. Second, and more important, the right wing of the nonsocialists was making plans to preserve the independence of the Russian Far East, alter its political form, and thus offer an alternative to the Moscow-dominated Far Eastern Republic.

The elections were scheduled for January 9 through 11 in Vladivostok, with twenty-six seats to be decided.[81] It is surprising that the nonsocialists decided to participate, considering the total number of representatives to be elected throughout eastern Siberia was 427.[82] They could not possibly hope to have any influence against such odds, since most of the delegates would be from Communist-dominated regions. Nevertheless, the nonsocialists were busy organizing, selecting their candidates, and campaigning for office.

Three nonsocialist groups emerged with lists for the election: the Trade-Industry group, a carry-over from political activities in the summer of 1920, and two more significant new parties, the Democratic Union and the National Democratic Union, representing respectively the moderate and conservative wings of the nonsocialists.

The members of the Democratic Union were formerly associated with the Cadet and Progressive Democratic parties and were now closely associated with the newspaper, *Vecher*. The leaders were liberal intelligentsia. Boldyrev, although not formally a member of this group, joined its list and, along with L. A. Krol and S. F. Znamenskii, was elected to the Constituent Assembly. The slogan of their campaign was "Neither communism, nor reaction."[83]

The members of the National Democratic Union came mainly from the Trade-Industry group and were associated with the rising, dynamic leadership of the Merkulov brothers, Spiridon and Nikolai, sons of an Amur valley peasant.[84] These two men represented both a major strength and weakness of their movement. Few of their colleagues and almost no others had any respect for them because of their weak characters and unscrupulous ambition. On the other hand, they owned the newspaper *Slovo*, had considerable financial reserves, were gifted speakers, and provided vigorous, dedicated, and shrewd leadership. Spiridon, the more dominant and educated of the two brothers, was trained in law and had served in the Ministry of Agriculture in St. Petersburg as a specialist on the Russian Far East.[85] Nikolai, a former captain of a ship on the Amur, owned a small match factory near Vladivostok. Boldyrev noted his close ties with members of the Japanese staff. Other leaders included I. I. Eremeev, former mayor of Vladivostok under Rozanov with long-standing commercial interests in a Japanese commercial firm;[87] D. I. Gustov, a tobacco manufacturer;[88] N. A. Andrushkevich, editor of *Slovo*; and S. P. Rudnev, a former jurist.[89] The followers of the National Democrats were primarily small shopkeepers, property owners, and other conservative elements. From this group the Merkulov brothers, Gustov, and Rudnev were elected to the Constituent Assembly.

The Trade-Industry group elected only one delegate, Kappelite Commander Verzhbitskii. As Rudnev pointed out, this illustrated the common interests of the commercial elements and the newly arrived Kappelites.[90] The SRs elected one delegate, F. S. Mansvetov, and the Mensheviks one, M. S. Binasik. Of the total of over 22,000 votes cast, the Communist votes numbered 12,588 and, as a result, they captured fifteen of the twenty-six seats available.[91]

The Constituent Assembly was scheduled to open on February 12 in Chita. When the Vladivostok delegates left, only one nonsocialist, Znamenskii, went with them. At a meeting on January 12 the nonsocialists decided that it was senseless to "risk their necks" by going to Chita when the odds were so heavy against their accomplishing any satisfactory results.[92] Mansvetov sent a wire from Chita urging them to come, and they decided to make the journey but were subsequently persuaded to remain in Vladivostok by Eremeev, "the best worker the Japanese" had.[93] An informant of Charles Smith (see Appendix 2), identified only as the chief of the Vladivostok customs, said that the Japanese instructed the nonsocialists to remain in Vladivostok because Japan intended to help them establish an independent buffer under its protection.[93] This is plausible in view of the Japanese tacit approval of White[94] plans for an overthrow of the Antonov regime.[95]

An Attempted Right-Wing Coup

There were plans afoot by a number of nonsocialists and other non-Communists to alter the course that the Maritime Province seemed to be taking. Semenov was heavily involved in a multitude of negotiations with various parties, including the Japanese and some Chinese.[96] I. I. Serebrennikov, a member of the ill-fated Provisional Siberian

Government and later an émigré in Manchuria, noted that there was a veritable procession of people to Port Arthur to see Semenov. He added that he believed they went, not to plan a coup, but to seek money, which Semenov spent freely.[97] This was in part true. The Kappelites especially were insistent that Semenov return their funds. There is ample evidence, including Semenov's admission, that plans were being laid for White action. Hardly a day passed that the Far Eastern press did not mention rumors of a spring offensive by the Whites, with Japanese assistance.

Important planning was being done by the group of nonsocialists led by Eremeev, the Merkulovs, and others. Reacting to the November Chita unity conference, they publicized their position in a resolution of November 6, 1920, signed by the "Committee for the Preservation of the Russian Far East." The group repudiated the Far Eastern Republic because it was Communist-dominated, and also because they felt that there should be no separate Far Eastern state. The Russian Far East belonged to the Russian people, they said, and called upon the Allied governments to defend and maintain law and order in the region until "the Russian government shall be in a position practically to exercise its rights and obligations in the Far East,"[98] that is, until communism had been destroyed.

The right wing actually began planning the coup sometime in late 1920. Ivan Kondratych Artemev, former president of the Khabarovsk Stock Exchange, received Japanese approval from General Oi for the "nationalists" to meet to "discuss their affairs."[99] The Committee for the Salvation of the Fatherland was formed, with Eremeev as chairman.[100] Its most active members were Spiridon Merkulov, who carried on the struggle in the Popular Assembly, his brother Nikolai, who was the "soul of all kinds of meetings," and Andrushkevich, who wrote many articles, protests, and appeals.[101] Meeting daily, the committee was very active, working overtly and covertly against the FER and the Antonov government. They corresponded regularly with conservative organizations, especially in Harbin, which in turn sent their representatives to Vladivostok to work with the committee. An anti-Bolshevik propaganda drive was begun, especially through the churches where priests gave pro-White sermons.[102] To carry on their political activities, including a projected nonsocialist congress to be held in Vladivostok in early March, two interrelated problems had to be solved—the need for military and organizational support and the need for money.

The committee represented conservative financial and political interests, making it suspect to liberals and moderate socialists. It was, moreover, caught in the middle between the Semenovites and Kappelites, who extended their mutual distrust to anyone having anything to do with the other. Yet, the committee tried to obtain financial and moral support from both groups. Rudnev heard that 6,000 rubles, collected for the Kappelite relief fund, went for the proposed nonsocialist congress.[103] Early in March Eremeev and N. Merkulov visited Semenov in Port Arthur to solicit funds and support of his forces in Grodekovo.[104] Their report, that Semenov promised his support if he could lead the movement, caused an uproar and the dispatch of another mission, led by Vasilii Fedorovich Ivanov of Harbin. On his return, Ivanov assured the committee that Eremeev and Merkulov had misunderstood Semenov, who wished to lead only the armed forces—not the civil government as well. An agreement was made with Semenov on this basis and financial aid was assured.[105] Attempts to obtain Japanese aid failed, probably because Semenov was not given full leadership.[106] By this time, however, the conservatives had sufficient funds to proceed with their plans. They themselves had donated money or had collected it from merchants in Vladivostok. In addition, the Merkulovs had substantial wealth, and Gustov used his tobacco factory as collateral for a loan earmarked for the forthcoming congress.[107]

The Nonsocialist Congress did not convene until March 20 because of the prolonged negotiations with Semenov.[108] Its original aim had been to unify the nonsocialist forces and thus broaden the political base of the movement to include the moderate nonsocialists, who were invited to participate as delegates, but refused and sat with the public in the galleries. As Kurtev told Charles Smith, the moderates knew of the negotiations with Semenov and refused to have anything to do with him.[109] Interestingly, some moderate socialists invited the nonsocialist leaders to participate in their plans, but the nonsocialists did not want to associate with the "Gaida crowd."[110]

The congress in Vladivostok, to say nothing of its goals, presented a threat to the Antonov government. It protested and sent an armed militia to break up the first session. Initially it succeeded, but the nonsocialists appealed to the Japanese command, who placed the Nonsocialist Congress under Japanese protection and told the Maritime government not to interfere,[111] further lessening the prestige of the Maritime government.

The arrangement made with Semenov had displeased the moderates, but so, too, did the reactionary tenor of the congress. Its delegates selected for their executive committee a Non-Socialist Council of six conservatives headed by Spiridon Merkulov.[112] Yet, the moderates could subscribe to the resolutions passed by the congress: a temporary government in the Far East based upon a popularly elected assembly until a legal government could be established in Russia by a constituent assembly, and no civil war.[113]

On March 30 and 31, the last two days of the congress, some anti-Communists attempted to overthrow the government, bringing discredit to the congress. The Maritime authorities, expecting a coup, had taken preventive measures by centralizing the military forces loyal to the FER and the Antonov government under a Maritime Council of Defense. N. K. Iliukhov, who headed this group, has claimed that the Communists knew of the precise plans and took strong measures to prevent the overturn. They put their military units in battle readiness, occupied significant buildings, and patrolled the streets.[114] About one hundred White leaders, mostly Kappelites, including General A. N. Lokhvitskii, and some civilians, including K. T. Likhoidov, were arrested.[115] The Maritime authorities claimed to have proof that the coup had been organized by Lokhvitskii at Japanese urging.[116] However, according to Lokhvitskii's adjutant, Lieutenant Meshkov, the Kappelites at Razdolnoe learned of the orders to arrest these Whites on March 29 and set out to prevent them,[117] thus becoming involved.

Lokhvitskii and other Kappelites were in Vladivostok planning for a new government, but the attempted coup was probably a Semenovite venture encouraged by the Japanese through N. Merkulov and perhaps other council members.[118] The leader was Colonel P. E. Gludkin, a Kappelite commander known for his strong character and bravery, but also for his Semenovite sympathies. He was ambitious and had the backing of Semenov and the Japanese as a successor to their enemy, General V. M. Molchanov, the commander of the Third Corps at Nikolsk.[119] The Japanese undoubtedly knew, or thought they knew, what was happening and cooperated with Gludkin, but when they realized how poorly organized and ill-supported the adventure was and how well-organized the government was in meeting this challenge, they helped put an end to the attempted coup.[120]

The Communists responded by again taking measures to break up the White armies in the Maritime Province. Early in April FER Commander in Chief Eikhe ordered A. Lepekhin, commander of the Vladivostok militia, to disband these forces.[121] Eikhe stated in an interview that the White soldiers meant well but resisted only because of misguided leadership and pressure by the Japanese.[122] On April 5 on instructions from Lepekhin, chief of the Nikolsk Garrison Nechaev proposed to Kappelite commander Verzhbitskii that the men who wished to return to Soviet Russia could do so under the personal guarantee of their safety by the FER; if they did not wish to cross Siberia, arrangements would be made for their departure to Odessa. Those desiring to remain could do so without arms and under the control of FER agents.[123] Lepekhin went to Grodekovo to make similar proposals to Semenov's commander in chief, General Savelev.[124] Neither attempt succeeded—the Whites had their own plans.

The attempted coup also prompted further diplomatic efforts to pressure the Japanese to withdraw from the Russian Far East. Two notes were directed to the Japanese by the Far Eastern Republic. The first, signed by Boris Skvirskii, was sent on April 29 to the Japanese foreign minister and protested Japanese actions in the March 30–31 events, accusing the Japanese armed forces of disarming the militia instead of attacking Whites. It also protested further interference in Maritime domestic life and the build-up of Japanese troops after March 31.[125] The other note dated April 24, from the FER Constituent Assembly to the Japanese government, described the situation in broader terms, reminding the Japanese of the reasons they had given for the intervention, and told them that their presence was no longer necessary. The note also pointed out the hardships the Japanese were causing the Russians by their continued presence and asked them to withdraw and extend diplomatic recognition to the Far Eastern Republic.[126] Similar dispatches sent to the governments of the United States, Great Britain, and France, placed the moral responsibility on these governments for the Japanese presence in the Russian Far East and, therefore, for pressuring the Japanese to withdraw.[127] There was even an appeal addressed to "All the Governments and Nations of the World."[128] None of these notes achieved significant results.

The Successful White Coup in Vladivostok

The Kappelite leaders were forced to act because of their serious economic situation, the prospect of increasing desertions to the partisans[129] and Semenovites,[130] and Semenov's influence with the nonsocialists. They preferred to join the FER than to be under Semenov's command and sought, therefore, to exclude Semenov entirely from the Maritime Province, establish a new government in Vladivostok that could give them financial relief,[131] and broaden the nonsocialist movement to include the moderates. To achieve these last two goals, they instigated a meeting of leaders of both wings of the nonsocialists. Plans for a coup and the make up of the government were discussed, but the moderates opposed these plans as a Kappelite adventure that would play into Japanese hands. They also considered the Merkulovs unacceptable as members of a new government and made several other objections.[132]

The moderates then made their own plans, placing their faith in elections being planned for June or July by which, in cooperation with moderate socialists, they hoped to force a genuine coalition on the Antonov government and use the Kappelites as a militia.[133] By refusing to work with the conservatives and thereby delaying decisive action, the moderates drove the Kappelites into an alliance with the conservative nonsocialists.

The Kappelites felt they could not wait until June or July. Their sense of urgency caused them to enter into secret negotiations with the Merkulovs, who were double-crossing Semenov. The Non-Socialist Council had promised the Ataman that he would be commander in chief of the armed forces, and it continued to assure Semenov's representative, General Savelev, that the agreement was still in effect so that they could rely upon the Semenovites for financial assistance and armed units. At the same time the Merkulovs, without the knowledge of the council, planned with General Verzhbitskii and other Kappelite commanders to exclude Semenov once the coup succeeded.[134] Semenov's group was meanwhile double-crossing the nonsocialists by forming its own government in Harbin. When the overturn occurred, this government intended to become the civil authority in Vladivostok and Semenov would head the military.[135]

The planning for the successful coup of May 26–27, well under way by mid-April, was done almost exclusively by S. Merkulov and the top Kappelite commanders, who organized a People's Revolutionary Committee (Narodno-revoliutsionnyi komitet, or Narrevkom—not to be confused with a similarly named Bolshevik organization). The political preparations were made by Merkulov and the military by General Dmitrii Antonovich Lebedev,[136] Kolchak's chief of staff and "a specialist in coups."[137]

The planning for a new government was not done in the daily sessions of the Non-Socialist Council; S. Merkulov, who headed it, dictated decisions that had been made elsewhere. Rudnev has described how the decision was made for the selection of the future government. At the regular meeting of the Non-Socialist Council in the first half of April, Spiridon Merkulov made the unexpected proposal that the future government should be elected in view of the impending overturn. Rudnev objected, stating that such an action was too sudden and that not all the members were present. Spiridon Merkulov proceeded with his plan and, after he and Eremeev had been named, proposed that his brother Nikolai also be a member of the new government. Rudnev objected on the grounds that Nikolai could better serve as a liaison with the Popular Assembly and that there would be strong criticism if both brothers were in the government. As an alternative, Rudnev suggested General Vasilii Boldyrev, which made Merkulov furious, and after an exchange of words Rudnev left the council and remained out of touch with it until after the coup.[138] D. I. Gustov had done so shortly before this for much the same reason.

The decision in favor of the coup was made by Verzhbitskii, backed by Kappelite and Semenovite commands, and by S. Merkulov, but without the knowledge of the Non-Socialist Council. White forces began moving into Vladivostok in mid-April, taking with them what weapons they had and obtaining others as they could. They had tried to obtain additional weapons from various parties—Japanese, Chinese, and others—but with no success.[139] The Whites entered into this venture ill-equipped, but they hoped to seize the arms of the Vladivostok militia.

The change in power in the Maritime Province occurred very much as it had in January 1920. By the time of the May 26 coup, Vladivostok was isolated. On May 23 and 24 the Whites in Razdolnoe and Nikolsk had disarmed the militia and had assumed control of the cities and the rail line; the same occurred on May 25 in Ugolnaia and at other major points.[140] The Maritime government's hands were tied. Vladivostok had only a small militia, which it dispatched to Nikolsk, the first city that fell, but it was prevented by the Japanese from retaking it[141] and Antonov was not allowed to call for reinforcements from the Khabarovsk area where Communist forces had been grouping all winter.

The Whites began their offensive in Vladivostok shortly before noon on May 26. Within a short time they had taken the western side of the city, its most important section, including the governmental headquarters located in the Naval Staff building. The governmental and Party leaders had expected the coup for some time and had made more elaborate preparations, including spending the last few nights at the Naval Staff building for their protection. When the action began, the leaders left the building and concentrated their forces in the eastern section of the city. The government's forces began a counteroffensive

and were pushing the Whites back when the Japanese appeared, disarmed them, and ordered them back to their barracks. From late afternoon through the first night the Japanese patrolled the streets. During
this time Antonov and other leaders were vigorously protesting the
Japanese disarming of the militia and their failure to disarm the
insurgents. The next morning the Japanese returned the weapons to
the militia, with orders not to use them. The Japanese then disarmed
some of the Whites. When it was apparent, however, that the Whites
were on the defensive, the Japanese intervened again, this time in
favor of the Whites, and by that evening the city was theirs.[142] As one
observer wryly put it, the battle was between the Reds and the Whites,
but the decision rested with the Yellows.[143]

Communist and White sources agree that Japanese troops provided
the decisive blow to Antonov's power.[144] But did this mean that there
was a change in Japanese policy or that this was part of a larger
Japanese plan? Officially, Japanese policy had not changed since
Japan had altered its justification for being in Siberia from helping
the Czechs to protecting Japanese citizens in the Far East and hin-
dering the spread of communism and anarchy. Both civilian and
military leaders publicly maintained this stance.[145] Yet, there were
further examples of a dual policy, indicating that the military and
civilian leaders continued to differ. Perhaps the most telling statement came from an interview with General Tachibana, the new commander in chief of the Japanese Expeditionary Force, who replaced
General Oi. Tachibana arrived in January, but returned to Tokyo
in May for an important conference on Asian questions. He was indignant at the charge that there was military interference in Japan's diplomacy. He maintained that military diplomacy could not
be tolerated and

The military authorities have never encroached on the sphere of the Foreign
Office because they are well aware of the evil effects attendant on so-called
military diplomacy. If the military men ever played the part of diplomats in Siberia, certainly it was only because the Foreign Office failed to take the necessary steps for the maintenance of national prestige as well as interest.[146]

And so, while military leaders publicly stated that Japan's policy was to promote order in Russia and to observe neutrality in Vladivostok, their actions consisted of disruption and interference in Russian domestic life—causing candidates to withdraw from the January election lists, prohibiting rolling stock from leaving the area under their control, and the like.[147]

While the Japanese had larger plans for the Russian Far East in the spring of 1921, it is doubtful that there was a secret agreement between the French and Japanese military leaders as Communist sources, complete with documentation, have claimed.[148] There was much intrigue at Japanese headquarters in Harbin, Mukden, Port Arthur, Vladivostok, and Peking, and the Japanese military appeared to have put together a general anti-Communist movement involving the cooperation of the Chinese and the military leadership of certain White Russian leaders, like Baron Roman Fedorovich von Ungern-Sternberg. This bizarre figure was known as the 'mad Baron" because of his strange ideas and behavior, including cruelty that exceeded even Semenov's. Ungern had established himself with Japanese aid in Urga, the capital of Mongolia, which was a center of intense Japanese-Chinese-Russian rivalry, but Ungern had his own dreams of creating a greater Mongolia (Semenov had a similar dream) to use as a base to liberate Russia from Communist rule and even from decadent Western influence. At this point in early 1921, Ungern was planning an attack on the Far Eastern Republic. This was part of a larger Japanese plan in which Semenov also figured, but the Japanese were unable to force him upon the Merkulovs and their military allies, the Kappelites.[149] Nevertheless, by benevolent neutrality or by outright aid, such as harboring White troops in their barracks and obtaining the release of White prisoners after the attempted coup, the Japanese promoted nonsocialist activities.[150]

At the time of the Merkulov coup, Commander in Chief Tachibana was in Tokyo, but undoubtedly he was in touch with events in Vladivostok.[151] This was probably why the Japanese did not act in a more consistent and decisive manner, but perhaps the larger reason was that they had to maintain some semblance of neutrality. They could allow the coup to crystallize, but they could not show too much favoritism toward the insurgents because of the possible negative response from the United States, Soviet Russia, and other interested parties. The important point is that the coup did succeed through the good graces of the Japanese military leadership, that the political situation was still in flux, and that the Japanese military still had a peace-keeping role in the unstable Maritime Province.

5

The Provisional Priamur Government
and Its Failure
to Unify the Non-Communist Population
May 26-October 1921

Fear and optimism had motivated the Whites to seize power. After
the Chita unity conference in November 1920 the leaders of the Far
Eastern Republic (FER) planned to call a constituent assembly in
February to delineate the political structure of the buffer republic.
The Maritime Province was nominally a part of the FER, and the
Whites were naturally concerned about the nature of the republic and
who would control it. In spite of assurances by some Communist
leaders that it would be an independent republic, other Communists
again demanded that eastern Siberia be sovietized. The left wing took
advantage of an absence of the pro-buffer group within the Dalburo to
pass a resolution favoring the liquidation of the FER and sovietization
of the territory. The moderate Bolshevik, Nikiforov, went to Moscow
to appeal to Lenin and the Central Committee for the continuation of
the buffer state. Nikiforov returned to Chita, armed with a new directive assuring, for the time being, the buffer status of the FER.[1] From
the Whites' perspective, this still did not solve the problem of Communist domination, which was amply demonstrated in the sessions of
the Constituent Assembly from February to April 1921. Even though
there was a build-up of White military forces in the Maritime Province
early in 1920, which might assure some form of autonomy for the area,
there was a greater increase in Communist forces near Khabarovsk.

The Whites believed that the Maritime Province would be absorbed fully into the FER by force if Chita found it necessary.

News of numerous peasant uprisings in western Siberia and Russia proper and of the important Kronstadt insurrection confirmed the White expectation that communism was crumbling from within. Many anti-Communists in the Maritime Province felt that once a White regime was established, especially after four years of unsuccessful Bolshevik rule, people would rally to it. This was self-delusion; the White regime represented the last fling of a desperate people who became increasingly demoralized as more of their expectations did not materialize. With the exception of the peasantry, which tended to become more conservative, the Whites had even less support than the regime they overthrew.

The Merkulov Government

On May 26 the Council of Representatives of the Non-Socialist Population became the Provisional Priamur Government.[2] Spiridon Merkulov, as chairman of the council, became self-appointed head of government. The other members were his brother, Nikolai, responsible for military and naval affairs, I. I. Eremeev, head of the Department of Internal Affairs, manager of financial matters, and again mayor of Vladivostok; E. M. Aderson; and A. Ia. Makarevich. N. M. Sokolov was the secretary for the group.[3] Within three days of the coup the existing Popular Assembly was dissolved and new elections were called for.[4] Until the new Popular Assembly met on July 20, 1921, the government consisted only of a governing board with no legislative branch or cabinet.

The major energies of the government in June were spent negotiating with Semenov and trying to prevent a coup in his favor. Nevertheless, a viable government had to be created and talent sought to fill numerous posts. In spite of the hostility he felt for him, Spiridon Merkulov appointed S. P. Rudnev to reorganize the government and fill vacant posts. Rudnev was a respected and able leader, and he was sufficiently dedicated to the White cause to overlook their personal differences. On June 1 he assumed the post of Director of

Governmental Affairs, rather like a temporary prime minister, and remained at this post until a major cabinet reorganization in September.[5] Merkulov asked another adversary, General Boldyrev, to return to the Russo-Japanese Conciliatory Commission as its chairman. Both the extreme right and extreme left found Boldyrev useful because of his patriotism, moderation, and respect by the Japanese and others. He assumed this important position on June 18 on the condition that he could also carry on independent political activity in opposition to the government.[6] Admiral Iu. K. Stark was put in command of the Siberian Flotilla, and he arrived from Harbin on June 18, 1921, to assume his post.[7] Other talent was sought, such as the able George Guins, former member of the Omsk government, then living in Harbin, but Spiridon Merkulov and his associates had difficulty attracting such people to his government because of their narrow outlook and questionable characters.[8]

The new government did not consider itself the permanent government for the Maritime Province; rather, it would rule for the benefit of the non-Communist population until a permanent Russian government could be established by a constituent assembly.[9] Of special interest was the name this government chose for itself—Provisional *Priamur* Government, referring, presumptuously, to the Priamur governor-generalship of tsarist days,[10] which consisted of the Maritime, Amur, Sakhalin, and Kamchatka administrative units of the Russian Far Eastern Region. The authority of the new government barely reached past Spassk, about 125 miles north of Vladivostok.

While the aim of ending the civil strife and of peace and reconstruction were publicly stressed, the theme of struggle was also evident. The Kappelite leaders and Merkulov did not intend to vegetate while waiting for the Communists to crumble from within; both were hostile to the FER and intended to carry on a struggle against it. Merkulov's statements were somewhat ambiguous on the subject— he talked about struggling against Soviet Russia and the FER, because, he said, there was no difference between the two.[11] He also indicated that this would be accomplished by sending about one thousand soldiers to the Khabarovsk-Blagoveshchensk area, where people were ready to rise up against the Communists and only needed a little assistance.[12] General Verzhbitskii was more aggressive. In his statement, read by General Molchanov to the Second Non-Socialist Congress (held in the latter part of June), Verzhbitskii expressed his hope of starting an offensive to liberate Russia from communism.[13]

Equally contradictory were the new government's statements on civil rights. The government was openly hostile toward the Communists and their sympathizers and excluded them from political activity, but having experienced the harassment of the Antonov government, the members of Merkulov's government were sensitive to questions of press censorship, arbitrary arrests, and the like. The new leaders wanted to win the support of their liberal opponents and to rule with a broader base because they believed their interests coincided with those of the vast majority of people in the area. Spiridon Merkulov attempted to allay public suspicion of his government, but at the same time he showed his determination to continue in power, warning the population that hostile activity against the government would not be tolerated. He stated that there would be no press censorship "for the moment" by the government, that no searches or arrests would be made without specific orders from the Department of Justice, and that fair treatment would be given to arrested persons.[14] For about a month the government respected civil rights for all but Communists, and it moved toward restoring traditional institutions of government and law.[15] Nevertheless, it implemented some repressive policies from the start and used more as time passed. The labor organ, *Rabochii*, first published on June 8, 1921, was suppressed.[16] It was, in fact, a Communist-supported newspaper replacing the Party organ, *Krasnoe znamia*, which had gone underground. By mid-June Merkulov was even intimidating the moderate press by warning the editors of such newspapers as *Vecher* and *Golos rodiny* not to print anything against the government, under threat of closure.[17] By the end of July the threats were formalized into a three-month jail sentence and a fine of 3,000 rubles to those editors publishing articles that may "bring discredit to the government or reduce its authority in the eyes of its citizens or which spread false information."[18] At the end of June the government was also arresting followers of Semenov because of their potential threat.

There was constant antagonism between labor, which was heavily influenced by the Communists, and the government. The first confrontation between the two occurred at a conference of workers at their usual meeting place, Narodnyi Dom. The meeting concerned whether to boycott the elections for the Popular Assembly. A militia official ordered the conference to disband; when it refused, militiamen immediately dispersed the meeting.[19] The antagonism between the Merkulov government and labor grew in intensity, resulting in clashes and arrests in August and September.[20]

The government's statements and actions in the economic sphere were also inconsistent. The financial situation in Vladivostok was disastrous; just as the Medvedev and Antonov governments were plagued by high expenditures and insufficient income, to say nothing of graft, the Merkulov government was similarly afflicted. One of the principal reasons the new government gave for its overthrow of the Antonov government was the latter's fiscal irresponsibility and graft. The original declaration of May 26 and V. Kolesnikov's financial report to the Popular Assembly in September were more like exposés; besides the charge of graft, the former government was indicted for the sale of state goods from the Vladivostok warehouses.[21] Yet, as A. I. Pogrebetskii pointed out, the Merkulov government liquidated state property, increased taxation, and did not pay wages and salaries to government employees.[22] Regardless of who or what party ran the government, its problems were insoluble. The Merkulov government recognized the serious financial situation and tried to obtain foreign support, especially from the United States and Japan; the former refused, and the Japanese attached too many conditions and demanded very high interest.[23] Some money was gained by selling concessions, mainly timber. Almost all went to the Japanese, and, as a result, Japan maintained military and economic control of Russia's coast.[24]

The Merkulovs were not squeamish about how they got their money, nor, according to Artemev, were they careful about getting it to the treasury. The government encouraged the opium trade by creating a special office, the "Inspection of Opium Affairs," and by licensing poppy cultivation and smoking. These efforts provided the government with a constant source of income.[25]

The White coup and the aid given it by the Japanese effectively ended Communist authority. Most of the Communist leaders had been arrested by the Whites, but just as the Japanese command forced the Antonov government to free the Whites arrested in March, now it forced the Whites to free the Communists, a move precipitated by a threat from the government in Chita to hold all Japanese there as prisoners unless the Vladivostok political prisoners were freed.[26] Under Japanese protection the Communist leaders were able to communicate with the FER capital and then leave Vladivostok, some with P. A. Tseitlin for Khabarovsk.[27] After several weeks there Tseitlin returned to Vladivostok as the official FER representative in the Maritime Province.[28] Most of the militia and military leaders, as well as some lesser Communist leaders, headed for Anuchino or other partisan strongholds.[29]

Many of the important governmental and Party leaders went to Chita, including V. G. Antonov and V. A. Maslennikov, who reported the circumstances of the coup and the situation in the Maritime Province to the Dalburo.[30] They were then ordered to establish a government in Iman, an area unoccupied by Japanese troops.[31] From this sanctuary their shadow government could serve as an alternative to the newly established Provisional Priamur Government and sign decrees and protests. Most of the socialist members of the Popular Assembly that served under Antonov went to Iman, where they reconvened the assembly in August.[32] Earlier they had voted not to recognize the new government and to boycott its elections,[33] but after an initial outburst of activity, the Antonov government faded into obscurity.

The Whites had shattered the Communist organization and driven what was left of it underground. It will be recalled that with the unification of eastern Siberia around the Chita government, the Maritime Party organization had been substantially weakened by an exodus of its leaders to Chita. Until the coup the most important Party leaders in Vladivostok were V. G. Antonov, V. A. Maslennikov, A. A. Voronin, and P. A. Tseitlin. When these men left for Chita or Khabarovsk, the Maritime Party organization was further weakened and the leadership went to members who generally were less experienced or well known.

In the course of events of May 26 and 27, 1921, a group of Communists created an oblast Revolutionary Committee (Revkom) to carry on the work of the Party in its new, illegal status. V. P. Shishkin, a member of the Party since 1918, was elected chairman, and other members included K. P. Serov, R. Shishliannikov, V. A. Vrublevskii, and Ia. K. Kokushkin.[34] The range of activities included forming revkoms in other White-held cities, such as Nikolsk,[35] reorganizing the Party in Vladivostok, renewing partisan warfare in the areas away from the railway lines and population centers, and organizing political forces and the laboring class in Vladivostok.

With its first directive the Revkom formed a resistance movement in the Maritime Province. It ordered various armed units and individuals within the city to take their weapons, mobilize all possible vessels, and go to Petrovka, located at the head of the Ussuri inlet. From this point they would go inland to join partisan forces.[36] Most of the ships of the Siberian Flotilla were away from Vladivostok at the time, but several in the harbor sailed to the coastal partisan base at Olga.[37]

At the original organizational meeting a division of labor was made to utilize most effectively the abilities of the Communist leaders. The partisan leaders N. K. Iliukhov and V. P. Vladivostokov, who had been in Vladivostok as members of the illegal Defense Council, were sent to organize the partisans.[38] Shishkin remained to oversee organizational activities in Vladivostok, and Serov stayed to work with the Vladivostok unions against the Merkulov regime.[39]

Throughout the Maritime Province the Party was put on a military footing. In Vladivostok, Party reorganization was carried out largely in June, but the measures taken were not always successful because of the effective counterintelligence force.[40] The Party carried on agitprop activities throughout the southern Maritime Province: public organizations were utilized and resolutions were formulated against the Merkulov government and in support of the FER;[41] sabotage was used to destroy mines and factories and to disrupt rail traffic;[42] and special effort was made to infiltrate and propagandize the Kappelite forces, which met with some success,[43] but was cut short with the Merkulov counteroffensive against the Party in October.

The White seizure of the southern Maritime Province precipitated the second partisan struggle (the first having ended with the fall of Kolchak and Rozanov). Since early 1920, the partisans had retained their bases, and later, fearing a White coup, had begun transporting arms and other supplies illegally from Vladivostok to such areas as Suchan.[44] Until May 26, 1921, there was no obvious enemy and many partisans had returned to their villages. With no legal military forces and with the lack of an administrative base where activities could be carried on with relative ease, a new organization had to be created to coordinate the partisan military struggle. At Anuchino, Iliukhov and Vladivostokov received an order from the Dalburo to form the Revolutionary Military Council of Partisans in the Maritime Province (Revvoensovet), which was to be subordinate to the FER military authorities. Military efforts were to be directed against the White government and its armed forces, while conflict with the Japanese was to be avoided.[45] The basis for the authority of the Revvoensovet had already been laid by the oblast Revkom, which had sent directives to various Communist leaders, putting them in battle readiness. As leaders of the insurgent movement, they were to await the arrival of the commander of the partisan detachments.[46] Iliukhov was the commander of all the partisan detachments until mid-July, when he was replaced by A. Lepekhin, former commander of the militia in Vladivostok.[47]

On June 10 Shishkin gave instructions on tactics to use against the Whites to all regional organizations. The partisans were ordered to concentrate on sabotage against the mines and other productive enterprises within their reach, and especially against railway communications.[48] The partisans carried these orders out quite effectively; they did not stop railway traffic completely, but there are numerous press accounts of bridges blown up and other damage done, particularly from July through September.[49] This sort of terrorism and increased khunkhuz banditry was a constant irritant to the government and a danger to individual lives.

Communist leadership and activity were significant in the labor movement, where they had considerable support. They were responsible for the boycott of the elections to the Popular Assembly and the general strike in late July. The Revkom planned the strike[50] to test the resolve of the Japanese to defend the Merkulov government,[51] and when the strikers presented their demands, which included restoring the rights and freedoms under the FER constitution and freeing political prisoners,[52] to the government, they gave it four days to comply. Had the government acceded, it would have committed suicide. The demands were ignored, and the strike commenced, lasting from July 27 to 8:00 A.M. on August 1. This was a violent period, which included much sabotage inside and outside of Vladivostok.[53] Although it was well planned and succeeded in crippling economic and political activity, it failed to topple the Merkulov government. However, Communist writers delighted in relating how the Merkulovs sought refuge on a Japanese ship during the strike, returning only when it was safe.[54]

* * * * *

The Merkulov coup elicited a strong reaction from the FER and Soviet Russia—both governments issued sharply worded protests. On June 1 Chicherin directed a note from the government of the RSFSR to the governments of Great Britain, France, and Italy protesting Japan's complicity in the Merkulov coup and in machinations in other areas, such as Central Asia. He considered these Allied governments equally hostile and accused them of collaborating with the Japanese and therefore responsible for Japan's actions.[55] FER Foreign Minister Ignatius L. Iurin sent a lengthy note to the Japanese government on June 2. Using confident and threatening language, Iurin accused the Japanese government of knowledge of the coup and of aiding the insurgents long before the actual event. He demanded that the Japanese command renounce the Merkulov regime, permit the former government to restore its authority, and arrest those responsible for the overthrow.[56]

More realistic action was taken by the Politburo in Moscow. Krasnoshchekov had previously warned the Soviet authorities that the FER was in danger from internal unrest and external threats. On May 6, for example, he cited the extensive White activities from Central Asia to the Maritime Province and stated that the FER was in jeopardy. He requested diplomatic and material aid and the use of Soviet troops in meeting the dangers his state faced.[57] The Merkulov coup finally caused the Politburo to act decisively. On May 28, 1921, it resolved to dispatch arms and other supplies to Chita, including armored trains, at least one hundred military-political workers, and one of its Siberian divisions for use by the FER. It also sent Vasilii Konstantinovich Bliukher, a leading general in the Red Army, to become commander in chief of the FER forces and minister of war.[58] Most important for the immediate future of the FER, it resolved to concentrate on the defeat of Baron Ungern-Sternberg, who had launched his attack on the Transbaikal area with the object of destroying the FER.[59] This aid proved to be of inestimable value to the FER from July through the winter of 1921–22.

Negotiations with Semenov

Most of the residents of Vladivostok were apathetic toward the Merkulov government. At first the Whites were greeted with some enthusiasm and flag waving; however, the Russians kept two flags, one red and the other tricolor, to hand out as the occasion demanded.[60] The population lapsed into passivity after the May 26 coup—they had no confidence in the government or in its ability to survive and simply wanted to be left alone. The negotiations between the government and Semenov, who had come from Port Arthur,[61] caused some stirring because most people in Vladivostok had little liking or sympathy for the Ataman. In their eyes he was much worse than the White government that had been imposed on them by the Kappelites.

As previously noted, in exchange for financial support for non-socialist political activities and support of his loyalists for the coup, Semenov was supposed to become commander in chief of the armed forces and retain his title of Field Ataman of the Cossacks. He has claimed that the Merkulovs wired him before the coup not to come to Vladivostok because he was being excluded from the government. Semenov questioned General Savelev on this matter and was assured that the agreement was still in effect, the army expected his arrival, and the coup must proceed. Semenov asserted that when he requested permission to depart for Vladivostok from the Japanese they told him he was unacceptable because of his lack of support there. He found it difficult to charter a vessel, and a storm during the voyage caused a further delay, which was critical to his cause.[62]

There is no doubt that Semenov had been double-crossed. Troops loyal to Semenov had contributed to the success of the coup, and they expected him to be the leader of the armed forces.[63] But the Kappelites told S. Merkulov that his group would be allowed to head the government only if they would exclude Semenov from the government and appoint General Verzhbitskii commander in chief instead.[64]

If the Kappelites had their plans, so too did Semenov. He formed a cabinet from his supporters in Harbin, and soon they appeared in Vladivostok. Semenov did not arrive until June 3, when the opportunity for an initiative on his behalf had passed; nevertheless, he proclaimed himself commander in chief and Field Ataman of the Cossacks and renewed his claim to be Kolchak's successor,[65] a claim clearly in conflict with the Provisional Priamur Government. The atmosphere in Vladivostok from Semenov's arrival to his departure on June 25 was very tense—only the presence of Japanese troops prevented an armed conflict. Meanwhile, there were many plans and consultations within the government and aboard Semenov's chartered vessel, the *Kiodo Maru*, over the future of the Ataman.

Semenov's plan, after establishing his power in Vladivostok, was to launch an offensive against the FER both in the direction of Khabarovsk and west across Manchuria. He realized shortly after arriving at Vladivostok that his position was weak and that he had better salvage what he could. At any rate, negotiations had to be carried on to allow both sides to extract themselves from the impasse. Semenov was not allowed off the *Kiodo Maru*. Kappelite leaders threatened to join the partisans in the hills or go to Khabarovsk before they would subordinate themselves to Semenov. The Consular Corps and the Vladivostok city duma both protested Semenov's arrival,[66] and on June 10 the Cossack Conference in Grodekovo, formerly the heart of Semenov's base of power, declared its opposition to Semenov's presence in the Maritime Province.[67] The Japanese had fully supported Semenov, but now recognized the impossibility of imposing him upon the Whites. They were only lukewarm to the Merkulov government and never did extend diplomatic recognition to it. Now they tried to mediate between the two parties to effect a reconciliation.

By the middle of June Semenov had given up any idea of establishing his base in Vladivostok.[68] On June 15 he had a five-hour conversation with S. Merkulov, and he agreed not to participate in the government nor lead its troops. Rather, he would organize his forces for an offensive against the Transbaikal region. He did not have the means, however, for such a large undertaking and sought 400,000 gold rubles and half the value of the cargo held in the Vladivostok warehouses from the Merkulovs. The government's response was that it would divide the cargo if Semenov would give the government half of what he carried out of the Transbaikal region,[69] referring, of course, to the gold the Kappelites had turned over to Semenov for safekeeping.

On June 16 Merkulov authorized Rudnev to offer Semenov a large sum if he would leave Vladivostok and plan his offensive somewhere other than in the Maritime Province.[70] Semenov responded with his own demands and the ludicrous ultimatum that if the government would not satisfy these demands, he would declare the Merkulovs enemies of the people and feel free to act in any way he saw fit. Semenov again demanded 400,000 gold rubles, a sum the government could not possibly pay, and also asked for the right to move to the Transbaikal territory via Grodekovo and Pogranichnaia.[71]

The Merkulovs sought support for their position by arranging for the nonsocialists to meet again in Vladivostok. The Second Nonsocialist Congress, chaired by Ivan Artemev, opened on June 17. During the days that it met, its members debated the merits of the government's position. Simultaneously negotiations were being carried on between the two parties, and the Japanese were trying to work out a compromise. Early in the congress Semenov had considerable support for his position—an offensive against the FER was attractive, and the Merkulovs' highhanded ways were resented. On June 22 Prince A. A. Krapotkin offered a resolution of confidence in the government. Resenting one of Semenov's general's (Tolmachev) seeking Japanese aid in the disposition of the goods in Vladivostok and Semenov's ultimatum to the government,[72] the delegates passed it.

The negotiations that had been taking place were no closer to a solution satisfactory to both parties. On June 25 in a well-planned and well-executed move, Semenov secretly left the *Kiodo Maru,* assisted by the Japanese and his loyal supporters, and went to Grodekovo.[73] This was unnerving and embarrassing for the Merkulovs and the Kappelites because Semenov had slipped out from under very tight security arrangements, and the government had no idea what he was up to. In retaliation the frightened government began arresting his supporters and taking other measures, but the worst fears did not materialize. There was intensive politicking by the two sides in the next month or two, and one major clash occurred between the Kappelite militia and a force of Semenovites on their way to join Semenov in Grodekovo.[74]

July and August must have been very depressing for the Ataman. He was an ambitious man, but he was also genuine in his desire to defeat communism by launching an offensive against the FER. His struggle with the Merkulovs had cost his cause time and had contributed to the defeat of Ungern-Sternberg in Mongolia because much needed supplies and reinforcements could not be sent. Semenov had gone to Vladivostok perhaps with the expectation that a combination of his supporters and the Japanese would put him in charge of both government and armed forces; at least he expected to have a base of operations in the Maritime Province. The dispute with the government had cost him support among the nonsocialists as well as among the Cossack population in Grodekovo and along the Ussuri River, who feared an outbreak of civil war among the Whites themselves. After an intense struggle within Cossack circles, representatives from the

Cossack units held a conference and in July passed a resolution condemning Semenov for not leaving the Maritime Province, as they had recommended in a June 10 resolution, and for other acts not in Cossack interests. The resolution stripped Semenov of his honorary title of "Field Ataman," which the Cossacks had awarded him earlier in the year.[75]

Finally, Semenov attempted to make an arrangement with Manchurian warlord Chang Tso-lin for assistance in transporting his troops across Manchuria for the offensive against the FER; due to pressure from Peking and Washington, this aid was refused.[76] The Japanese at this time were not prepared to back a Semenovite venture and, therefore, did not intervene with Chang on Semenov's behalf. The United States, meanwhile, had called a conference to meet in Washington to discuss Pacific affairs, including the Siberian situation. To preempt the purpose of this conference and make a more favorable arrangement with the FER, Japan had arranged to meet with FER representatives at Dairen. Thus Japan's efforts were directed toward diplomatic, rather than military methods. With his support melted away and having no more money for the maintenance of himself and his army, Semenov sent his chief of staff, Ivanov-Rinov, to Vladivostok to negotiate his departure from the Maritime Province,[77] and on September 13 Semenov's army subordinated itself to the Provisional Priamur Government.[78] On September 14, 1921, Semenov left Grodekovo, and a few days later he left the Maritime Province, ending his political life in Russia.[79] He resided and intrigued in Japan and Manchuria until the end of World War II, when he was captured by Soviet troops, tried, and executed.

In addition to the conflict with Semenov, the Merkulovs were also challenged by the moderates, including the Democratic Union, the Peasants, the SRs, and others. They supported the government regarding the exclusion of Semenov but wanted to retain the Popular Assembly and install a coalition cabinet. S. Merkulov had originally expressed his desire to retain the Popular Assembly, and the moderates had pressed him to do so, but overnight he changed his mind, dissolved the assembly, and called for new elections.[80] This action caused frantic activity by Boldyrev, A. N. Kruglikov, and Kurtev, who held several private conferences with Merkulov, who remained resolute.[81]

The moderate parties organized the Conference of Democratic Parties and Organizations of Vladivostok to uphold the rights of the Popular Assembly and to support moderate demands.[82] The conference drew up a list of demands, which Boldyrev then presented to S. Merkulov. They called for a responsible cabinet headed by a prime minister and made up of a coalition of two nonsocialists, two Peasants, one Cossack, and two others to be decided upon later. The Popular Assembly was to be reinstituted so that it could dissolve itself legally in preparation for the new elections. Finally, Semenov was to be excluded from the territory under the government's jurisdiction and a policy of civil peace with no offensive action against the FER was to be established. The government ignored the demands. The conference invited Kappelite Generals Verzhbitskii, Molchanov, and F. A. Puchkov to attend its final session. They stated their disapproval of any changes in the government, undoubtedly because of the negotiations in progress with Semenov.[83]

Elections for a New Popular Assembly

Elections for a new Popular Assembly were held in the second week of July 1921. The election laws were substantially the same as for the election of June 1920 except for a change in the age requirement and the prohibition against Communists and their sympathizers. A total of 160 seats were to be filled, Vladivostok being awarded 35 of them, but only about 70 delegates were actually elected because seats were assigned to villages and cities, such as Khabarovsk, which were under Communist control and did not recognize the Merkulov government.[84]

Although the Communists had been prohibited from participating in the election, they could have run on a union list; however, through their influence, the workers held a conference on June 26 and voted 222 to 7 to boycott the elections.[85] Understandably, fewer votes were cast than in June 1920, and the Popular Assembly was more conservative. In June 1920 the votes in Vladivostok totaled 28,853; in this election the total was 19,334, several thousand of which were Kappelite votes.[86] One observer noted that Kappelites came to the polls bearing the number "7," the number of the National Democratic list.[87] This accounts for the large conservative vote, which was reasonable because the government was installed by the Kappelites, and it was to their benefit to support it. Out of the seventy-odd seats that were filled, the National Democrats and their allies gained over forty; the more moderate Democratic Union gained eight; the Left Peasants, ten; the SRs, four, and the remaining seats were scattered among the other names on the election list.[88]

The Popular Assembly as envisioned by the Merkulovs was to be neither an effective body nor one of long duration. On July 8, 1921, the government issued Ukase No. 27 containing the regulations for the assembly. The limitations in this document were reminiscent of the restrictions on the Duma under the tsar. Legislative initiative belonged to the Popular Assembly, the Provisional Priamur Government, and the Council of Department Heads, but any legislation had to be approved by the government. When the Popular Assembly was not in session, the government could issue ukases and resolutions, but when the assembly opened, the government's actions had to be presented for approval. However, certain regulations could not be changed by the Popular Assembly, such as the ones concerning the Popular Assembly itself, elections, and the government.[89] The Popular Assembly was to meet for a one-year term only. This was understandable because the first obligation of the Popular Assembly, as stated by S. Merkulov in his speech before its first session, was to draw up election laws for a constituent assembly.[90] This cause was constantly in the minds of non-Bolsheviks since Lenin had dissolved Russia's only Constituent Assembly early in 1918. The Constituent Assembly would determine the final form of government for eastern Siberia, write a constitution, and thus establish a new political form in direct competition with Chita.

The Popular Assembly opened with religious services, the first official body to do so since tsarist times. According to Boldyrev, a quorum was not present because the Peasant Group had not yet arrived; nevertheless, it began its session, and Prince Krapotkin was elected its president. Spiridon Merkulov outlined the goals of the assembly and called for cooperation with the government, and General Verzhbitskii welcomed the assembly on behalf of the army. Other speeches full of high-sounding phrases were delivered, but nothing of substance was accomplished in this session nor in the first months of the Popular Assembly's existence.[91] Rather, it turned into a debating society in which the opposition, usually led by F. S. Mansvetov, a Socialist Revolutionary, attacked a particular policy of the government or hurled charges of corruption at it. The government's supporters would respond, and name-calling would erupt.

Not surprisingly, the first obligation, to write election laws for a constituent assembly, was forgotten. The Whites now had a government, but there were no spontaneous popular uprisings leading to the breakup of the FER as expected, and very few people, even within nonsocialist circles, showed any enthusiasm for the Merkulov government. It would have served no useful purpose to call a constituent assembly for such an inconsequential territory with a government whose days were clearly numbered. Even if the Merkulovs were replaced, who would lead the new government? The best-known non-Communists in the Russian Far East—George Guins, former member of the short-lived Omsk government; Nikolai VLvovich Gondatti, former governor general of the Priamur region; and General Dmitrii Leonidovich Horvath, the most influential Russian in Harbin—had refused to hold office, and, as Andrushkevich lamented, no member of the Romanov family showed the slightest interest in leading the White cause in Siberia.[92] Robbed of its role by circumstances, all the assembly could do was meet and debate.

The next major political change occurred in September with the selection of a full cabinet. The Merkulovs, responding to pressure from moderates and nonsocialists, instructed V. F. Ivanov to form a cabinet.[93] Ivanov, a lawyer and an accomplished orator, had been valuable to the government in the Popular Assembly.[94] According to Rudnev, the Merkulovs did not really want Ivanov in that position, but they accepted him because his name was advanced by the new Non-

Socialist Council.[95] The new cabinet included Ivanov as prime minister and director of internal affairs, V. Kolesnikov as director of foreign affairs, and K. T. Likhoidov as director of finance. The other members were lesser-known figures selected from both conservative and moderate nonsocialists.[96] The military leaders did not sit in the cabinet, but rather were responsible directly to the Merkulovs.

This cabinet did not bolster morale or dampen rumors that the Communists would march into Vladivostok momentarily. These rumors, particularly widespread during August and September 1921, were strengthened by two factors: the negotiations between the FER and Japan, and a coup that was, in fact, being planned by the Communists.

Negotiations at Dairen

The negotiations at Dairen between the FER and Japan represented one phase of a larger, more complex diplomatic struggle between Russia, the United States, and Japan. Russia had two objectives: to utilize the American-Japanese rivalry to force Japan out of the Maritime Province and to obtain U.S. recognition of the Soviet government. This desire for recognition underlay Lenin's granting of concessions to American business concerns. Publicly Lenin justified his policy as providing needed economic development, but in Party circles he stressed its tactical nature.[97] Two large concessions were granted by the Communists in the Russian Far East—one to Washington B. Vanderlip on the Kamchatka Peninsula, and the other to Sinclair Oil on northern Sakhalin. The Kamchatka Peninsula legally did not belong to Soviet Russia but was claimed by the newly formed Far Eastern Republic on April 6, 1920, a claim approved by the Soviet government in its telegram of May 14, 1920.[98] The inclusion of the Kamchatka Peninsula in the FER was reiterated in the declaration of the Chita unity conference at the end of October 1920,[99] but by then negotiations were under way in Moscow to grant mineral rights to Vanderlip.[100] The close working relationship between the two governments, however, allowed an easy transfer of the Kamchatka Peninsula from the FER to Soviet Russia. On December 15, 1920, they signed a treaty establishing their mutual borders, and Kamchatka was excluded from the territory of the FER.[101] Nothing concrete was or could be accomplished by this transfer because the Japanese were effectively in control of the peninsula. A concession was similarly granted by the FER to the Sinclair Exploration Company to exploit the oil reserves on the northern (Russian) half of Sakhalin and to develop two ports on the eastern coast of the island.[102] This also was a paper agreement because the Japanese occupied the Russian half of the island in July and August 1920.[103] Both Vanderlip and the Sinclair agreements were conditional upon diplomatic recognition of the Soviet government by the United States.[104]

The United States distrusted the Soviet government, but pursued a policy of promoting Russian territorial integrity, largely because of its objection to Japanese expansion in the Far East. In numerous diplomatic moves the United States government attempted to put pressure on Japan to withdraw from Siberia. On May 31, 1921, after the White coup, the State Department sent a memorandum to Japan reminding it of previous commitments to withdraw and its failure to live up to these commitments.[105]

Two other diplomatic activities, one American and one Japanese, were even more important. The first was a series of moves aimed at displaying American interest in the FER and establishing unofficial contacts with it. A fact-finding mission was dispatched to the Russian Far East led by Lieutenant Colonel William J. Davis, the assistant military attaché in the American embassy in Tokyo, and James F. Abbott, the commercial attaché there. The two men spent several days in May and all of June in Chita and sent back a flattering (and naïve) report stressing the FER's independence, its Siberian character, and its friendliness toward the United States.[106] This was followed by an "exchange" of unofficial representatives. The State Department sent an observer to Chita—John K. Caldwell, consul at Kobe, Japan, and former consul in Vladivostok.[107] In exchange, FER representatives, ostensibly a trade delegation, were given permission to appear unofficially at the forthcoming Washington Conference on armaments in November.[108] The Washington Conference was called primarily at the instigation of the United States to deal with postwar questions in

the Far East. Although the Siberian problem would be considered,
Russia was not invited, which brought numerous protests from Moscow
beginning on July 19, 1921.[109] Nevertheless, Soviet interests would
be unofficially represented by the FER delegation, an American move
designed to put pressure on the Japanese. Of all the Russian groups
outside of Soviet Russia claiming to represent Russian interests,
the FER representatives made the most diplomatic gains with the
United States, receiving a hearing with the Russian Division of the
State Department[110] and appearing at the Washington Conference.
The FER delegation also made speeches and published numerous
pamphlets describing, among other topics, Japanese misconduct in
Siberia, the commercial potential in the Russian Far East, and the
institutional structure of the Far Eastern Republic.[111]

The second notable diplomatic activity was the continuing Japanese effort to obtain some concessions in Siberia. There were reports
of talks between Japanese and FER representatives prior to the White
coup of May 26, 1921. This coup may be viewed in part as pressure
applied upon Chita by the Japanese for a more favorable agreement.
As remarked before, this brought an inevitable protest from the FER
on June 2, but the protest to Japan also stated the desire to "discuss
the abnormal conditions . . . [and] arrive at a decision satisfactory
to both."[112] On July 13 the FER sent a formal note to Japan asking
for negotiations.[113] Meanwhile, informal discussions were being held
in Harbin between Japanese Vice-Consul Shimoda and FER Deputy
Foreign Minister Kozhevnikov and Councilor O. Somov.[114] These
diplomatic moves resulted in the Dairen Conference, which opened on
August 26, 1921. Chita sought Japanese withdrawal from territory it
claimed; Japan, feeling the pressure of the forthcoming Washington
Conference, sought a favorable political and commercial agreement.

The negotiations at Dairen were prolonged and barren; they are of
interest here only insofar as they reflect Japanese aims and affect
Vladivostok's interests. The major conflict, which ultimately brought
the talks to an unsuccessful conclusion on April 16, 1922, concerned
the evacuation of Japanese troops. The FER position was that evacuation should begin immediately and be completed no later than one

month after an agreement was concluded. This was one of twenty-nine articles contained in a draft treaty presented to the Japanese delegation on September 6.[115] Other articles called for mutual recognition, the exchange of diplomatic and consular personnel, and the recognition of the Open Door principle. Several articles of the draft treaty indicated that Japan would be able to gain favorable commercial arrangements.[116]

Japan's counterproposal was handed to the FER delegation late in September. These were the famous Seventeen Demands, reminiscent of Japan's diplomatic style as embodied in the more famous Twenty-One Demands presented to China in 1915. Both involved Japan's attempt to press demands upon a weaker opponent in strictest secrecy, and the result of both would have been a considerable loss of sovereignty to their victims. The Seventeen Demands (plus three secret demands) were, in the main, conditions for withdrawal that had been drawn up at a cabinet meeting on May 13, 1921, and as such represented an extreme expansionist policy. Vladivostok would have been affected in several ways. Without consulting the Provisional Priamur Government, Japan would have transformed Vladivostok into an international port and turned the territory it claimed over to the FER. Japan would have gained nearly unrestricted access to the natural resources of the entire area east of Lake Baikal and complete freedom to exploit the northern half of Sakhalin Island for a period of eighty years. In addition, the new state would be crippled militarily; its coast would be demilitarized and Japanese military missions would be able to roam at will. The only mention of evacuation was contained in the secret articles. The Japanese would evacuate the Maritime Province "at a time which in its own judgment will be convenient, when this shall be necessary."[117]

It was no wonder that the negotiations soon became deadlocked and the delegations stopped meeting in mid-October. These negotiations made the city's population very uneasy, for had the two sides come to an agreement calling for Japanese evacuation, Red troops most assuredly would have swept through the southern Maritime region with little difficulty. Japanese residents in the Russian Far East for many years were also concerned because the Japanese intervention had transformed them into unwanted aliens. In late November a number of Japanese residents met in Vladivostok and called for the organization of a self-defense corps, improved Russo-Japanese relations, and Japanese protection of their interests.[118]

The Reds Prepare a Coup

While Communists at Dairen were trying diplomatically to remove the Japanese and the Merkulov government, the Maritime Communists were laying the groundwork for a *coup d'état* in Vladivostok. In mid-July the Dalburo directed the Revvoensovet of Partisan Detachments to organize a "spontaneous" uprising within the Kappelite forces in conjunction with a Communist coup in Vladivostok. It also recommended the creation in Vladivostok of a military center headed by experienced Party leaders. N. K. Iliukhov was to direct this illegal staff, and V. P. Shishkin and P. A. Tseitlin were to assist him. According to Iliukhov, his staff was very successful in establishing cells in almost all Kappelite detachments and in gaining sympathy of some officers. In August the question of the uprising was discussed and within a month preparations for it were completed. The Dalburo and the Revvoensovet were both informed of this.[119]

The coup was set for mid-October; however, the government's counterintelligence discovered the plans before the uprising could take place. Communist sources differ as to why the information leaked out, but they all blame a certain Darello (or Dorello or Derello) who had replaced R. Shishliannikov in the oblast Revkom some time in the late summer or early autumn.[120] Iliukhov accused him of being a double agent planted by the government.[121] K. P. Serov of the Revkom stated that Darello divulged information under torture.[122] Whatever the truth, after his arrest on October 15, he revealed a great deal of information about the Communists' plans, and the government began rounding up the conspirators. Iliukhov has described how he and Shishkin, after learning of the betrayal, sent orders to Party members to change their locations and to all activists within the Kappelite units to stop recruiting and be on guard. By then it was too late and arrests began within the military units as well.[123]

Once again the Merkulov government had shattered the Communist organization. After this, the Communists gave up any idea of attempting a coup in Vladivostok and concentrated instead on building up the partisan forces outside the city. Iliukhov and Shishkin were directed to leave Vladivostok, and only a skeleton Communist cell remained.[124]

August and September were grim months for the Merkulov government. The conference at Dairen had made it appear as if its days were numbered and there was little for support or confidence in the government. The khunkhuzes were terrorizing the southern Maritime Province, and the partisans were very active, dynamiting the railway lines on an average of six times per week.[125]

Not even the arrival on September 23, 1921, of refugees from European Russia, including soldiers and sailors, was cheering news. There had been a great deal of diplomatic activity and rumor regarding the transfer of Wrangel's defeated army to Vladivostok in order to renew the offensive against the Bolsheviks, but there was little enthusiasm for the project. It was reported that the services of Wrangel's army of 42,000 men, half of whom were officers, were offered to the Provisional Priamur Government if it would share the expense of the army's transportation. The French government was no longer willing to support the Wrangelites,[126] the British were not interested in the adventure, and the United States would not even allow Wrangel to use its channels of communication to negotiate with Vladivostok.[127] Even the Merkulovs were not enthusiastic. Foreign Affairs Department Head Kolesnikov wired the Russian Consul in Paris that the government simply did not have the financial resources to pay the transportation costs, let alone the upkeep once the army arrived.[128] The Soviet leaders were upset by the rumors and made charges of collusion on the part of the Allies, especially the French and Japanese. It was about this same time that the FER and Soviet leaders charged that a secret agreement had been made between the Japanese, the French, and Semenov.[129] This seems doubtful. There may have been discussions, but the best argument against the existence of any formal agreement is that nothing resulted.

In any case, Wrangel's army was not transferred to Vladivostok. Only about nine hundred persons, most of them originally from Siberia, were transported to Vladivostok from the Crimea at British expense. These refugees included about two hundred sailors and eighty to one hundred officers from the former Caspian Fleet, a number of Ural Cossacks, and women and children.[130] This was hardly a formidable armed force, although the personnel of the Siberian Flotilla was substantially augmented by the addition of so many skilled seamen.[131]

Government and military leaders had little choice of direction in the fall of 1921. Either the government would be overthrown, die a slow death, or pursue a more aggressive policy in order to restore confidence and, if possible, generate some enthusiasm among the population.

6

The Winter Offensive and Its Aftermath
November 1921-May 1922

THE WINTER offensive of 1921–22 expanded the territory under the jurisdiction of the Provisional Priamur Government, an aggression agreeably coincident with the aims and necessities of the Japanese expansionists. Now that Semenov had been outmaneuvered and had retired from the scene, they had to deal with the Merkulov regime. The Japanese might have been more willing to back the Merkulov government had it enjoyed more public support. However, it was not popular, was too attached to the Kappelite command, and had faced too much opposition, including opposition from the Semenovites. Nevertheless, this government was all the Japanese military had, and they had to manipulate it as best they could to pursue their goals.

The principal diplomatic events of this period were the Dairen Conference (August 26, 1921, to April 16, 1922) and the Washington Conference (November 12, 1921, to February 6, 1922). The winter offensive of the Provisional Priamur Government served the interests of the Japanese expansionists at Dairen, who wanted to see the talks there fail. But if an agreement with the Far Eastern Republic (FER) were to emerge, they wanted it to contain as many of the Seventeen Demands as possible. Therefore, the more pressure applied to the FER, the better for Japanese expansionist goals. To this end the early success of the White movement was useful. The White expansion also helped Japanese interests at the Washington Conference because it demonstrated that Siberia was still unsettled and required Japanese troops to protect Japanese lives and to keep order. It was clear why Japanese military officers were behind most of the White moves and also why Japanese participation in such activities was denied by Japan's diplomats, who wanted to ease their troops out of Siberia and improve Japan's relations with the world's powers.

The height of the White offensive was the capture of Khabarovsk in December 1921. It would appear to the casual observer that the goal of the Whites from the beginning had been to march on Khabarovsk and farther—to Blagoveshchensk, Verkhneudinsk, even to Moscow. This is a view shared by both Communist and non-Communist writers.[1] Evidence, however, points to White expansion proceeding in stages, some unrelated in origin to others, and that the offensive against Khabarovsk was not decided upon until mid-November.

The first plans for expansion were made shortly after the May 26 coup. The Merkulov government claimed the Kamchatka Peninsula and in June 1921 formed the Okhotsk-Kamchatka Conference, headed by Rudnev, to coordinate the government's plans for the area. The creation of the conference, according to Rudnev, originated with two representatives who came to Vladivostok to represent the population of Kamchatka.[2] The outcome of the conference's planning was the expedition sent to Kamchatka in August to enforce the Priamur Government's claim to the peninsula.

This expedition apparently originated with Bochkarev, a Cossack and former Kalmykovite officer.[3] According to Rudnev, he seemed to unite the two most typical traits of the Cossacks—reckless courage and a passion for accumulating wealth.[4] Bochkarev, by all accounts, was a scoundrel interested only in plunder, but the idea of an expedition to seize Kamchatka Peninsula found much support in the ruling circles of Vladivostok, who viewed the Kamchatka Peninsula as a last retreat. They realized its importance to the Japanese, who controlled it at the time, and thought there was a possibility of establishing a protectorate under the Japanese if the Communists took control of Vladivostok.[5] There is some evidence that the Japanese gave aid to the Kamchatka venture.[6] At any rate, the expedition could not have proceeded without the Japanese permitting it, and it must have pleased them because the establishment of White power on Kamchatka Peninsula made the FER-RSFSR treaty and the Vanderlip concession appear as meaningless as they were.

The expedition occupied Petropavlovsk on September 10, 1921, bringing the area nominally under the control of the Provisional Priamur Government. Bochkarev was the military governor, and Khristian Birich, a Vladivostok landlord, was the civilian governor. Drinking and plundering seem to have been the major activities of the Bochkarevites,[7] and some people thought that Bochkarev had been sent to Kamchatka to free Vladivostok of him and his unruly followers.[8] They made so many enemies that they were overthrown the following summer; Bochkarev was killed by some villagers, and Birich was executed by the Communists in Vladivostok in 1923.[9]

The Merkulov government similarly claimed the northern half of Sakhalin Island, but it was not necessary to send an expedition because the Japanese had already installed first a military government and then a civilian government there. Instead, a representative was sent to establish a claim,[10] which the Japanese permitted to show that as it was not under the control of the FER, the FER could not grant mineral concessions on the island.

The White expansion in the Maritime Province itself was more serious. The original plan, limited in scope and primarily defensive, had as its goal the seizure of the partisan strongholds around Olga, the Suchan mines, and the Anuchino valley. The object was to stop partisan and khunkhuz attacks on the rail lines and on the Maritime population. This is not to say that the partisans and khunkhuzes worked together or even cooperated. As previously pointed out, some khunkhuzes were originally poor Chinese hired and armed by the Japanese to stir up trouble. By their very nature, however, they were not always reliable and sometimes plundered on their own or with the partisans.

The first major partisan stronghold the Whites seized was the Suchan region. White soldiers had occupied Suchan peacefully in mid-August, but had not intended to do any more than bring the coal mines under Vladivostok's control.[11] The offensive of early November, however, was designed to destroy the partisan headquarters in the area and drive out the partisans led by M. P. Volskii. General N. P. Sakharov and a force of about six hundred fifty men easily and effectively accomplished this goal.[12] Another offensive in the Prikhankai region south of Lake Khanka by two- to three-hundred men resulted in the removal of the partisans there led by E. V. Lebedev.[13] This early and rapid success led to the formation of plans for an offensive in the southern Maritime Province.

On November 10, 1921, General Verzhbitskii, head of the military and naval departments and commander of the White forces, ordered a general attack on the remaining partisan strongholds in the southern Maritime Province. Admiral Stark and his Siberian Flotilla were to attack and seize the port of Olga, capturing any vessels there; the First Corps was to link up with General Sakharov and his men north of Suchan; the larger Second Corps would march on Iakovlevka and Anuchino; General Molchanov and his men were to destroy the partisans northeast of Suchan, including around Frolovka and Sergeevka; and another unit would clean the partisans out of the area south of Suchan.[14]

The first step in this large operation was the seizure of Olga, whose importance was twofold. An important supply source for the partisan base at Suchan, it also served as a port for the several ships with Bolshevik-dominated crews that either left Vladivostok or were at sea at the time of the White coup. These ships and the ships of the Amur River Fleet together made up the navy of the FER. The vessels working out of Olga patrolled the coast, but, more importantly, gathered intelligence on White activity and relayed this information via an effective communications network to Chita.[15]

Admiral Stark and his party arrived at Olga on November 14 and met little resistance. About three hundred partisans protected the area, but the Whites easily took the base, seized all the ships the Communists held there, and inflicted heavy casualties on the partisans.[16]

Anuchino was the nerve center of the Communist and partisan

operations in the southern Maritime Province. The FER armed forces were not allowed in the territory south of Iman because of the April 29, 1920, agreement and because of the presence of Japanese forces at Sviiagino Station. All activities below Iman were directed, and for the most part supplied, from Anuchino. Logically this was the major target of the November offensive, and most White troops were thrown into this enterprise.

Anuchino was defended by about one thousand partisans.[17] The aim of the operation was to annihilate the partisans and destroy their bases. The Whites began to group for the offensive on November 15 and launched the attack a few days later. They met little resistance and soon swept through their assigned regions; Anuchino fell without a struggle on November 23, 1921.[18] Within three weeks the White army easily forced the partisans out of their strongholds and destroyed their bases and supply and communications networks. General Molchanov did not consider the Anuchino operation successful because the partisans had not been annihilated, but nevertheless White spirits were lifted immeasurably and their prestige was raised somewhat in the eyes of the Maritime population.[19]

Success again increased ambition. White leaders now turned their eyes farther north, and so, too, did their protectors, the Japanese, who suggested that the Whites attack Iman and seize the city for the Provisional Priamur Government.[20] This was readily accepted and plans were quickly made. Such an undertaking now transformed the White movement into an offensive operation. White authority extended along the Ussuri Railway line only as far as Spassk. The Japanese controlled the railway line up to and including Ussuri Station, but the villages and towns along the way did not recognize Vladivostok's authority and would have to be seized militarily. This was accomplished even more easily than the march through the partisan territory to the south. There was less military resistance, except between Ussuri Station and Iman, where the FER People's Revolutionary Army (PRA) had about five hundred fifty men.[21] This was a neutral zone guarded by the PRA, while the area north of Iman was FER territory defended by the PRA. In effect, therefore, Ussuri Station was the front line of defense, but it was obviously weakly guarded. By December 5 the Whites had taken Iman and were laying plans to march farther north.[22] On December 8, 1921, Verzhbitskii issued an order to attack Khabarovsk,[23] which the Whites occupied just two weeks later on December 22. This victory raised White spirits to new heights. Khabarovsk now was seen as only another step—there was even talk of marching on Moscow. The White drive did in fact push beyond Khabarovsk almost to In Station, but by the end of December Molchanov was ordered to limit his activities to the Khabarovsk area, that is, to turn to a strictly defensive operation.[24] Once this happened, the spirit that had kept the Whites going was broken and was never regained. Even if Molchanov had been allowed to pursue the Reds, he probably could not have gone farther than Blagoveshchensk; the Whites were at the end of their tether, and the Reds were preparing to reverse the situation in their favor.

Strengths and Weaknesses of the White Offensive

At this point it is necessary to analyze the nature of the White offensive, why it succeeded as it did, and why the partisans and PRA failed to stop the White offensive much earlier, or at least to offer some resistance.

From the beginning the White operations were kept secret from the public, the Popular Assembly, and even some members of the government. This served three purposes: the first was military—the enemy was caught by surprise, adding considerably to the success of the offensive; the second and third were political—the Merkulov government seized power with a promise of no civil war and could not admit to the incitement of one, which, of course, it was doing, as its opponents were quick to point out[25] (the first official statement regarding the White offensive was not made until December 9,[26] and yet the government had been on the offensive from early November); the third reason involved wishful thinking, self-delusion, and faulty intelligence. The Whites hoped to create a reverse partisan situation, believing there was widespread hatred of Communist rule and that, given the hope of overthrowing the Communists, the peasants would rally to the White cause. The plan was to attack the Communists, incite local uprisings, and move in to liberate the areas. The Whites involved in the operations were called *belopovstantsy* (White insurgents), a term representing both the hope that there would be popular insurgencies and propaganda to give the impression that these insurgencies were, indeed, occurring. It fooled no one; people soon knew that these were White army operations.

There could have been no White offensive without able leadership and willing armed forces. The over-all planning was done mainly by the Kappelite leaders and the forces used were mainly Kappelites with some Semenovites. The leaders realized they could not win over the peasantry without strict discipline and popular goals—they could not repeat the ways and errors of the Semenovites, Kalmykovites, and similar groups. There would be no requisitioning of peasant property; all goods taken were paid for with yen or silver and strict rules were enforced against pillage and rape. FER taxes were abolished in the FER territory occupied. Popular slogans were used, such as "Down with the plunderers—hands off peasant property!"; "Hail to the All-Russian National Constituent Assembly!"; and many, many more.[27] The Whites were unsuccessful in their attempt to rally the peasants to their cause, but at least the peasants did not actively oppose White control.

The Whites had a larger armed force in the Maritime region than the Communists, a force estimated variously at between ten and fifteen thousand, but the White units were never up to strength. Therefore, it is probably more realistic to say that they fielded an army of seven- to nine-thousand men, while the Communists had a partisan force in the southern Maritime Province of perhaps two thousand at the most, and FER units in the northern Maritime-Priamur region probably totaled no more than a few thousand.[28] The Whites also had the military advantage because they were better organized. At the time of the White offensive General Bliukher, FER commander in chief and minister of war, was at Dairen, and Seryshev, the FER commander of the Eastern Front, as it came to be called, was in Chita. The leadership of the FER People's Revolutionary Army was inexperienced and lacked authority.[29]

There could have been no White offensive without Japanese approval and aid. The Japanese certainly approved, possibly even suggested,[30] the original aim of clearing the southern Maritime Province of partisans, and urged moving north once it was accomplished. Japanese aid, however, was not dependable; a great deal was promised, but much less was given, and then it was given only in small portions.[31] White Chief of Staff General Puchkov has stated that the Japanese gave the Russians small quantities of arms from the weapons stored in Vladivostok[32] and General Molchanov reported that they sold the Whites some weapons prior to the May 26, 1921, coup for 30,000 rubles.[33] They also had weapons purchased in Shanghai and thousands of rifles and other supplies taken from the partisans and FER forces in the course of the offensive.[34] The Whites, therefore, had sufficient arms and ammunition, with the expectation of more from the Japanese, to enable them to struggle for two months all the way to Volochaevka.

Japanese support for the offensive was likewise inconsistent. Sometimes they stopped trains, at other times they let them pass. B. B. Filimonov has described how the Japanese gave Colonel Popov a brief interrogation on December 1, informing him of certain restrictions, and then invited him to their officers' mess and drank to the White success. In late November the Japanese disarmed the Whites at Ussuri Station and made them return to their barracks, but let them leave the same evening to protect the rear of their advancing comrades. Filimonov concluded that such actions served two purposes— to show the FER that the April 29 agreement was being kept and to remind the Whites that the Japanese were still in control.[35]

There were other weaknesses among the partisans that aided the White drive through the Maritime Province. It has already been seen how the transfer of Party leaders to Chita weakened the Vladivostok government; the same was true of the partisans. Former partisans noted how in each of the partisan areas attacked by the Whites, the partisan leadership was weak. From October 1921, when the Merkulovs crushed the Communists in Vladivostok, until January or February 1922, the partisan leaders were torn by personal rivalries, factionalism, and, at least among some, an independent spirit leading to insubordination.[36]

In December Aleksei K. Flegontov was sent into the Maritime region by the Dalburo to head the partisan Voensovet (Military Council). His task was to pick up the pieces and build a new partisan movement, which was fairly well accomplished by March or April. He also was instructed to bring the partisans firmly under the political and military direction of the Communists.[37]

The People's Revolutionary Army (PRA) was similarly disorganized and leaderless. The military authorities were clearly taken by surprise—Bliukher was at Dairen and Seryshev was in Chita. Two popular, talented leaders heading the forces of the PRA in the Priamur area was a basic cause of disunity and with both absent, a less experienced leader was in charge of the FER forces. Pokus has pointed out that the FER leaders did not expect the offensive when it came and further did not expect it to take the course that it did. They believed the Whites would cross Manchuria and attack along the railway line or through Mongolia as Ungern-Sternberg did.[38]

PRA units were only about 40 percent of their strength because of a recent demobilization of the older men, and there was a serious shortage of supplies.[39] This latter problem was worse because the FER supply line was extremely long, the railroad was in poor shape, and there was a shortage of rolling stock. Disturbances behind FER lines along the Amur River also made rail transportation more difficult.[40] The Whites agitated behind enemy lines in the Amur region, but General Molchanov complained later that the Cossacks there only killed a few commissars.[41]

It was fortunate for the FER that the Whites stopped their advance. The Communists had evacuated Khabarovsk hastily, were in the process of leaving Blagoveshchensk, and had mobilized Party workers for front line service, but the larger task of retrenchment and reorganization necessitated a breathing spell. The success of their counteroffensive was due to the White slowdown, the return to the front of Seryshev and Bliukher, and the arrival of reinforcements from Chita and Soviet Russia. These tipped the balance in favor of the Reds and boosted their morale at the same time.

The first blow to the Whites' morale was the failure of their attack at In Station on December 28.[42] To the Reds this proved that the Whites were not invincible. Another blow was delivered in Khabarovsk. The popular Red partisan leader, D. I. Boiko-Pavlov, had laid careful plans to attack the city on January 11 and 12; he was successful and inflicted heavy losses on the Whites.[43] The attack also drew General Molchanov and his troops from the front. While Molchanov was in Khabarovsk, the Whites suffered a more serious defeat at In Station, and the way was clear for a Red offensive against Volochaevka,[44] considered important psychologically and strategically for the Whites. The PRA attacked and by February 12 had seized Volochaevka. This was the turning point of the struggle against the Whites and is, therefore, one of the most celebrated events in Communist literature on the civil war in the Russian Far East.[45] Defeat meant retreat for the Whites, and retreat turned into rout. Communist forces retook Khabarovsk on February 14, 1922. General Molchanov then tried to make a stand at Bikin Station south of Khabarovsk and to use it as a base to retake Khabarovsk, but again the Reds overwhelmed the Whites. The battle of Bikin on February 27 was the last struggle of the winter offensive.[46] Within the next two weeks the Whites retreated into Japanese-held territory and the situation returned to what it had been before the Whites began their offensive, except that the White cause appeared even more hopeless than it had in the fall of 1921.

One more conflict did take place before the front stabilized. In the last days of March and early April there was a confrontation near Spassk and also a diplomatic exchange between the advancing PRA and the Japanese. FER Foreign Minister Ia. D. Ianson[47] sent a note on March 23, 1922, to his Japanese counterpart, Uchida, denouncing the April 29, 1920, agreement on the grounds that the Japanese had violated the terms by allowing armed Whites within the thirty-verst zone. Furthermore, Ianson stated, the FER had never ratified the agreement.[48] This was the legal pretext for PRA armed troops to enter the neutral zone between Iman and Ussuri Station in pursuit of the retreating Whites. The Japanese had disarmed many of the Whites at Shmakovka, but some units refused to give up their arms and continued on their way. This was the actual incident that the PRA used to declare the April 29 agreement void. The PRA was ordered to clear the Maritime Province of the Whites and to occupy Nikolsk and Vladivostok. In case of difficulties with the Japanese, a representative of the PRA, E. V. Lebedev, was instructed to negotiate with them. He was to inform the Japanese that: (1) they should remember that negotiations were in progress at Dairen, having as their goal the establishment of friendly relations between the two governments; and (2) the PRA's only aim was the liquidation of armed insurrection directed by an illegal government from Vladivostok, and it did not want conflict with the Japanese. Lebedev was not to recognize the April 29 agreement nor to conclude any agreements with the Japanese restricting the movement of the PRA, but he was also told to avoid clashes with the Japanese forces—an impossible assignment. The Japanese informed Lebedev that the April 29 agreement was still in force, and they opened fire on the PRA. This convinced the Reds to retire once again behind the neutral zone;[49] nothing further could be done by the FER army without the withdrawal of the Japanese.

The White march north had been an ill-conceived, ill-prepared adventure that had no real hope of succeeding. It was an enormous gamble based on two false assumptions. The first was that the population would rise up at the enemy's rear and help to defeat it. Shortly before the Khabarovsk offensive a conference of members of the government and high-ranking officers was held. General Shilnikov reported that there was widespread disaffection in the Transbaikal region and that uprisings could be expected. The people, he said, were merely waiting for an outside stimulus and the weapons the Whites would bring.[50] It never happened. The local population was generally passive, favoring neither side. It was tired of war, had little faith in the Whites' ability to succeed, and did not embrace the Whites because they never knew when the Reds might return.[51]

Furthermore, they regarded the Whites as outsiders since most of the Kappelites had come from the area around the Urals. One reason for the opposition to the Merkulov government was that it was installed by militarists from outside the Maritime Province who were using Vladivostok for their own ends.[52]

Further, the Whites believed that the Japanese would turn over the military supplies in Vladivostok once they saw the success of the offensive. This did not happen, and the men at the front were forced to retreat when they ran out of cartridges.[53]

Supply in general was a problem. The winter of 1921–22 was one of the coldest on record, with temperatures dipping for prolonged periods to forty and fifty degrees below zero Fahrenheit. Frostbite put troops from both sides out of action, but it was particularly hard on the Whites because of their shortage of winter clothing. They also lacked manpower reserves to back up their army. The Semenovites generally were uncooperative and refused to go to the front; four Semenovite generals were arrested in November for opposing Kappelite leaders and their plans.[54] General Molchanov complained that Vladivostok was full of monarchist officers, but he could not get them to leave the city.[55] Furthermore, volunteers from the Maritime population did not reinforce the White army.

The Reds Reorganize

When the White army withdrew into safer territory, it gave up much of the region in the southern Maritime Province away from the Ussuri Railway that it had taken from the Reds several months earlier. The Communists retook Anuchino and again made it their stronghold and the nerve center of their struggle against the Whites. Three organs of power were centered there: the Voensovet of the partisan detachments, the Maritime Oblburo (Oblast bureau) of the Party (formerly the Maritime Obkom), and the Narrevkom.

The Voensovet (Military Council) had been organized earlier by A. K. Flegontov, who headed it until he was replaced in April by partisan leader M. P. Volskii. Joining Flegontov were K. F. Pshenitsyn, long active in Communist military efforts first in the Transbaikal region, then in the Maritime Province, and A. T. Iakimov, a trusted Communist from the Transbaikal region and the Voensovet's link with the PRA military command in Khabarovsk. By April the partisans were well organized, divided into regions headed by such familiar figures as G. M. Shevchenko, E. V. Lebedev, and others. They set as their task agitprop activities among the local population and the White forces.[56]

The Oblburo was now the most important Party organization in the Maritime Province. The groundwork had been laid by Pshenitsyn, who became its secretary, and Pavel Nikitenko. The Dalburo had directed both men to the Maritime Province in November or December at about the same time as Flegontov.[57] I. V. Slinkin, a member of the FER government, also joined the Oblburo.[58] By late March 1922, when it was reorganized by the Dalburo, the Oblburo was ready to carry out its tasks: undermining Japanese and White power; directing the activities of the Voensovet and Narrevkom; and strengthening the authority of the Narrevkom wherever possible.[59]

The Narrevkom (People's Revolutionary Committee), consisting of Slinkin (chairman), Flegontov, and Pshenitsyn, was created by the Dalburo on March 22, 1922, to replace the defunct Antonov government and to serve as the temporary political authority until the Japanese and Whites could be forced out.[60] In early April the Narrevkom ruled through its plenipotentiaries, who enforced its directives in the local organs of government, the zemstvo boards.[61]

It is obvious from the membership of the three leading organs of power that control rested in the hands of a small group of trusted Communists. The Dalburo wanted to assure loyalty and complete subordination in all fields of activity. It was particularly interested in assuring that the partisans not become an independent armed force as the Communists laid the groundwork for the transformation to Soviet power.[62]

White Political Strife

The failure of the White offensive was a severe blow to the Merkulov government. The big question once again was how long it would last. Reinforcing the doubts about the longevity of the Provisional Priamur Government was the growing opposition to it, which reached crisis proportions even before the failure of the winter offensive.

The political crisis in Vladivostok in the winter and spring was very complex, but basically it involved the estrangement of the Merkulovs from the groups that had put them into power. There was increasing discord in the last months of 1921 between the Merkulovs and nonsocialists primarily because of the arbitrary and autocratic manner in which the brothers ran the government. Three members of the executive council, Aderson, Makarevich, and Eremeev, complained to the Non-Socialist Council that the Merkulovs were forging their names to documents. The three did not want to make the charges public for fear of damaging the nonsocialist cause, but they expressed their desire to resign from the government. They were persuaded to remain in the executive council to observe and moderate the Merkulovs' activity.[63] In October for similar reasons the nonsocialists had forced the Merkulovs to accept as head of the Finance Department Likhoidov, who had been the chairman of the Popular Assembly, but he also was unable to keep the Merkulovs' hands out of the till.[64] The problem became particularly acute during the winter offensive. The Merkulovs kept the operation secret from their colleagues and from the Popular Assembly, but they also had to pay bills and salaries. They issued assignats for this purpose, but the financial picture and political rivalries had become so serious that the Merkulovs ordered that none be paid without one of their signatures—a measure aimed at Likhoidov and the nonsocialists. Those closest to the Merkulovs could get the assignats signed and thus cashed. Speculation and graft resulted. There was open trading in assignats, the average price being about one-fourth of their face value. The trade was lucrative for some, including N. Merkulov's sixteen-year-old son; he would buy assignats at the low price and cash them at face value. Criticism naturally arose, but Merkulov said that he had nothing to do with it and that it was his son's business.[65]

N. Merkulov was also in charge of military supply. Apparently many of the goods delivered to the army were of poor quality and in insufficient supply. Rumors of graft reached the front, seriously affecting morale.[66]

The nonsocialists and the Popular Assembly were uneasy about the army's activities in the southern Maritime Province. They were not informed of the scope of the plans and the intentions of the leaders and were also concerned about the arrests of the Semenovite generals in November. Semenov still had some support among the nonsocialists, and they objected to such arbitrary acts. Boldyrev noted that the Merkulovs and the Kappelites were becoming too confident and allowing their success and power go to their heads.[67]

The conflict between the Merkulovs on the one side and the nonsocialists and Popular Assembly on the other finally broke into the open. Before adjourning on December 24, 1921, the Popular Assembly ordered a parliamentary commission led by Boldyrev to Khabarovsk to find out what the "White insurgent" activities were all about, to examine the conditions of the front, and to convey the greetings of the Popular Assembly members.[68] The Merkulovs and, indeed, the Kappelite command thought the Popular Assembly was meddling and causing unnecessary opposition. Whereas Chairman Andrushkevich announced that the assembly would adjourn until January 24, the Merkulovs on December 28 said the assembly would not reconvene until February 14.[69]

Meanwhile, the offensive had slowed down and showed signs of being reversed, causing another shifting of alliances. As long as the offensive was progressing satisfactorily, the Kappelites were willing to support the Merkulovs, but when the supplies gave out, they blamed the Merkulovs for failing to provide them. The Merkulovs countercharged that the failure of the offensive was the fault of the Kappelites who had originated the idea. Other charges were exchanged, and the Merkulovs became estranged from their main supporters, the Kappelite generals. While the parliamentary commission was in Khabarovsk, it received word that the Popular Assembly would reconvene sooner than expected, so its members returned home.[70]

In Vladivostok a cabinet crisis had erupted. Likhoidov expressed his wish to resign because he no longer desired to cover up for the

Merkulovs' financial manipulations. Ivanov wanted to resign as chairman of the Council of Department Heads for the same reason. The break came on January 11 when the council refused to approve two directives of S. Merkulov. The resignation of the two men and their dismissal by the Merkulovs occurred almost simultaneously. Both Ivanov and Likhoidov were popular among the nonsocialists, but their replacements were not.[71]

The Popular Assembly reconvened on January 23. To honor Likhoidov and insult the Merkulovs, the assembly returned Likhoidov to the chairmanship. The first order of business was Boldyrev's report, which criticized the offensive and the government's role in it. It praised the "White insurgents," but also recommended that the offensive be concluded and that funds be provided for the care of those wounded and suffering from frostbite. A commission was then formed to establish new taxes for the support of the army.[72]

The Kappelites and nonsocialists by this time were determined to force the resignation of the Merkulovs. Andrushkevich had stated: "We created it [the government] and now we can kill it."[73] The opposition tried to force the Merkulovs to resign—pleading with them, reasoning with them, and ultimately threatening them—but they refused. A new progovernment faction was being formed among the Popular Assembly members headed by Rudnev, but the others were insignificant, lesser-known figures.[74] More important in bolstering the Merkulovs' resolve were their new sources of strength—Admiral Stark and the navy, former Semenovites, and the Japanese.

Admiral Stark had been brought to Vladivostok by the Merkulovs, but as commander of the Siberian Flotilla, he was subordinate to General Verzhbitskii. The natural rivalry between services was particularly acute between the army and the flotilla. The army was Kappelite-dominated but the navy had been a strong center of support for Semenov.[75] Stark sided with the Merkulovs over who was to blame for the failure of the winter offensive, contending that the Merkulovs, having taken power on a peace platform, were basically cautious, but that they had been forced into the disaster by the Kappelite command. Stark reported that the counterintelligence had learned of a coup being planned by the opposition. He issued a declaration on January 21, 1922, stating that the existing government must be preserved and unity retained and formed a military council and a militia from naval forces. Stark claimed that he thus averted a coup, but this did not, of course, end the dissension among the Whites.[76]

The Merkulovs still feared a seizure of power by Semenov, or at least they used this alleged threat in their attacks on the Non-Socialist Council.[77] In fact, however, the growing opposition between the Kappelites and the Merkulovs was drawing the latter closer to the Semenovites. Their distrust of the Kappelites was kept alive by attempts of the Kappelite command to force the Semenovites into participating in the White offensive, the arrest and imprisonment of some of their leaders, and by the failure of the winter offensive. As the Semenovite support was not unified, it constituted the weakest new element of support for the Merkulovs.

The Japanese had little or no regard for the Merkulovs personally, but it was to their advantage to support the status quo in the southern Maritime region in the first few months of 1922. The Whites were retreating rapidly in February and March, and political stability was necessary to stop the Communists from seizing the entire area. Early in March pressure forced S. Merkulov to retire from office;[78] the Kappelite command had finally convinced him to resign, but he later changed his mind.[79] According to the secret Japanese telegrams (see Appendix 2) the Japanese military command informed Merkulov that they would tolerate no new government at this time. In exchange for financial support, he then agreed to resume his post.[80] Shortly after this there were rumors of Japanese loans[81] and negotiations regarding the sale of the Ussuri Railway to the Japanese.[82] The Japanese had intervened decisively at Spassk and forced the PRA to withdraw behind the former neutral zone, thus dashing PRA plans to move on to Vladivostok. This convinced the partisans, who had been filtering into Vladivostok, to leave the city and wait for a more opportune time effect its seizure.[83] The Whites had evacuated Olga and Suchan, but during April they restored a shaky hold on these areas[84] and on the coast of the southern Maritime region and had organized an expedition

to clean the Bolsheviks out of the Iakutsk region. Bolshevik power
had been overthrown in a sparsely populated Iakutsk, which had then
sent two representatives to Vladivostok to recognize the government
and seek its support.[85]

The March governmental crisis passed. Merkulov resumed his
duties and chose as his new prime minister S. I. Efremov, former head
of the Department of Trade and Industry, but this did not satisfy the
opposition to the government.[86] In March and April 1922 negotiations
were reported between moderate elements in Vladivostok and FER
representatives, the former seeking a democratic government similar
to the Medvedev and Antonov governments.[87] Throughout April and
May there were rumors of an imminent coup,[88] but tensions increased
in Vladivostok for other reasons. Higher taxes for military support
agitated the local population, business concerns, and foreigners. The
Consular Corps issued a statement saying that foreigners would ig-
nore the new property tax; some business firms indicated an intention
to move their enterprises to Harbin rather than pay increased taxes,[89]
and complaints were heard among the local population in general,[90]
including Japanese residents who considered moving to Japan to
escape the high taxes, and not just because of the uncertainty of
their existence in Russia.[91] There were numerous reports of civil
servants and others not receiving salaries for several months.[92]

Fear of a general mobilization of the population grew in the
southern Maritime Province. In February the army had already regis-
tered the male population for possible service, but more ominous was
the Order of the Provisional Priamur Government No. 294 of April 24,
1922, that rescinded a regulation allowing members of the White army
to leave the service on May 1, 1922.[93] According to one report, 80
percent declared their intent to leave.[94] The government and military
leaders before this had often boasted that military service was volun-
tary but voluntarism was now a thing of the past, and mobilization
was expected, but mobilization by an unpopular and doomed government having no money to finance an army would gain few, if any,
willing recruits.[95]

By this time no one seriously entertained any hope that a non-

Communist government would survive in Vladivostok. In January, when it was obvious that the White offensive was not being supported, Rudnev suggested to the government that Eremeev take an armed force of Kappelites to the Kamchatka Peninsula and that the population be transferred there gradually. No one openly opposed the idea, but it was not subsequently discussed,[96] even though a leading Kappelite officer, General Pavel Petrovich Petrov, had also entertained this and similar ideas.[97]

The Dismal Diplomatic Scene for the Whites

The eruption that had been expected for several months occurred at the end of May. Before proceeding to that, it is necessary to consider briefly the diplomatic activities that affected the southern Maritime Province and the Merkulov government.

At the suggestion of FER Foreign Minister Ianson, negotiations between the Far Eastern Republic and Japan resumed at Dairen on November 14.[98] For Japan the time was propitious. The Washington Conference had opened on November 12 and renewed negotiations would indicate that Japan was acting in good faith to achieve an agreement. More important was the White offensive under way in the southern Maritime region. General Bliukher met with the Japanese military representatives led by General Takayanagi, a proponent of expansionist policies, to discuss the evacuation question. The Japanese military leaders apparently felt confident and stood firm in their demands of September.[99] FER delegate F. N. Petrov noted how arrogant the Japanese military representatives were, and how they wanted to demand, rather than negotiate.[100] The FER was not intimidated. On December 5, 1921, a Soviet representative, Iu. I. Markhlevskii, arrived at Dairen to guide FER negotiations.[101] With the PRA doing so poorly in the White offensive, the FER welcomed this Soviet support. By February 20, 1922, the negotiations were deadlocked.[102] By this time, however, the Japanese negotiating position was considerably weakened. The tide had turned in the White-PRA struggle, and Japan had taken a more conciliatory stand in Washington.

The Washington Conference opened on November 12, 1921, but the

Siberian question was not considered until January 23, 1922. Siberia was to have had equal weight with the questions regarding China, but, as it turned out, Siberia received scant attention. On January 23 Baron Shidehara read a prepared statement on Japan's position,[103] making it clear that Japan considered withdrawal from the southern Maritime region and withdrawal from northern Sakhalin as two distinct issues. Japanese would continue to occupy northern Sakhalin until satisfactory compensation had been received for the Nikolaevsk massacre. Regarding Japanese occupation of the southern Maritime region, Shidehara put Japan on record as respecting Russian territorial integrity and seriously intending to withdraw. Shidehara noted that the Dairen negotiations were being held to settle certain outstanding questions, such as a commercial agreement, protection of Japanese lives, and the prohibition of Communist propaganda outside of Russian territory. The next day, January 24, 1922, Secretary of State Hughes read a statement giving the United States' position. It followed familiar lines, stating in strong terms the desirability of Japanese withdrawal from both the southern Maritime region and northern Sakhalin in the shortest time possible.[104]

With the failure of the White offensive and the pledge to the other powers to withdraw from Siberia, Japanese Foreign Minister Uchida wired Japanese delegate Matsushima at Dairen on March 20, 1922, to resume negotiations. This time Japanese demands were much softened in tone and, by the end of March, full accord had been achieved. And then, on March 27, 1922, Uchida sent new instructions. These included a draft military agreement and a warning to the Russians that the Japanese would break off talks by April 15 if the general and military agreements were not signed.[105] (It was shortly after March 27 that the Japanese stood firm at Spassk, stopping the PRA in its drive to Vladivostok.) Again the issue of when the Japanese would withdraw hindered an agreement. The FER delegation wanted a firm commitment on the precise day by which this would be accomplished. Japan's ultimatum was countered by an FER ultimatum. No agreement was reached, and the negotiations ended on April 16, 1922.[106] The only positive result for the FER was that V. G. Antonov (who had been overthrown in May 1921 by the Merkulovs and Kappelites) was able to go to Tokyo as the representative of Dalta, the official FER news agency.[107] This allowed the FER to have an unofficial representative on hand when the Japanese had important matters to discuss.

The real loser in the rupture of negotiations was Japan. The FER could afford to have no treaty because time was on its side. It had the full support of Soviet Russia, which was becoming stronger materially and diplomatically. Eventually Japan would have to withdraw because of domestic and foreign pressures. Japanese diplomats could have reached a favorable agreement, but were stopped by the military leaders who acted as advisors at Dairen.[108] The military demands were sufficient to destroy a viable basis for agreement. In the end, however, the military came away empty-handed.

One final diplomatic sidelight must be added. When it was clear that the White offensive was failing, the Vladivostok leaders made an attempt to secure Allied aid or, at least, to find out the attitude of the powers regarding the Provisional Priamur Government's position in the Russian Far East and Soviet Russia's position in Europe. General Boldyrev had connections with the French command and was to meet with French Marshal Joffre, who was scheduled to visit Japan in January and February and Peking in early March.[109] Boldyrev arrived in Peking in mid-March only to find that Joffre would see him for just a few minutes before departing for Vancouver, Canada. Boldyrev had no real hope for any encouraging words from the marshal but was affronted by his treatment; consequently, he did not talk to Joffre, but did converse with some unnamed important Allied personnel on several topics of importance to Vladivostok. He asked them their opinion on: (1) a temporary separate status for the Maritime Province, with an economic agreement between it and the FER; (2) the ending of Japanese intervention in the Russian Far East; and (3) the future status of the Railway Zone and the growth of Chinese influence there. Boldyrev was told that the Allies certainly had no objection to a Maritime government–FER agreement, but that they considered it highly unlikely. The Allied spokesmen said the withdrawal of Japanese troops was only a matter of time, due to the

Washington Conference and public opinion. Regarding the Railway
Zone, they told Boldyrev that the situation was still in flux, but that
both American and Chinese influence was growing there.[110] Boldyrev's
trip bore no results, but this must have been an expected disappoint-
ment to the White leaders. On his return trip he happened to be in the
same car with Soviet representative Vladimir Vilenskii. Boldyrev
mentioned a possible economic agreement with the FER, but the suggestion was met with hostility.[111]

The spring of 1922 was a depressing time for the White leaders
as their hold on the southern Maritime region became more precarious.
There was no realistic way they could hold onto their power, and yet
they continued to struggle among themselves for the prize of governing a doomed regime. If the situation had not been so serious and
depressing, it would have seemed like a comic opera, each event
being more ludicrous than the one before.

7

The "Last Russia"
June-October 1922

THE TENSION that had been building for the previous several months finally erupted in late May 1922. The Whites had been in power a year and May 26 should have been a time for celebration; it was, rather, a time for recrimination.

On May 26 the military forces under generals G. A. Verzhbitskii and V. M. Molchanov staged a parade with Spiridon and Nikolai Merkulov,[2] but a meeting of nonsocialist organizations the same day represented a truer picture of the spirit of that occasion. Chairman K. T. Likhoidov refused to permit a representative of the government greet the gathering.[3] Spiridon Merkulov, sufficiently inebriated so that his eyes were bright, his voice loud, and his steps uncertain, gave a speech, which was met by hisses and jeers. He in turn attacked his audience and at the end declared that all who favored the national idea should rise and follow him. No one moved. He then ordered the militia to disperse the meeting.[4] On May 30 the Popular Assembly turned down a government-sponsored tax on apartments.[5] This precipitated decisive action by the government, whose intelligence organizations, according to Admiral Iu. K. Stark, knew of a coup being planned by military and Popular Assembly leaders.[6] General P. P. Petrov was directed by Kappelite leaders to Harbin to ask General M. K. Diterikhs to come to Vladivostok and assume full command of the military, even arresting the Merkulovs if necessary. This was in response to a

government conspiracy to dismiss the Popular Assembly and certain
military leaders.[7]

On May 31 the Merkulov government dissolved the Popular Assembly,[8] and on the same day it dismissed General Verzhbitskii as commander in chief and General Puchkov as his chief of staff. Needing
military support to counteract the Kappelites, the Merkulovs replaced
Verzhbitskii with Semenovite General F. L. Glebov, hoping to rally
disaffected Semenovites in Grodekovo and Nikolsk. Glebov was
already at First River trying to rally forces behind the government.
Colonel P. E. Gludkin was sent to Nikolsk to replace General I. S.
Smolin as commander of the garrison there, but Smolin resisted, and
in the resulting conflict Gludkin was killed and other casualties were
suffered by Semenovite officers.[9] More immediate protection was
gained from naval forces. Admiral Stark was at Olga when the conflict
broke out. His chief of staff, Captain N. Iu. Fomin, was summoned by
the Merkulovs and told that the Popular Assembly had been dismissed
but that its members, ignoring the order, were meeting illegally. The
flotilla remained loyal to the government. Fomin called for the cannon
ship, *Manchzhur*, to dock near government headquarters, provided an
armed guard to protect the members of the government, and sent a
naval detachment to dismiss the Popular Assembly. By this time,
however, the Kappelites already had a military unit protecting the
assembly.[10] Throughout the conflict the Japanese gave repeated
warnings that they would allow no shooting, so that shows of force by
both sides remained just that, and civil war among the Whites was
averted.

Shortly after the Popular Assembly had received the declaration of
dissolution, it issued its own ukases. Its first act on June 1 was to
withdraw authority from the Provisional Priamur Government and declare itself the supreme power until the establishment of a permanent
government. It then passed a resolution stating that only ukases of
the Popular Assembly were official. The first ukase ordered the arrest
of both Merkulovs, the second ordered the arrest of the chairman of
the Council of Department Heads, S. I. Efremov, and the third ordered the commander of the armed forces to arrest the Merkulovs.[11]

Verzhbitskii had resigned his post in favor of General Mikhail Diterikhs, but until the latter arrived from Harbin, General Viktorin M.
Molchanov was the temporary commander in chief.[12] The next few
ukases established a temporary executive authority headed by I. M.
Starkovskii.[13]

Had General Molchanov acted immediately upon the order to arrest
the Merkulovs, the overturn of their rule probably would have been
quick and decisive, but for some reason the order was not carried out,
and the Merkulovs had time to consolidate their forces.[14]

The next day the Popular Assembly met again. By this time a wire
had been sent to Diterikhs to come to Vladivostok to assume command
of the military. Interestingly, the wire was signed not only by the
Kappelite leaders, but by Stark's chief of staff as well.[15] But the Kappelites had also decided that the temporary government selected the
previous day was not strong enough and pressed for the naming of a
new one, putting forth as candidate for head of the government General Diterikhs. This suggestion surprised and appalled those who
knew him, and there was an uproar in the assembly.

General Mikhail Konstantinovich Diterikhs

General Mikhail Konstantinovich Diterikhs had been an officer in
the Imperial Russian army, but after the Bolshevik coup he joined the
Czechoslovak corps as chief of staff. He rejoined the Russian military service under Kolchak and was commander in chief for a few
months from July 1919. After Kolchak's defeat Diterikhs retired to
Harbin, where he kept in close touch with White military leaders.[16]
He was known as a monarchist and a religious mystic and would, as
·Anichkov has noted, have been preferable as an archbishop.[17] Colonel
G. V. Enborisov commented on Diterikhs's strange habit of appearing
suddenly, then disappearing when things went wrong or when he had
made a mess of things, only to reappear again later.[18]

Diterikhs was opposed on two grounds—his personality and because he was a military man chosen by the generals. Only two members spoke for Diterikhs—Prince A. A. Krapotkin and V. F. Ivanov.
N. A. Andrushkevich was suggested as a candidate, but he refused on

the grounds that he did not consider himself strong enough.[19] Deputy Sazonov, an eighty-year-old Siberian regionalist, proposed turning power over to his small organization. A white and green flag was hoisted over the Zolotoi Rog Theater building where the Popular Assembly met, but Sazonov's proposal was rejected and the flag was removed.[20] The Whites needed a Napoleon to save their cause. Instead, with Boldyrev and his group abstaining, they finally elected Diterikhs to head the government with Likhoidov and Eremeev as his assistants. Until Diterikhs's arrival, Molchanov was to act in his behalf.[21]

On June 3 Admiral Stark returned to Vladivostok and immediately acted on behalf of the Merkulov government. He replaced Glebov as commander of the armed forces and met with Molchanov that day and the next, but they could come to no agreement.[22] On June 4 S. P. Rudnev sponsored a private meeting of several leaders aboard the *Manchzhur* to end the impasse, and the following proposals were accepted: (1) that S. Merkulov resign because of ill health; (2) that the old cabinet remain as before and that Eremeev now head the government; (3) that an amnesty be declared for all persons involved in the "near coup" (*nedovorot*); and (4) that the Popular Assembly be dissolved and a constituent assembly be called to decide a final form of government.[23] N. Merkulov and Admiral Stark assumed the responsibility of convincing Spiridon Merkulov to resign. According to Andrushkevich, S. Merkulov at first acquiesced, but the Japanese talked him out of it.[24] It did not really matter, for Molchanov also refused to abide by the agreement, stating that no alterations in the existing situation could be made before the arrival of General Diterikhs.[25]

What was the "existing situation"? Government in Vladivostok was paralyzed because nobody was certain who constituted the government. Armed conflict seemed imminent, but was prevented by repeated Japanese warnings, which reduced the conflict to secret meetings and public debate. Nikolai Merkulov would appear on his balcony every afternoon at 4:00. Using language derived from his experience as a boat captain, he harangued about what scoundrels the Kappelite and Popular Assembly leaders were.[26] Speeches and argumentation could be heard in almost any quarter of the city during these difficult times and the protagonists carried on a debate in the newspapers. The citizens of the city were amazed but generally remained apathetic.

Although there were more than two sides to the struggle, the progovernment and proparliament press were the major contenders. The Merkulovs were supported by the naval forces and by many Semenovites, most of whom viewed this support as a means of facilitating Semenov's seizure of power.[27] The Popular Assembly had been in league with the Kappelite commanders, but the Kappelite commanders now looked to General Diterikhs. The moderates favored neither the government nor the military, but were powerless to alter the course of events. A number of nonsocialist leaders met during these "June days" and offered their own solutions to the problem. So, too, did the Vladivostok City Duma, the Siberian regionalists, and organizations within Vladivostok, such as the Chamber of Commerce.[28] But it was the army and the navy that held the power and had to be reconciled before a satisfactory settlement could be made.

It is understandable why the arrival of General Diterikhs was anticipated with mixed feelings. He was summoned by the army, but it was hoped his arrival might relieve tensions and restore an equilibrium to the troubled population. After arriving on June 8, Diterikhs held numerous meetings with individuals and groups and by June 10 it was clear that he had reached a decision regarding the future course of the government. He submitted a written statement to the Popular Assembly detailing his position. He wanted the government to rescind its decree dissolving the Popular Assembly and asked the Merkulov brothers to resign and pass their power temporarily to him, as commander in chief, until the convocation of a Zemskii Sobor, or land assembly, within two or three weeks. Diterikhs further wanted the Popular Assembly to dissolve itself.[29] The same day the government published a resolution it had passed after a meeting with Diterikhs, to remain in power until the proposed Zemskii Sobor met to decide the form of the new government, and the Popular Assembly was to cease. An amnesty was declared for all who had participated in the

"near coup," and freedom of speech and assembly was guaranteed for
all but Communists and their sympathizers.[30] The major difference
between Diterikhs's statement and the government resolution was
whether the Merkulovs would remain temporarily in office. This
was clarified the next day.

On June 11 the government appointed General Diterikhs commander
of the army and navy. Immediately he published his first order giving
his view of the events of the past ten days. He compared the action
of the Popular Assembly to the action of the Duma in deposing the
tsar—both were illegal and revolutionary. Therefore, he could not
accept a post from the Popular Assembly because this would be tan-
tamount to approval of its acts. This explained his request to the
Popular Assembly to dissolve itself. He further stated that the Provisional Priamur Government had charged him with responsibility for
the armed forces; therefore, he ordered the troops to return to their
barracks, to submit to him, and to follow his example by obeying all
laws. Finally Diterikhs noted that within fifteen days the government
would summon the Zemskii Sobor to establish a new government.[31]

The Zemskii Sobor had no relationship to a *zemskaia uprava*, or
zemstvo board. Rather, it was an institution dating back to the reign
of Ivan IV in the mid-sixteenth century and was comparable to similar
institutions in Europe during early modern times. Basically these
"estates-generals" represented royal attempts to seek broad support
from several estates, not just the nobility, for actions of national
importance. The last Zemskii Sobor met in Russia in the mid-seven-
teenth century during the reign of Alexei, Peter the Great's father.
One could hardly expect twentieth-century Russians to identify with
this archaic institution, especially since it had no resemblance to a
democratically elected representative body. But this, apparently, is
precisely why it appealed to the mystic Diterikhs.[32]

The idea of calling the Zemskii Sobor may have originated with
the troubled Cossacks as a way out of the events of early June 1922.[33]
The government liked the idea and on June 6 published an ukase
stating that within fifteen days the Zemskii Sobor would be convened;
the ukase also gave details of its organization.[34] While the government

was pleased with itself, leaders of the Popular Assembly were indignant, disillusioned, and dejected. They asked the military leaders their attitude, and Molchanov ordered the military to submit. The "near coup" had ended and the Merkulovs were still in power. The Popular Assembly dispersed quietly.[35]

Japan's Decision to Withdraw

Important decisions regarding Siberia were being made by the Japanese government. Hara Takahashi, premier since September 1918, had been assassinated on November 4, 1921. Although Hara had opposed the Siberian intervention and pressed for withdrawal, he could not control the military leaders, so he temporized. His death had opened the way for a solution to the impasse, but positive steps could not be taken until the formation of a new cabinet, which did not occur until the following June. On June 11, 1922, Admiral Baron Kato Tomosaburo was chosen premier. Kato had attended the Washington Conference, where the Japanese had committed themselves to a policy of withdrawal from Siberia, and he vowed to carry on in the spirit of the Washington Conference.[36] On June 23 the premier submitted the proposal for withdrawal from Siberia to the cabinet, winning its approval and the approval of the Diplomatic Advisory Council.[37] On June 24 the Japanese government issued the following terse statement:

The Japanese Government have decided to withdraw all Japanese troops from the Maritime Province of Siberia by the end of October 1922. Suitable measures will be taken for the protection of Japanese subjects.[38]

Upon hearing the Japanese announcement, the Provisional Priamur Government immediately called a conference. The tone of the meeting was pessimistic. According to General Pavel Petrov, the Merkulovs and other leaders felt the situation was hopeless. They had no money, no military supplies, and no enthusiasm. Diterikhs was silent, except for occasional declarations to the effect that the army would go where directed. There were attempts to put aside the idea of the Zemskii Sobor, but, as Petrov commented, Diterikhs thought this institution might find some way out.[39]

In such a hopeless situation the logical move would have been to direct all efforts toward resettling the people who wanted to emigrate, yet few White leaders, caught as they were in a web of hope, duty, and paralysis, thought along these lines until mid-October. Some did not believe the Japanese would actually leave, reasoning that since the Japanese had stayed this long after the Czechs left, they would remain because their interests obviously dictated it.[40] There was also the hope that the Japanese would finally release arms so that the Whites could defend themselves—rather like a "fortress Vladivostok" approach. Some even still retained the hope that there would eventually be widespread uprisings in Transbaikalia, if only the Whites could wait.[41]

Duty motivated some White leaders to remain until the last.[42] Whatever the reasons, the White government continued to drift, while the partisans increased their pressure on the Whites in Suchan, Olga, and other areas, and the territory under the government's control diminished in size. In the third week of July the Whites evacuated Olga and the partisans immediately reestablished their control there.[43]

Spiridon Merkulov had promised the convocation of the Zemskii Sobor by June 27. On that day the government announced that it would open on July 15, and it listed the representatives who were obliged to attend. No thought was given to elections, except within certain organizations. Rather, the 280 delegates would come from organizations representing groups and classes, including all members of the Provisional Priamur Government, the department heads and their assistants; certain bishops; commanders and representatives of the army and flotilla; Cossack leaders; representatives of nonsocialist organizations; and others.[44] The Vladivostok City Duma, representing 200,000 to 300,000 persons, was allowed only 8 representatives, yet a street improvement association representing a handful of people was allotted 1 representative.[45] The peasants were not well represented and labor was grossly underrepresented. Communists and their sympathizers, of course, were not allowed. Petrov commented that the Zemskii Sobor, was in reality, a nonsocialist congress with a different name.[46]

The Zemskii Sobor

On July 23, 1922, the Zemskii Sobor was ceremoniously convened in a hall lined with imperial tricolored flags. It had two tasks before it. The first was to act on a report of the government regarding its past activities. Many nonsocialists felt that the Merkulovs should have been arrested and other members of the government prosecuted in order to clear the air and restore confidence in the Whites. This did not occur. Diterikhs did not want to hurt the White movement by scandalizing it.[47]

The second task was to establish a new government. The feeling that emanated from the speeches and procedures was very much of old Russia, religious in tone. At the August 3 session the Committee of Monarchist Organizations of the Far East sponsored a resolution recognizing that supreme power rested with the Romanov family. This passed by a vote of 207 to 23. A greeting was sent to Dowager Empress Maria and Grand Duke Nicholas, for which Maria thanked the assembly by wire, and a delegation was selected to travel to Europe to negotiate with the Romanovs.[48]

Until the Romanovs arrived, a regent would have to be elected to rule the White-held territory. Again the Whites called upon Nikolai Lvovich Gondatti to lead them. At first agreeing, Gondatti then refused because of the recognition of the Romanovs.[49] The only other choice was Diterikhs. On August 6, 1922, by a vote of 219 to 19 the assembly elected the general *pravitel* (ruler) or, in effect, military dictator. Two days later he was installed in a solemn ceremony.[50]

Diterikhs believed that he was reinvigorating the state by returning to proved historic values and his speeches were replete with references to God, Holy Russia, Christian Russia, and the like. Almost all institutions now had the word *zemskii* in front of their name. The new term for the White-held territory was the Zemskii Priamurskii Krai, considered the base for the mission of the Whites—the defeat of bolshevism.[51] It should also be pointed out that service, both civilian and military, was obligatory for all.[52]

Diterikhs created a new organ, the Zemskaia Duma, to advise him when the Zemskii Sobor was not in session. It consisted of thirty-four representatives, some of whom were from the Zemskii Sobor, while the remaining ones were chosen by Diterikhs. V. P. Razumov was selected to be chairman.[53] Two new collegial groups replaced the former Council of Department Heads: the Council of External Zemskii Affairs of the Priamur Krai and the Maritime Landed (*pomestnyi*) Council. Each consisted of four members who headed traditional departments, such as finance and internal affairs. The theory behind these was that the latter would strengthen the base of the White movement while the former could move quickly to broaden the base by administering the territory acquired. It is interesting to note that Nikolai Merkulov was selected to fill the position of director of foreign affairs and Spiridon was named Diterikhs's political representative in Washington. The latter appointment was a shrewd, well-planned ploy to remove the most objectionable Merkulov from the political scene. In a little over a month he was on his way to Canada with 30,000 rubles, his pay-off for leaving.[54]

The organization of local government was the most bizarre move Diterikhs made. In theory, while the Zemskii Sobor was charged with larger administrative problems, the Tserkovnyi Sobor (church assembly) was to organize the population on the local level. The local unit of organization was the parish, which would be administered by a council headed by a priest for church affairs and a president for civil affairs. Religion was the criterion for citizenship.[55]

These changes may have looked appealing on paper, but they were an ill-conceived waste of effort. The people, even most leaders, did not understand them or their medieval names. Furthermore the reforms did not reinvigorate the population and administration as Diterikhs had hoped. The White exodus was beginning. People were deciding whether to remain and take their chances with Soviet rule, or choose the uncertain course of emigration. Desertions from the White forces, never before a serious problem with the volunteers, were growing as both officers and enlisted men joined the partisans or left Russia.[56] Bad timing and the radical nature of the reforms resulted in administrative chaos.[57] Diterikhs compounded the problem in the latter part of August when he moved his headquarters and the Zemskaia Duma to Nikolsk, leaving all other governmental institutions in Vladivostok. Diterikhs's justification for this move was that he wanted to be closer to the front; however, it was believed that he simply wanted to be out of Vladivostok, away from his detractors, "scum" as he was quoted as calling them.[58]

Diterikhs also undertook a reorganization of the military services, again using archaic terminology. He renamed the army the Zemskaia Rat and he became its *voevoda*, or leader. During August the former three corps were regrouped into four *rat*, or groups, and further subdivided into regiments and *druzhiny*. The White units in Siberia from 1919 to 1922 constantly diminished in size and occasionally were reorganized and regrouped under larger units, but subgroups kept the same names and often the same leaders they had had when they were first organized during the civil war. As of September 1, 1922, there still was a Moscow Cavalry Regiment, a Volga Rifle Regiment, and a Petrograd Cavalry Battalion, and the Semenovites and Kappelites remained as divided as the day when the first Kappelites entered Transbaikalia.[59] The object of the reorganization was to prepare the White forces for defending and enlarging the White-held territory now that the Japanese had decided unequivocally to withdraw.

On August 15 General Tachibana stated that Japanese evacuation would begin on August 26. It was to be a four-phase operation with the southern Maritime region divided into zones, from which all Japanese troops would be withdrawn at a given time.[60] No completion date was specified—the Japanese had said earlier that all their forces would be out by November 1—but it was reassuring to the Communists, and portentous for the Whites, that the first Japanese troops left Vladivostok on September 3.[61]

The reorganization of the military was not the only measure the Whites took to save their cause. The Zemskii Sobor had sent a delegation to Tokyo to persuade the Japanese to postpone withdrawal. The delegation met with Japanese officials early in September, but failed in their purpose. They also tried to persuade the Japanese to turn over the arms stored in Vladivostok. While in Tokyo the

delegation called on U.S. Ambassador to Japan Charles Warren, asking him to intercede in their behalf, but he replied that the United
States was neutral on the question and refused the request.[62] The
delegation returned to Vladivostok empty-handed.

Japan's Final Diplomatic Effort

The Japanese were preparing to resume negotiations, broken off
at Dairen in April, regarding a normalization of relations with the
Far Eastern Republic. Inquiries were made by FER representative
V. G. Antonov in Tokyo as early as May 20 and again on June 12.
The FER made two stipulations: a representative of Soviet Russia
be included in the negotiations and a specific date for evacuation be
set by the Japanese.[63] On June 24 Japan announced its decision to
withdraw from the Maritime Province by the end of October. Japanese
leaders were sufficiently astute to realize that after their forces had
evacuated, the Far Eastern Republic would lose its most compelling
raison d'être and would probably be dissolved. It was to Japan's
advantage to arrive at an immediate settlement with Russian leaders,
and so they acquiesced to the demand to include Soviet Russian representatives in the talks. As an incentive to reach a rapid agreement,
the Japanese said that if a treaty could be signed by August 15, the
military supplies they controlled would be turned over to the Communists rather than the Whites.[64]

Both Japan and the FER were eager for a conference. The Japanese announcement of June 24 that they would evacuate and the date
for the withdrawal given on August 15 undoubtedly surprised[65] and
certainly pleased the Communist leaders. It also made an agreement
a less pressing matter for the Russians than for the Japanese. The
conference opened on September 4 at Changchun, a Japanese-controlled city in Manchuria located below the junction of the South
Manchurian and Chinese Eastern railways. The Japanese assumed
that the negotiations would pick up where they had left off at Dairen;
that is, what had been agreed upon at Dairen should be the basis
from which negotiations should proceed. Further, they intended to

sign a general agreement with the Far Eastern Republic alone, not with the FER and Soviet Russia, and did not intend to discuss the withdrawal from northern Sakhalin. This problem was to be negotiated after a basic agreement was reached and at a separate conference in which compensation for Japanese losses at Nikolaevsk would be discussed.[66]

Soviet Russia's negotiating position vis-à-vis both the international scene and the Far East had improved daily since May. Soviet confidence and the importance of normalizing the situation in the Far East is exemplified by the man selected to represent Soviet interests at Changchun, Adolf Abramovich Ioffe. A Marxist since 1903, Ioffe was a close associate of Trotsky and followed Trotsky's lead in joining Lenin in 1917. By 1922 Ioffe was one of Soviet Russia's leading diplomats. He headed the Soviet delegation to Brest-Litovsk in 1918, was ambassador to Germany for several months in 1918, and headed negotiating teams to draw up peace treaties with the Baltic nations and Poland. Ioffe also had a hand in the Soviet-German rapprochement, which produced the Rapallo agreement of April 16, 1922, and he was a member of the Soviet delegation to the Genoa Conference in April and May 1922.[67] With this experience and string of successes, Ioffe was sent to Changchun to present the Soviet position to Japan. Using delaying tactics, Ioffe demanded the recognition of Russia by Japan and the withdrawal of the Japanese from the northern half of Sakhalin Island. These two issues caused the break-up of the conference on September 26, 1922; Japan was not yet prepared to deal with Soviet Russia as an equal in the Far East, and the Japanese position regarding Sakhalin was too far from the Russian position. Japan sought compensation for the Nikolaevsk massacre of May 1920, and the Russians disclaimed any responsibility for the tragedy, countering with the demand for compensation from Japan for its four-year occupation of Siberia.[68] The breaking off of talks at Changchun would have been more pleasing to the Whites had it interrupted Japanese withdrawal; but Japanese Foreign Minister Uchida stated that the evacuation would proceed on schedule, as indeed it did.[69]

Communist Preparations for the Final Encounter

While the Communists were making their diplomatic moves leading to the Changchun Conference, they were preparing their military and political organizations for the final encounter with the Whites in the southern Maritime Province. The tasks of the Party lay primarily in the agitprop and organizational realm, and all their activities were carried on in the name of the FER, not Soviet Russia, although the close friendship of the two states was stressed.

In Vladivostok special emphasis was placed upon the trade unions. The Communists could not function legally, but their work in the unions gave them a political outlet, while at the same time allowing them to direct labor activities. The Party concentrated on keeping the FER name and platform constantly in the minds of the unions, excluding labor participation in the Zemskii Sobor, and later, in October, directing a general strike in Vladivostok. They agitated where White power was weak or nonexistent for the same ends and for the elections to be held in mid-July for the FER Popular Assembly.[70] The Party also had to be vigilant with its own membership to assure adherence to the accepted line. A letter of August 16 from the Oblburo to the local Party organs noted the presence of right opportunists among them who seriously considered the possibility of a democratic parliament remaining in Vladivostok. The letter warned against leftist tendencies as well and reminded the local leaders of the guiding principle of centralism.[71]

Party leaders also guided the administrative and military organizations in areas formerly held by the Whites. Once the Communists had seized power, they ruled in the name of the People's Revolutionary Committee (Narrevkom) through existing local governments or newly established local revkoms. Thus the Narrevkom's primary function was the destruction of local autonomy and White agitation and the establishment of Communist power. A secondary function was the recruitment of all able-bodied men to fight the Whites at the front.[72]

Defeat of the Whites was the most important Communist goal now that the last interventionist power was leaving. Between the Spassk engagement with the Japanese in March and April and the renewal of armed conflict in September, the Reds were reorganizing their forces. In June Bliukher was replaced as commander in chief of the FER People's Revolutionary Army (PRA) and minister of war by General K. A. Avksentevskii, who was replaced in August by General I. P. Uborevich.[73] Reinforcements were brought in by the FER from troops previously stationed in the Transbaikal region, while the PRA was augmented by a division of the Red Army to protect the FER-Manchurian border.[74] The PRA could not act openly against Japanese forces. Communist leaders did not want to provoke Japan and thus alter plans for evacuation nor would they risk harming the FER-Soviet position at the bargaining table. Until the PRA could operate openly as a military force, its troops could engage in military operations only as part of the partisan forces, who were actively pressing the Whites from all sides and operating in the rear.[75]

The partisans were an important cause of White demoralization; their hit-and-run tactics along the railroad lines and even within population centers allowed the Whites no respite.[76] The partisans carried on a propaganda campaign in villages and near White units[77] so, as desertions became a greater problem for the Whites, the partisans benefitted most directly by increasing the size of their units. This is not to say that Communist and partisan propaganda was the major cause of White desertions; the hopelessness of the White cause played a larger role, and many White officers and enlisted men fled rather than face the last encounter.

The Whites began their offensive operations against Communist positions at the end of August, just a few days before the opening of the Changchun Conference. The two events had little in common, that is, the Japanese had nothing to do with the White offensive. The Whites were making a desperate gamble—to attack Red positions before the Japanese pulled out their forces and thus to take the PRA off guard and prevent it from attacking.

The Battle Resumes

The battle plans of the Whites were reminiscent of the winter

Vladivostok harbor in winter
Courtesy of Walter A. Grayson and the Hoover Institution

offensive, but the gamble was greater now. The Whites would soon be alone, with no Japanese lines behind which to retreat. The Whites' spirit was not as high as it had been during the winter offensive—desertions do not result from optimism—and the Whites were facing a stronger, better organized, more confident enemy. Nevertheless, the Whites rushed headlong into the decisive encounter. General Molchanov, with between twenty-five hundred and three thousand men, was to take Spassk to use as a base for moving farther north; General Smolin, with about twelve- to fourteen-hundred men, was to clean the Bolsheviks out of the region south of Lake Khanka; General Glebov, with perhaps fifteen hundred men, was to seize the Razdolnoe-Shkotovo-Suchan region; General Borodin, with about one thousand to twelve hundred men, was to move against Suchan; and General Savelev was to organize White partisan groups to operate behind enemy lines. All of the operations were directed from the Voevoda's headquarters in Nikolsk. Vladivostok was protected by the militia and a reserve force of about seven hundred men.[78] Admiral Stark's orders were hopelessly unrealistic. Appointed chief of the rear when Diterikhs moved to Nikolsk, Stark was responsible for part of the protection of Vladivostok, the defense of the entire coast including the Kamchatka Peninsula, and the supplying of a White thrust into Iakutsk led by General Pepeliaev.[79]

The first stage of the White offensive progressed reasonably well. General Smolin cleaned the partisans out of the Prikhankai region within a few days. General Nikitin was to drive northward and occupy the railway line as far as the Ussuri Station, which would then serve as a base for moving on to Iman. He was successful for the first few days and did reach Ussuri, but by September 11 he had been driven back to Spassk. But the major effort of the Whites during the last two weeks of September was the drive into Anuchino. After two weeks the partisans turned the Whites back,[80] and a Red drive began that did not stop until the People's Revolutionary Army entered Vladivostok on October 25, 1922.[81]

Diterikhs recognized the gravity of the failure to take Anuchino. On September 28 he ordered all educational institutions closed until

January 1, so the youth could "fight for freedom," and closed all amusement establishments—theaters, movies, gambling houses, opium-smoking dens, and the like. The sale of alcoholic beverages was prohibited. Vladivostok was ordered to raise 1,500,000 gold rubles and Nikolsk 500,000 gold rubles. The cities were ordered to contribute 4,000 and 700 men respectively, equip and send them to the front by October 10, and raise a militia for home defense.[82] The wealthy complained about the levy because its confiscatory nature affected them most.[83] Artemev protested because the amusement houses brought in much-needed revenue. Diterikhs's reaction was surprise and indignation; he asked if it was possible that the main sum of their budget had been derived from gaiety and drunkenness.[84] The most tragic aspect of the order was the mobilization of children and young adults; those who could not escape were taken to the front to fight experienced PRA troops. According to Diterikhs, of the 3,000 soldiers who fought on the Whites' side in the last engagement, only 670 returned. The Communists took no prisoners.[85]

The battle of Spassk, termed the "storming of Spassk" by Communist writers, broke White resistance. Spassk was a major fortified area on the Ussuri Railway line, and the Whites put their full energies into defending this position. It was taken by the PRA on October 9. The last White stand, a useless shedding of blood, occurred between October 10 and 14 halfway between Nikolsk and Spassk. After this the White units evacuated the Maritime region as rapidly as they could, going to Pogranichnaia or to Poset, from where they could be transported to foreign ports.[86]

An interesting sidelight to the White defeat concerns the insufficient supply of weapons and ammunition. The Whites had counted on the Japanese giving them the materiel stored in Vladivostok. Several delegations went to Japan to convince Japanese leaders to turn the goods over to White authorities. Diterikhs even gave the Japanese an ultimatum to turn over the weapons or he would take action—an empty threat as there was no action he could take. The Whites also approached individual Japanese commanders. General Tachibana told Artemev that he could not distribute the goods because they had been secured by order of the Consular Corps.[88] Stark reported that one warehouse full of weapons and ammunition was turned over to the Whites on October 15 because of an old friendship,[89] and there is evidence that some war materiel got into White hands before this. N. Merkulov carried on a long series of negotiations with Chang Tso-lin from late August into October for the sale of the Vladivostok stores.[90] Perhaps the Whites thought that Chang, who had a close relationship with the Japanese, could put pressure on them to open the warehouses to the Whites. It is reasonable to assume that the Whites were making arrangements for their people to enter Manchuria, but it is also likely that the series of visits between Merkulov and Chang or his representatives involved war materiel as well.[91] On October 1 and 2 two railway cars crossing the border at Pogranichnaia were found to contain rifles, hand grenades, and ammunition;[92] other such materiel was strongly suspected to have reached Mukden.[93] The White government needed the money, but it also needed weapons. Anichkov noted that one colonel went to the front, but could not obtain a weapon and so returned to Vladivostok.[94] The Whites did not have enough arms, and an important reason for their rapid retreat in October was that they ran out of shells at the front, just as they had during the winter offensive.

Recognizing that all was lost, Diterikhs issued an order on October 15 calling for an end to the struggle and urging that all efforts be made to evacuate. In spite of this, Stark still felt there was a chance to resist, and because Diterikhs had assigned him full command of the rear, he assumed that he had the authority to go ahead with his plans. He reasoned that he still had several thousand men he could use. Generals Lebedev and Glebov expressed a willingness to continue the struggle, and Vladivostok still had a human reserve of about two hundred thousand people. He felt that the Japanese would turn over the weapons in the city and might even postpone final evacuation if the Whites showed some resistance. Stark signed a series of orders for publication the next day. General Diterikhs, however, returned to Vladivostok and put an end to Stark's madness by urging immediate evacuation.[95]

By this time panic had seized the city. A Communist-led general strike brought a halt to commerce and municipal services—electricity, transportation, and so forth. People planning to leave were selling what they could at bargain prices.[96]

The Whites commandeered all vessels they could find to help evacuate those wishing to leave the city and the Japanese also provided ships. The first ship carrying refugees left for Poset on October 16; Diterikhs left with his staff on October 19.[97] In the midst of all this activity, on October 20, 1922, the Siberian regionalists created a new government, the Council of Representatives of Autonomous Siberia, led by eighty-year-old Sazonov. Their army consisted of three or four squads of Orenburg Cossacks led by General N. S. Anisimov. This last non-Communist "government" occupied the empty governmental offices and declared that it intended to carry on the struggle against bolshevism.[98] As Boldyrev pointed out, the population remained completely indifferent, no longer surprised at anything, an understandable state, considering what they had been through the previous five years.[99] Within two days Sazonov and his colleagues were on a ship leaving Vladivostok.[100] General Glebov's Cossacks terrorized and looted in the last two days before leaving on the nights of October 24 and 25, when the last ships carrying refugees departed. By midday the last Japanese troops had also left, and the way was open for the People's Revolutionary Army and partisans to march into the city.[101]

The civil war had finally ended. The sense of relief was evident in the way the people welcomed the Red troops when they entered Vladivostok. The soldiers sang as they marched triumphantly through the city, and the people turned out to greet their new masters with flowers and the red banners they had used before but had put away when the Whites seized power in mid-1921.[102] The Communists used the next few months to eradicate pockets of resistance in the Iakutsk and Kamchatka regions, as well as in Vladivostok itself. The reports of American Vice-Consul Winslow's successor in Vladivostok, Pinkney Tuck, indicate that Soviet retribution, including deportation, arrests, and imprisonment, was widespread and affected thousands of people who had led or cooperated with the Whites. Some White leaders remained either through choice or the lack of means to emigrate. General Boldyrev chose to remain, was arrested on November 5, 1922, and imprisoned for several months before being released.[103] Even Medvedev, who had cooperated with the Communists throughout 1920 and 1921, was arrested and exiled to a northern region.[104] Thus the first stage in the establishment of Red power in the Russian Far Eastern region had been completed. By force of arms this region was now fully under the authority of the government of the Far Eastern Republic. The second stage involved the mechanics of political absorption by the Soviet government in Moscow.

Soviet Russia Annexes Eastern Siberia

The Far Eastern Republic had served its purpose as a buffer state and was now no longer useful. On November 14 the FER government issued an act declaring that it was transferring all of its authority to the Popular Assembly of the Far Eastern Republic. On the same day the Popular Assembly passed a decree creating and transferring its power to the Dalnevostochnyi Revoliutsionnyi Komitet (Dalrevkom). This was, according to Communist accounts, in response to an overwhelming mandate of the Russian Far Eastern population, as exemplified by decrees passed by numerous public organizations.[105] In reality, the formation of a revkom was a typical move preparatory to the assumption of power by the Communists and reflected the Party's effective mobilization of public opinion. The FER then sent a telegram to the Presidium of the All-Union Central Executive Committee notifying it of the organization of the Dalrevkom and asking for a union of the Russian Far East with Soviet Russia.[106] On November 15, 1922, the chairman of the Central Executive Committee acknowledged the uniting of the territory with Soviet Russia.[107] The process was now complete. With the exception of the northern half of Sakhalin Island, which Japan did not return until a treaty had been negotiated in 1925, Russia's Asian borders were returned to their prerevolutionary limits.

Epilogue: An Interpretation

THE RAPID disintegration of Admiral Kolchak's government and the consequent collapse of White hopes in Siberia augmented the revolutionary tide in eastern Siberia, but the Red Army did not pursue the defeated Kolchakist forces past Lake Baikal. Communist military weakness and the struggle against Polish forces in the Ukraine and against the Wrangelite army in the Crimea account only in part for this. The Soviet government also faced formidable obstacles within the Russian Far East to an expansion of its authority there.

Sympathy for communism was weak in Siberia for several reasons. There was virtually no industry, and so there was no significant proletariat, except in important railway centers and port cities. The independent-minded Cossacks were a privileged group, favored with land by the tsarist regime in order to settle this distant border region. And since serfdom and landlordism had not taken a firm hold in Siberia, peasants were generally better off than their counterparts in European Russia. Neither Cossacks nor peasants sympathized with the Communists' seizure of land. Siberia's bourgeoisie, located primarily in such commerical centers as Harbin (which Russians considered as their city), Khabarovsk, and Vladivostok, were naturally very anti-Communist.

One of the most important Siberian anti-Communist leaders to emerge was Grigorii Semenov. As a Cossack, he was supported by much of the Cossack population in the Transbaikal region and along the Ussuri River, but he had little support outside the Cossacks, except for the Japanese. Non-Cossack peasants, already resenting the Cossacks because of their privileged status, had further reason to distrust and hate them because of their Japanese ties and their brutality. Thus Semenov's constant presence within or on the periphery of the political arena of eastern Siberia was a divisive factor in the anti-Communist cause.

Refugees from European Russia and western Siberia began pouring into eastern Siberia after the defeat of Kolchak in late 1919. These refugees included leaders of tsarist and post-tsarist governments and soldiers who had fought under various White banners. Some Cossack units numbered among the White units, but the largest group among them were the Kappelites, who were workers from the Ural Mountains region. Unfortunately for the anti-Communist cause, military power was divided between the two groups—the Semenovites and the Kappelites. Personalities aside, the differences between them, which proved irreconcilable, lay in their origins and goals. The Semenovites were conservative and generally had narrow Siberian and Cossack interests, while the more moderate Kappelites wanted to return to their homes in European Russia. The Kappelites blamed the Semenovites for having contributed to Kolchak's defeat by withholding supplies in the rear and by not coming to his (and their) aid as an organized military force.

Most Siberians were apathetic toward all parties unless their personal property and lives were in jeopardy. They had little interest in Bolshevik propaganda, but they also resented Cossack overlords and even the Kappelites, whom they considered outsiders who forced themselves onto the political scene in the Russian Far East. The general populace would like to have been left alone, but in such chaotic times the best they could do was to survive and allow the main antagonists to fight it out among themselves.

It is unfortunate that the Russian experience with political parties and representative institutions was so new. Russia did not have a long parliamentary tradition that produced a sizable group of moderate political leaders who could work together with a spirit of trust and compromise. Rather, the moderates were divided between liberals (mainly Cadets) and socialists (for the most part Socialist Revolutionaries and Mensheviks), and a suspicion existed between the two that was never successfully overcome. No strong moderate leader emerged, and the revolutionary situation caused attitudes to polarize, with the result that most of the political activity was on the extreme Right and extreme Left.

The Right in eastern Siberia became increasingly active in late 1920 and early 1921. The more moderate military force, the Kappelites, joined the Right and succeeded in establishing in power a new, conservative government led by the Merkulov brothers. This new government would have had more support if an accommodation between the Kappelites and the Semenovites had been made. The Semenovites were bitter, however, because their leader could neither head the military forces of the new White government nor use the southern Maritime Province as a base from which to launch an offensive against the FER. As a consequence, the Semenovites generally sat on the sidelines and gave little or no support to the government or to its policies. The Kappelite leaders could have gained support from the general population had they created a more moderate government with popular leaders and policies. They were anxious, however, to stop the movement toward Communist power in the Maritime Province and to lead their own anti-Communist offensive. And they found willing allies among the Merkulov-led rightists, but erred in their assumption that they could control the Merkulovs. Thus the Kappelites weakened their position by antagonizing both the Cossacks and the general non-Communist population in the Maritime Province.

The Whites in the Maritime Province based their hopes upon one of two alternatives. Anti-Communists generally looked for the Soviet regime to fall on its own. If this did not happen, all that was needed was a push from the outside—a misconception that led the Whites to seize power in May 1921 and then launch an offensive in the winter of 1921–22. This offensive failed for many reasons, including the shortage of materiel and weapons, but it might have been more successful if the Whites had stopped fighting among themselves, presented a program that was popular, and launched the offensive at the most opportune time. In the spring and summer of 1921, Baron Ungern-Sternberg was making his drive on Chita, and anti-Communist feeling was high in eastern Siberia because of dissatisfaction with the policies of the Communist-run Far Eastern Republic and also because of news from Soviet Russia of the Kronstadt rebellion and peasant uprisings. But the Whites had as their leaders men whose policies and even whose basic honesty were questioned. They launched their offensive without broad support or agreement as to its goals, and it came at a time when Lenin put the New Economic Policy (NEP) into effect. The NEP brought a more relaxed atmosphere to Soviet Russia and lessened hostility against Communist rule there and elsewhere, thus helping to erode White strength.

The second principal obstacle to the forcible spread of communism in eastern Siberia from 1920 to 1922 was the Japanese army, the largest and most powerful military element in the region. Its presence was purported to help the Czechoslovaks leave Siberia, but the Japanese decided to remain in Siberia even after this reason was no longer valid. They did so to seize Russian territory or, at least, economic concessions, but their will to remain was strengthened by the fear of communism spreading to Japan's sphere of interest on the Asian continent or to Japan itself. The military expansionists seemed bent on an all-or-nothing policy. Early in the Dairen negotiations Japan could have obtained certain economic and political advantages in Siberia, but the longer the talks lasted, the weaker Japan's bargaining position became. Finally when withdrawal was decided upon, it was unconditional, removing any advantage Japan had except for its continued occupation of the northern half of Sakhalin Island. The Japanese, however, considered this a separate issue, a bargaining point for settling Japan's claims arising from the loss of Japanese lives and property in the Nikolaevsk massacre.

It can be argued that Japanese intervention damaged the White cause. The Japanese government professed neutrality, but it was no secret that it favored and at times covertly aided the Whites. The

Whites were in a delicate position; they did not want to be associated with the Japanese, but needed an outside source of supplies. The Japanese aided the Whites just enough to make them confident and at times daring, and just enough to weaken their moral position in the eyes of their fellow Russians, but not enough to enable them to act independently and decisively. Meanwhile, the Japanese bided their time, used the Whites as they could, applied pressure wherever and whenever they could, and hoped to receive some reward for their effort. Instead, Japan received no political or economic concessions, and Japanese businessmen and civilians, some of whom were long-time residents in Siberia, left because they lost their property and feared for their lives. The intervention cost Japan over two thousand deaths, ten thousand wounded, and seven hundred million yen.[1] The intangible costs of Japan's Siberian policy were social unrest at home and the loss of prestige for the army and politicians associated with that policy.

One of the significant questions regarding the Russian civil war and intervention is how Lenin, with such a small following relative to the large Russian population, could seize and retain power. Numerous writers, such as E. H. Carr and William Henry Chamberlin, have answered this question as it pertains to European Russia, and most of the same reasons apply to eastern Siberia. As suggested above, the Reds won in part because of the failure of the Whites to offer a viable alternative. The anti-Communists were simply too divided by ideology, personalities, and interests. The lack of discipline among the Whites and the brutality of their rule, especially of such scoundrels as Semenov, Kalmykov, Bochkarev, and Rozanov, drove the population into the hands of the Communists. The Japanese presence strengthened this tendency. But there were also positive factors aiding the Communists.

The Bolsheviks won in eastern Siberia primarily because of the prestige they had gained from their success in European Russia and western Siberia. It was only a matter of time before Soviet power would be extended to the Pacific Ocean and eastern Siberia would be reunited with the rest of Russia. The Maritime Province was Russian territory, and Vladivostok was a Russian city regardless of which person or groups headed the Russian government. For almost all Russians in Siberia the existence of a separate state was viewed as temporary. Most of them preferred to gamble with Soviet rule rather than attempt independence and risk falling under Japanese domination. The only major group not sharing this view was the extreme Right. So it might be said that the Whites were going against the tide of history and the Reds with it.

Similarly, the Whites were popularly associated with the ideology and outlook of the past—with tsarism, landlordism, and other traditional features—while the Communists spoke of the future. There was enough truth in this view to make the people seek a new path, even to take a chance with the Communists, since the choice seemed to be between communism and tsarism. The Communists offered attractive slogans, they were more dedicated to their cause, and they demonstrated, in general, a higher level of morality in their conduct. And the Communists over-all were more confident. As Lenin proved, a handful of confident zealots with determined leadership could be more effective than legions of apathetic or defeatist people.

Another factor in the Communists' success was their superior organization and discipline when compared to their opponents. Some Soviet writers would have one believe that the Bolsheviks were always well-organized and always adhered to *the* correct policy, but this was not always the case in eastern Siberia. Occasionally Communist organization and communications broke down or were shattered by Czechoslovak, Japanese, or White actions, but at least the Communists had an organization and the leadership to restore their organization and communications.

The Communists were able not only to maintain their own organization, but also to manipulate effectively the proletariat and the partisans. Both the railway workers along the Chinese Eastern and Ussuri Railway lines and the workers, especially stevedores, in Vladivostok followed Communist direction throughout the 1920–22 period. The partisans, by nature an independent, irregular force, were unreliable before 1920, but from 1920 to 1922 the Communists concentrated on bringing them completely under control so that they could insure partisan loyalty to their own cause, as well as use them to maintain pressure on the Whites.

Communist success may also be attributed to their tactics, which were peculiar to eastern Siberia because of the presence of the Japanese army and moderate and rightist elements. The line adhered to by Lenin and Party leaders in eastern Siberia was not to show their true colors by engaging in wholesale confiscation of property and capital, but to press for the creation of a buffer republic as a temporary measure for dealing with the Japanese. Lenin favored this because it provided a method of avoiding war with the Japanese and, at the same time, avoiding civil war with the anti-Communists. But just as Lenin wanted to use the buffer state to his advantage, so, too, did others. The Japanese wanted it to serve as an Asian *cordon sanitaire*, a shield to keep communism out of Asia. Nor did the added advantage of Japanese control for economic gain escape the expansionist leaders. Non-Communist Russians in eastern Siberia were similarly attracted to the idea because it allowed them to remain in their native country, if not in their home territory, and to avoid being ruled by Communists. Although the non-Communists were favored in 1920 with superior numbers and means, they lacked the singleness of purpose to agree on the type of state they wanted and to pursue it successfully.

Even after Lenin had clarified his stand on the kind of state the buffer republic should be and on the location of its capital, the Bolsheviks in eastern Siberia were almost as divided on the issue as as were their opponents. Some wanted immediate sovietization and annexation of eastern Siberia by Soviet Russia and an immediate all-out struggle with the Japanese and their lackeys. This impatient "leftist" tendency was unrealistic because of overwhelming Japanese military superiority; nevertheless, this was a popular view with many Party leaders and followers. The "rightist" Bolsheviks favored a buffer republic true to its stated purpose. They generally felt that Siberia was too underdeveloped to be transformed into a proletarian state, but wanted an independent non-Communist state with close ties to Soviet Russia. It would serve the purpose of lessening Japanese hostility, while at the same time ending the civil war and intervention, allowing for economic development, and preparing the way for eventual sovietization. This alternative was attractive to liberals and non-Communist socialists, but it was evident quite early that this was not what the Communist leadership had in mind for the Far Eastern Republic. The "centrists" favored a Communist-directed buffer state that would serve only one purpose—as a diplomatic tool to assuage and remove the Japanese peacefully. Once this was accomplished, eastern Siberia could be united again with Russia. This "centrist," Leninist view prevailed.

On the issue of the location of the capital of the republic, however, Communist leaders in eastern Siberia remained divided until events forced Lenin to decide where it was to be. Verkhneudinsk (and later Chita) was selected over Vladivostok because of its proximity to Soviet Russia and distance from Japan. Thus the two "deviations" that were most difficult to overcome were the view that the capital should be in Vladivostok, rather than in Verkhneudinsk or Chita, and the "leftism" of those who continually pressed for immediate sovietization. Communists favoring Vladivostok were effectively silenced by the fall of 1920 when the enlarged Far Eastern Republic centered in Chita was created, but sovietization was a demand constantly heard until it was successfully implemented in late 1922 after the Japanese withdrew.

On June 24, 1922, the Japanese government announced the unconditional withdrawal of its armed forces from the Maritime Province. One of the most puzzling aspects of White rule was that their leaders did not prepare for this eventuality. The Whites' faith had been based upon the imminent crumbling of communism in the rest of Russia. When this did not occur, they hoped that a spark from the Maritime Province would engulf the Communist state in the flames of popular revolt. This hope died with the failure of the winter offensive. But many continued to believe that the cause of an independent buffer state was not lost, even though the state might be considerably smaller than originally envisaged. Some thought that Vladivostok might become a free city or internationalized port, as Danzig had. Japan's interest in such a plan was exemplified by one of the Seventeen Demands made at Dairen calling for the neutralization and internationalization of Vladivostok. Some White leaders continued to believe in miracles— that the Japanese would at the last minute change their minds and remain in Vladivostok, and that the Japanese would turn over the military stores to the Whites. And so, instead of planning the evacuation of all Russians who wished to begin a new life abroad, the White leaders carried out a last offensive, which turned into a useless, bloody rout. Instead of evacuating in an orderly fashion from the southern Maritime Province, the last Whites fled in panic, and some of them were unable to get out before the Bolsheviks arrived.

When the last Japanese troops had left Vladivostok, the victorious Red forces moved in, bringing to an end the civil war and intervention in Siberia. Within days the Far Eastern Republic, having served its purpose as a buffer state, was dissolved and the authority of Soviet Russia was extended to the Pacific Ocean.

Appendix 1

A. *Agreement between the Japanese Military Command and the Provisional Zemstvo (Medvedev) Government Vladivostok, April 29, 1920*

1. The Russian military command, on the one hand, and the Japanese military command, on the other hand, mutually agree by the issue of simultaneous corresponding orders to immediately end the military operations between the detachments of Russian and Japanese troops in various districts, and the military operations must cease on both sides from the moment the order is received and is mutually exchanged by the commanding officers.

2. The Russian military forces, regardless of the political parties or groups they belong to, must not be located simultaneously with the Japanese troops within the limits of the following districts:

    a. Within the limits marked by the line passing within 30 kilometers from the final point occupied by the Japanese troops along the Ussuri Railroad, on the one hand, and the line of the Russo-Chino-Korean frontier from the west and south, on the other hand.

    b. Within the line along the Suchan Railroad along the Suchan River from its end, 30 kilometers on each side.

3. The Russian military forces that are at the present time in the above-mentioned districts, within three days after the receipt of

this order, are to end military operations, and must be removed from these districts in the above-mentioned three-day period, but this limit may be prolonged by agreement with the local Japanese command.

4. The Russian armed forces which are being withdrawn behind the line of demarcation keep their arms, munitions, and supplies, the quantity being in accordance with the number of the troops on the day the orders are exchanged by the local command, regarding the cessation of military actions, and in accordance with the existing war-time regulations.

5. In case of necessity the troops, or portions of them, may be removed from the places where they were originally sent and transported by order of the Russian command to other districts outside the limits of the demarcation line, but without the right to transport them to the Provinces of Transbaikalia and Sakhalin. In case such a removal of Russian forces takes place they may be moved within the limits of the established 30-kilometer zone, and they may use the Ussuri Railroad on conditions stated in paragraph 4, but only by agreement with the Japanese command regarding the method of transportation.

6. In order to maintain general order and peace and for the performance of militia duty in the districts mentioned in paragraph 2 and along the railroad line, Russian military militia units are permitted, and the personnel, arms, and number of these in each individual district are determined by the Russian authorities with the knowledge of the Japanese command, and must be limited to actual necessary requirements.

The terms regarding the necessary military units for guard duty and military institutions and prison duty in the city of Vladivostok are defined by agreement between the two commands.

7. The guarding of railroads is carried on on the basis of decisions arrived at by the allied military committee in accordance with the decisions of the allied railroad committee regarding the control of railroads.

8. Arms, munitions, and other material necessary for military operations, factories manufacturing such, and warehouses where such

are kept, in the districts mentioned in paragraph 2, are subject to seizure by the Japanese command. The future fate of the above-mentioned supplies is subject to special decisions. The following are the exceptions:

a. Arms, munitions, and supplies necessary for militia and prison duty and also necessary for instruction in military schools and maneuvers in the city of Vladivostok in accordance with paragraph 6, are returned from the supplies seized by the Japanese command.

b. The Far Eastern Mechanical and Shipbuilding Works in Vladivostok remain at the disposal of the Russian authorities on condition that no munitions are produced in them and that the Japanese command has the right to supervise the execution of this condition.

c. All objects of military use not mentioned in paragraph 8, which have no direct relation to military operations, and also warehouses containing such, are not subject to seizure.

d. Military supplies used as means of transportation, which have been seized and which are not the absolute property of the Russian authorities, are subject to special registration.

9. The right to dispose of barracks which are at the present time occupied and which may be occupied in the future by the Japanese troops, belongs to the Japanese command until the evacuation. In case of necessity the Japanese command shall furnish to the institutions and military units mentioned in paragraph 6, barracks which are at their disposal within the possible limits.

10. The Russian authorities shall take all measures to protect railroads and telegraph lines in the districts enumerated in paragraph 2, and must use all efforts to reestablish normal communication, and the Japanese command shall give assistance in case of necessity.

11. Both contracting parties must take measures for the speedy realization of this agreement. For this purpose, in case of necessity, and also for the working out of details regarding the execution of this agreement, a special Russo-Japanese commission is established.

12. All the conditions established by the command are of temporary character, and are to be reconsidered at the request of either side, and may be changed by agreement.

B. *Supplementary Agreement between the Japanese Military Command
and the Provisional Zemstvo (Medvedev) Government
Vladivostok, June 15, 1920*

In accordance with paragraph 6 of the Russo-Japanese agreement
of April 29 the number and arms of the militia units are established by
the Russian authorities, with the knowledge of the Japanese command.

In order to execute the above the following project is proposed:

1. The number of militia within the district outlined in paragraph 2 of the Russo-Japanese agreement of April 29, 1920, is to be
4,250.

2. The entire militia is divided as follows:

   a. Administrative.

   b. Railroad.

   c. Special militia reserves for combating criminal gangs.

   d. Vladivostok Fortress militia.

3. The numbers of the above-mentioned divisions of militia are
to be as follows:

   a. Administrative militia (city and county), 2,300 men.

   b. Railroad militia, 300 men.

   c. Special militia reserves, 1,350 men.

   d. Vladivostok Fortress militia, 300 men.

4. The 4,250 men established by the commission are divided
within the districts of the Province as follows:

   a. Vladivostok district: City militia, 1,100 men. Reserves,
600 men. Fortress militia, 300 men.

   b. Khabarovsk district: City militia, 250 men. County militia, 100 men. Reserves, 250 men.

   c. Nikolsk-Ussuriisk district: City militia, 250 men. County
militia, 200 men (including Poset, Barabsh, and Grodekovo). Reserves, 300 men.

   d. Iman district: County militia, 200 men. Reserves, 200 men.

   e. Olginsk district: (including Suchan and Skhotovo), 200 men.

   f. Militia for Ussuri Railroad, 300 men.

5. The entire militia of the Provinces with the exception of the

fortress militia, i.e., railroad, administrative, and special militia reserve, are under orders and at the disposal of the ministry of the interior, through the government inspector of militia.

The fortress militia is under orders of the commandant of the fortress.

6. The functions of the various groups of militia are defined by the existing government regulations or by regulations which may be issued by the government.

7. The militia is to be armed as follows: Two-thirds of the city, county, railroad, and fortress militia is to be equipped with sabers and revolvers and one-third of the above with rifles.

8. The arms are issued by the Japanese command from the supplies of Russian arms which are under Japanese guard.

Appendix 2

Secret Japanese Telegrams

From 1920 to 1922 there circulated among officials of various governments documents purported to be intercepted communications between Japanese military leaders and occasional Japanese and Russian politicians in major centers of Japanese activity—Tokyo, Vladivostok, Harbin, Mukden, Port Arthur, Peking, and others. There are about fourteen hundred telegrams, dated between May 17, 1920, and June 26, 1922. Copies of all of them are in the U.S. National Archives in the "Confidential Records of the President of the Interallied Technical Board, 1919–1922," Record Group 76, and are reproduced on National Archives microfilm, but are scattered in the decimal classifications 861.00, 861.77, and 861a.01. These were forwarded to the State Department by John F. Stevens (president of the Inter-Allied Technical Board), who claimed they were obtained through a leak in the Japanese military staff in Harbin. S. Merkulov gave a group of the documents, identical to some of the Stevens group, to David B. Macgowan (U.S. consul at Vladivostok); FER contacts would often pass them on to Charles Smith (American representative on the Inter-Allied Railway Commission); and occasionally the texts or contents appeared in the Russian, Chinese, or Japanese press.

The telegrams contain a wide range of information on Japanese military and political activities in China proper, Mongolia, Manchuria, and the Russian Far East. They are generally damaging to the Japanese because they show the extent to which the Japanese military leaders would go to influence events in these areas. They also demonstrate the division that existed between Japanese military and diplomatic personnel. In addition, they are damaging to the reputation of Whites, as they show how the Japanese would occasionally twist the arms of White leaders by promises, bribes, and threats. They are damaging to the Communists for the same reason. Consequently, leaders of divergent political persuasions could select the appropriate documents and make them public to prove this or that point.

The major problem with using these documents as evidence is that their authenticity is questionable. Certain terminology concerning the Japanese political scene raised strong doubts as to their validity in the minds of the U.S. ambassador to Japan, Charles Warren (861a.01/ 182), and MacMurray of the Division of Far Eastern Affairs of the State Department (861.77/2703). On the other hand, Stevens, who could observe events close to him and compare references, for example, to troop movements or khunkhuz activity with reported activities, was convinced of their authenticity and said so on several occasions (861.00/7777; 861.77/1769). The group that Macgowan submitted to the State Department contained annotations, presumably written by a member of his staff, which, in general, confirmed the attitudes and events with which the annotator was familiar. Communist historians have accepted the validity of many of the telegrams and have printed some that are damaging to the Japanese and/or the Whites, in the following publications: Borba za vlast Sovetov v Primore, 1917–1922; FER, Japanese Intervention in the Far Russian East; "Iaponskaia interventsiia," Sbornik materialov po istorii revoliutsionnogo dvizheniia na Dalnem Vostoke; I. I. Mints, ed., Iaponskaia interventsiia, 1918– 1922 v dokumentakh; and others.

A question inevitably comes to mind with this type of evidence. If they were forgeries, to what extent were they forged, who did it, and why? I have attempted to verify facts and opinions and have come to the conclusion that telegrams like these must have been sent. In general, they are reasonable and reflect Japanese and Russian activities and attitudes fairly. If they were forged, they must have been selectively altered rather than created from nothing. The information is too wide-ranging and too much in accord with known facts to be otherwise. I have found them useful guides to Japanese and Russian machinations, and I have cited them when the information can be substantiated by other sources or when I am reasonably certain they accurately reflect an event or opinion.

Notes

Chapter 1

1. In the period under consideration the Maritime Province stretched from Vladivostok in the south to Khabarovsk and territory somewhat north to Nikolaevsk. See end paper map.

2. General information on Vladivostok has been obtained from numerous sources, the most important of which are: *Bolshaia sovetskaia entsiklopediia*, 2d ed., s.v., "Vladivostok"; *Encyclopaedia Britannica*, 11th ed., 13th ed., s.v., "Vladivostok"; *Vladivostok Daily News*, April 13, 1921; John and Dorothy Findlay, "Letters from Vladivostok, 1918–1923," *Slavonic and East European Review* 45 (July 1967): 497–531; and White, *Siberian Intervention*, chap. 2, passim.

3. Paul S. Reinsch (minister to China) to Robert Lansing (secretary of state), n.d. (received July 25, 1919) in U.S., Department of State, *Papers Relating to the Foreign Relations of the United States, 1919, Russia*, p. 513 (hereafter *Foreign Relations*).

4. Kalmykov, although not a Cossack, led a group of Cossacks in the Russian Far East and seized control of Khabarovsk in September 1918. Typically, he ruled in a cruel manner and cooperated closely with the Japanese until he was run out of Khabarovsk early in 1920 and was killed shortly thereafter. (See White, *Siberian Intervention*, pp. 198–99, 266–67, and Elena Varneck and H. H. Fisher, *The Testimony of Kolchak and Other Siberian Materials*, p. 233.) Ivanov-Rinov represented the Kolchak government in the Russian Far East from October 1918 until his recall for cruelty in May 1919, leaving an equally black mark on the White cause. He later served as a

Semenov henchman in 1921 and reportedly worked for the Soviets after the White movement failed in eastern Siberia. See chap. 5, p. 112, this volume. White, *Siberian Intervention*, p. 118, and Varneck and Fisher, *Testimony of Kolchak*, pp. 183–84.

5. One of the best sources on the Kolchak government and its involvement with the Allies is John Bradley, *Allied Intervention in Russia*, chap. 5.

6. Roland Morris (ambassador to Japan) to Lansing, Jan. 9, 1920, 861.00/6111, U.S. National Archives, Record Group 59: General Records of the Department of State (hereafter cited by file and document number only).

7. For competent assessments of the social cleavages in Siberia as an underlying factor in the growth of the partisan movement, see Donald W. Treadgold, *The Great Siberian Migration*, and White, *Siberian Intervention*, pp. 44–46 and 273–96.

8. For a description on the physical features of the Maritime region and adjacent areas see Erich Thiel, *The Soviet Far East*.

9. See map, p. 8.

10. I. G. Kushnarev, "Informatsiia o deiatelnosti Dalnevostochnogo podpolnogo komiteta RKP(b) Tsentralnomu komitetu RKP(b) i Sovnarkomu, polnomochnym predstaviteliam TsK RKP(b) i SNK Sibiri, ianvar 1920 g.," *Borba za vlast Sovetov v Primore, 1917–1922*, p. 303.

11. Numerous writers make this point, for example, Mirovoi, "Partiinaia organizatsiia i rabota na Dalnem Vostoke, 1920–1921 gg.," *Revoliutsiia na Dalnem Vostoke*, p. 313; Kushnarev, "Informatsiia," p. 301; and F. N. Petrov et al., *Geroicheskie gody borby i pobed*, passim, but especially pp. 96 ff.

12. Petrov, *Geroicheskie gody*, p. 101; Leonid M. Papin, *Krakh Kolchakovshchiny i obrazovanie Dalnevostochnoi respubliki*, p. 53, n. 2; Kushnarev, "Informatsiia," p. 299. Whether there is a relationship between the formation of the Siberian Bureau (Sibburo) of the Central Committee of the RCP(b) on December 17, 1918, and the Obkom in January 1919 is unclear. The Sibburo did direct agents to Siberia, but I have found no record of their influencing events as early as January 1919. Difficulty of transportation and communication seemed to preclude this possibility. In addition, the Sibburo focused its attention on the area in Kolchak's immediate rear and gave little attention to Siberia east of Lake Baikal.

13. Petrov, *Geroicheskie gody*, pp. 101, 352–81; Papin, *Krakh Kolchakovshchiny*, p. 53, n. 2.

14. *Oktiabrskaia revoliutsiia i grazhdanskaia voina na Dalnem Vostoke*, ed. S. Tsypkin et al., p. 116; Papin, *Krakh Kolchakovshchiny*, pp. 54–55. This is the source of both confusion and controversy. The confusion arises from the lack of precision in the use of the terms oblast and krai.

Before 1917, as previously pointed out, the Russian Far Eastern region, or krai, included four administrative provinces, or oblasts—Transbaikal, Amur, Maritime, and Kamchatka—and the northern half of Sakhalin Island. Most Soviet writers, both contemporary with the period and in more recent times, refer to a Russian Far Eastern Krai, which excludes the Transbaikal region. Thus the use of krai, depending on who uses it and when it is used, could include or exclude the Transbaikal region. Similarly, the term oblast is used carelessly. Reference is made continuously to the Maritime Oblast, a specific designation for the area (stretching from Vladivostok to the territory north of Nikolaevsk) indicated on the end paper map. But the term Far Eastern Oblast is also used often, generally when the Far Eastern Obkom is referred to, and designates most probably the old Russian Far Eastern region excluding the Transbaikal region.

The controversy involves the area of jurisdiction claimed by the Vladivostok Communist leaders through 1919 and well into 1920. In 1919 there was little dispute because the Vladivostok Party leaders were the most able, active, and important in the Russian Far East. But in the course of 1920 several events occurred that undermined their authority, causing it to shrink to Vladivostok and its environs. These events were: the establishment of Japanese military control over the southern Maritime Province on April 4–5, 1920; the establishment of a rival center of Communist power in the Transbaikal region in the form of the Far Eastern Republic; the eviction of the Semenovites and other Whites from the Transbaikal region; and the enlargement of FER power in the Russian Far Eastern region. These events will be described later. Suffice it to say at this point that because events did not work out in favor of the Vladivostok leaders, Communist literature from the early 1920s on is critical of them for their presumptuousness, a practice that continues among Communists.

It is more realistic to consider the area of effective authority of the Vladivostok Communists as being the Maritime Province; therefore, rather than use the term Kraikom to refer to the leading organ of Communist power in the Maritime Province, I shall usually refer to it as the Obkom, although it called itself a Kraikom and its influence did extend at times beyond the strict confines of the Maritime Province.

15. Nikolai K. Iliukhov and M. Titov, *Partizanskoe dvizhenie v Primore, 1918–1920*, pp. 18, 48; A. N. Iaremenko, "Partizanskoe dvizhenie v Primorskoi oblasti (1918–1920 gg.)," *Proletarskaia revoliutsiia* 7 (1922); Papin, *Krakh Kolchakovshchiny*, pp. 52–53.

16. Iaremenko, "Partizanskoe dvizhenie," pp. 74–75; Iliukhov and Titov, *Partizanskoe dvizhenie*, pp. 93–94; Papin, *Krakh Kolchakovshchiny*, p. 55.

17. Kushnarev, "Informatsiia," p. 303; Iliukhov and Titov, *Partizanskoe dvizhenie*, pp. 124–27; Iaremenko, "Partizanskoe dvizhenie," pp. 94–95; Papin, *Krakh Kolchakovshchiny*, pp. 57–58; Petrov, *Geroicheskie gody*, pp. 119–20.

18. Iliukhov and Titov, *Partizanskoe dvizhenie*, pp. 93 ff.

19. General Rudolf Gaida, an officer in the Czechoslovak Legion, joined the Kolchakist forces and impressed Kolchak so much that he was appointed commander in chief for several months in mid-1919. Gaida then split with Kolchak and in the latter half of 1919 organized coups in several cities with the connivance of Socialist Revolutionaries to overthrow Kolchak's government. The attempted coup in Vladivostok occurred on November 17 (Bradley, *Allied Intervention*, p. 127).

20. Partisan leader N. K. Iliukhov in the work he coauthored with I. P. Samusenko, *Partizanskoe dvizhenie v Primore, 1918–1922* (p. 164), initiated a major controversy by his assertion that a plan was worked out by partisan leaders at Belaia Pad in August 1919 and that Lazo approved and carried the plan to Vladivostok in November where it was approved and subsequently effected. Strong exception was taken to this "partisan approach," prompting a conference in 1964 at which surviving leading participants and scholars roundly denounced Iliukhov for his narrow approach. See K. I. Sedov, "Diskussiia o nekotorykh voprosakh istorii partizanskogo dvizheniia na Dalnem Vostoke v 1918–1922 godakh," *Voprosy istorii*, 5 [1964]:156–69. The general feeling of the conference seemed to be that Iliukhov and Samusenko failed to recognize the leading role of Lazo and other Party leaders in their main concern for their own and the partisans' role. Sedov stated that no documentation for Iliukhov's claims exists (and I have found none) and thus that Lazo must have been the originator of the plan at a later date. Other errors were pointed out, but for some reason no rebuttal was given.

21. Papin, *Krakh Kolchakovshchiny*, p. 124; Petrov, *Geroicheskie gody*, pp. 129–30.

22. Petr S. Parfenov, *Borba za Dalnii Vostok, 1920–1922*, p. 108.

23. Ibid.

24. Ibid., pp. 108–9.

25. Kushnarev, "Informatsiia," pp. 309–10; *Oktiabrskaia revoliutsiia*, p. 153; Petrov, *Geroicheskie gody*, p. 130, which bases its information on a manuscript by S. G. Cheremnykh, one of the delegates to the January conference in Vladivostok.

26. *Oktiabrskaia revoliutsiia*, p. 153.

27. Kushnarev, "Informatsiia," p. 310.

28. This question will be considered later. See Lenin's telegram to

the Revvoensovet of the Fifth Army, January 21, 1920, in V. I. Lenin, *Polnoe sobranie sochinenii*, 21 : 334.

29. Petr M. Nikiforov, *Zapiski premera DVR*, p. 162; see also Leonid Karpov, "Vosstanie," *Taezhnye pokhody*, pp. 199–202.

30. Iliukhov and Titov, *Partizanskoe dvizhenie*, pp. 127–28.

31. "Partizanskoe dvizhenie v Primore," *Krasnyi arkhiv* 82 (1937): 68–69.

32. *Japan Advertiser*, Feb. 7, 1920; Papin, *Krakh Kolchakovshchiny*, p. 125.

33. Nikiforov, *Zapiski*, p. 163.

34. *Borba za vlast*, pp. 322 ff.; "Partizanskoe dvizhenie v Primore," passim; *Sergei Lazo*, eds. G. Reikhberg et al., pp. 160–66.

35. Nikiforov, *Zapiski*, p. 161; *Borba za vlast*, pp. 316–19.

36. Nikiforov, *Zapiski*, pp. 163–64.

37. Petrov, *Geroicheskie gody*, p. 131.

38. David B. Macgowan (vice consul at Vladivostok) to Lansing, Jan. 5, 1920, 861.00/6069; K. N. Khartling, *Na strazhe rodiny*, p. 99.

39. Papin, *Krakh Kolchakovshchiny*, p. 126.

40. Khartling, *Na strazhe rodiny*, p. 138; *Japan Advertiser*, Feb. 7, 1920.

41. R. H. Allen to L. Farrand, Feb. 6, 1920, American Red Cross Papers (hereafter cited as ARCP), File 987.08.

42. Macgowan to Lansing, Jan. 30, 1920, 861.00/6274.

43. William S. Graves, *America's Siberian Adventure*, *1918–1920*, p. 317.

44. *Japan Advertiser*, Feb. 4, 1920.

45. Henry Rogers, ARC camp supervisor in Skhotovo, Siberia, to A. C. Lyons, ARC director of military relief in Vladivostok, ARCP, Military Relief, File 987.118. Lyons reported that about 600 Kolchak troops deserted, killing two of their officers, and that few troops remained.

46. Khartling, *Na strazhe rodiny*, pp. 96 ff.; *Japan Advertiser*, Feb. 7, 1920.

47. Parfenov, *Borba*, pp. 105 ff.; note 286, p. 552 by editor V. Vegman in Vasilii G. Boldyrev, *Direktoriia, Kolchak, interventy*. I find no official documents stating this, but numerous reports are available that indicate a hostile American and Czechoslovak attitude toward the Japanese. Also, the Consular Corps (Allied diplomatic representatives who had left Omsk when Kolchak's government fell and now represented various Allied nations in Vladivostok), when sent a query by the United Operative Staff as to what its reaction would be to an overturn, hesitated and then declared its neutrality,

apparently convincing Japanese officials to do the same. See Boldyrev, Direktoriia, p. 304, and Petr S. Parfenov, Uroki proshlago, p. 109.

Chapter 2

1. L. A. Krol, Za tri goda, p. 211.

2. U.S., Congress, "Japanese Aggression in the Russian Far East," Congressional Record, p. 3261 (hereafter cited as "Japanese Aggression in the Russian Far East"). This is a reprint of Far Eastern Republic, Japanese Intervention in the Russian Far East (Washington, 1922). Incidentally, when the zemstvo was formed in Vladivostok in 1917, Medvedev was also its chairman then.

3. Vasilii G. Boldyrev, Direktoriia, Kolchak, interventy, p. 318.

4. Petr M. Nikiforov, Zapiski premera DVR, p. 166; Boldyrev, Direktoriia, p. 305; Dalnevostochnoe obozrenie, Feb. 3, 1920.

5. Nikiforov, Zapiski, pp. 173–74. Nikiforov, like Kushnarev, was a realist who understood the trouble Japan could cause the Russians while its military forces were present. His approach to the task of establishing political power in eastern Siberia was cautious, favoring more moderate policies. Communist accounts speak of Nikiforov in glowing terms, and publication of his memoirs in 1963 indicates official approval. General Boldyrev, former member of the Omsk Directory and a political moderate, described Nikiforov as small in stature, with a typical worker's exterior, a man who spoke quietly, thoughtfully, and soberly (Boldyrev, Direktoriia, p. 320). N. A. Andrushkevich, an intelligent observer, but one with strong monarchist leanings, said Nikiforov was once no more than a highwayman, who at one time attacked a mail team near Irkutsk killing either the mailman or the coachman. Nikiforov was caught, sentenced to death, but his sentence was later commuted to forced labor. Andrushkevich, however, credited Nikiforov with being one of the more honest and intelligent Communists (N. A. Andrushkevich, "Posledniaia Rossiia," chap. 2, p. 20).

6. Nikiforov, Zapiski, p. 174; Petr S. Parfenov, Borba za Dalnii Vostok, 1920–1922, p. 113. Vasilii Grigorevich Antonov (1882–1967) had been a Bolshevik since 1906 and was the first editor of the Maritime Party organ, Krasnoe znamia, in 1917. A secondary figure from 1917 to 1920, his importance grew in 1920 when he replaced Medvedev as leader of the government when it was joined to the Far Eastern Republic. F. N. Petrov et al., Geroicheskie gody borby i pobed, p. 353. Further information on Antonov is given on page 80 of the text.

7. See note 139, p. 816 in Borba za vlast Sovetov v Primore, 1917–1922.

8. Boldyrev, *Direktoriia*, pp. 311 ff.; Parfenov, *Borba*, p. 113; Nikiforov, *Zapiski*, p. 172.

9. *Golos rodiny*, Feb. 8, 1920.

10. Vasilii P. Golionko, *V ogne borby*, p. 185; Nikolai K. Iliukhov and I. P. Samusenko, *Partizanskoe dvizhenie, v Primore, 1918–1922*, p. 174; A. N. Iaremenko, "Dnevnik Kommunista," *Revoliutsiia na Dalnem Vostoke*, p. 276.

11. Boldyrev, *Direktoriia*, p. 316; Parfenov, *Borba*, p. 113.

12. *Oktiabrskaia revoliutsiia i grazhdanskaia voina na Dalnem Vostoke*, p. 171; Parfenov, *Borba*, p. 147; I. Ia. Melekhin, *Taezhnymi tropami*, pp. 152–53.

13. Parfenov, *Borba*, p. 169.

14. Iliukhov and Samusenko, *Partizanskoe dvizhenie*, pp. 180 ff.; Melekhin, *Taezhnymi tropami*, p. 180; A. N. Iaremenko, "Partizanskoe dvizhenie v Primorskoi oblasti (1918–1920 gg.)," p. 83. Iliukhov and Samusenko must be used with caution here as before because of their excessively Iliukhov- and partisan-centered approach. See supra, p. 186, n. 20.

15. *Golos rodiny*, Feb. 8, 1920.

16. Boldyrev, *Direktoriia*, pp. 305, 307.

17. Andrushkevich, "Posledniaia Rossiia," chap. 2, pp. 16 ff.; also *Golos rodiny*, Mar. 2, 1920; Sergei P. Rudnev, *Pri vechernikh ogniakh*, p. 302.

18. *Dalnevostochnoe obozrenie*, Mar. 21 and 23, 1920.

19. This material is based upon a perusal of numerous Vladivostok newspapers, including their advertisements, and statements of various governmental representatives, both Communist and non-Communist, for example, the statement of P. V. Utkin, important Communist and editor of *Krasnoe znamia*, in Josephus Daniels (secretary of the navy) to Bainbridge Colby (secretary of state from March 22, 1920, to March 4, 1921), April 24, 1920, Naval Intelligence Report of March 4, 1920, in 861.00/6844 (Record Group 80).

20. This will be considered later in this chapter.

21. Iliukhov and Samusenko, *Partizanskoe dvizhenie*, p. 204. Kushnarev was probably the delegate Lazo mentioned, in his direct wire conversation with Blagoveshchensk on February 18, 1920, as having been sent to Moscow ("Partizanskoe dvizhenie v Primore," *Krasnyi arkhiv* 82 [1937]:63). Kushnarev's report is in Petrov, *Geroicheskie gody*, pp. 133–34.

22. "Partizanskoe dvizhenie v Primore," p. 61; *Oktiabrskaia revoliutsiia*, p. 164.

23. Nikolai K. Iliukhov and M. Titov, *Partizanskoe dvizhenie v Primore, 1918–1920*, pp. 207–9; Vladimir D. Vilenskii, *Za velikoi kitaiskoi stenoi*, p. 8.

24. *Krasnoe znamia*, Feb. 25, 1920.

25. *Krasnoe znamia*, Mar. 3, 1920; L. I. Belikova, "Borba Vladivostokskoi partiinoi organizatsii za vossoedinenie oblastei Dalnego Vostoka, ian. 1920-ian. 1921," *Materialy po istorii Vladivostoka*, bk. 2, 1919–1960, p. 60.

26. *Oktiabrskaia revoliutsiia*, p. 165; *Borba za vlast*, pp. 375 ff.

27. Larisa I. Belikova, *Bolsheviki Primoria v gody grazhdanskoi voiny i inostrannoi interventsii*, p. 68.

28. Allen to Farrand, Mar. 19, 1920, American Red Cross Papers (hereafter cited as ARCP), File 987.08.

29. Vilenskii, using his own name and his pseudonym, Sibiriak, wrote numerous articles and several books. Between 1918 and 1920 he divided his time between Moscow and Irkutsk, was Moscow's plenipotentiary in the Russian Far East in 1920, and between 1920 and 1922 negotiated for Soviet Russia with Japan and China. See Allen S. Whiting, *Soviet Policies in China, 1917–1924*, p. 290; Xenia J. Eudin and Robert C. North, *Soviet Russia and the East, 1920–1927*, p. 463.

30. Telegram of Lenin to Trotsky, copy to Smirnov, in V. I. Lenin, *Leninskii sbornik*, 36:97.

31. *Sergei Lazo*, p. 174.

32. *Iz istorii grazhdanskoi voiny v SSSR*, 3:710; *Borba za vlast*, pp. 386–87 (the texts of these two sources differ, but both substantiate the point made); *Iz istorii grazhdanskoi voiny v SSSR*, 3:711.

33. Nikiforov, *Zapiski*, p. 181; Parfenov, *Borba*, p. 146; Belikova, "Borba Vladivostokskoi partiinoi organizatsii," p. 61.

34. Mirovoi, "Partiinaia organizatsiia i rabota na Dalnem Vostoke, 1920–1921 gg.," *Revoliutsiia na Dalnem Vostoke*, p. 315.

35. Parfenov, *Borba*, p. 169; Nikiforov, *Zapiski*, p. 182; Iliukhov and Samusenko, *Partizanskoe dvizhenie*, p. 204. No text of the directives from Moscow is given except for a short excerpt in Leonid M. Papin (*Krakh Kolchakovshchiny i obrazovanie Dalnevostochnoi respubliki*, p. 136), and reports conflict as to their contents. Nikiforov, for example, contended that the directives called for the creation of a buffer state with its center in Vladivostok, but I believe, like Papin (pp. 135–36), that Nikiforov is in error.

36. Two informative articles on the Dalburo by Soviet scholar A. P. Shurygin are "Dalburo TsK RKP(b) v gody grazhdanskoi voiny 1920–1922 gg.," *Voprosy istorii KPSS* (Aug. 1966):55–62, and "Dalburo TsK RKP(b) v period grashdanskoi voiny i interventsii, 1920–1922 gg.," *Iz istorii sovetskogo Dalnego Vostoka*, ed. E. M. Shagin et al., pp. 36–53.

37. *Iz istorii grazhdanskoi voiny v SSSR*, 3:708.

38. The idea of forming a democratic buffer originated within the SR-Menshevik Political Center, which seized power in Irkutsk in early January

1920. Its idea was to have Irkutsk as the capital of the buffer, and this plan was approved by Soviet representatives at a meeting in Tomsk on January 19, 1920. However, before the representatives of the Political Center could return to Irkutsk with the news, their government collapsed under Red Army pressure. Krasnoshchekov had participated in the Tomsk negotiations, although he was not formally a member of the Political Center delegation. He was enthusiastic about the agreement and was, therefore, disappointed with the sovietization of Irkutsk. Undaunted, he seized the initiative and moved to Verkhneudinsk to establish his buffer there. See Papin, *Krakh Kolchakovshchiny*, pp. 90–108; *Poslednie dni kolchakovshchiny*, ed. M.M. Konstantinov, pp. 172–195; and Leon C. Martel, Jr., "Russian Foreign Policy and the Establishment of the Far Eastern Republic," pp. 38 ff.

39. Lenin to Revvoensovet of the Fifth Army, Jan. 21, 1920, in V. I. Lenin, *Polnoe sobranie sochinenii*, 51:334, and Lenin to Smirnov, Mar. 9, 1920, ibid., p. 156; also Lenin to Trotsky, Feb. 19, 1920, *Iz istorii grazhdanskoi voiny v SSSR*, 3:708.

40. Papin, *Krakh Kolchakovshchiny*, p. 136.

41. White, *Siberian Intervention*, pp. 368–69.

42. For Verkhneudinsk, see supra, p. 191, n. 39; for Vladivostok see *Golos rodiny*, Feb. 29, 1920.

43. Shiriamov was a member of the Maritime Obkom in 1919. Goncharov (born in 1886 and a Party member since 1904) came to political prominence from his membership in the military council of the Soviet Fifth Army. Petrov, *Geroicheskie gody*, pp. 187, 360.

44. It is unlikely that it was a coincidence the three members of the Kraikom (or Obkom) Politburo and the three Dalburo members from Vladivostok were the same, i.e., Kushnarev, Nikiforov, and Lazo. Vilenskii must have known about the Dalburo makeup and thought it would be a good idea to elevate the stature of the three in the Maritime heirarchy as well, hence the formation of the Maritime Politburo, an innovation in Communist organizational structure there.

45. Kushnarev did pass through Verkhneudinsk on his return from Moscow to Vladivostok. He conferred with Krasnoshchekov and undoubtedly was aware of his plans to proclaim a government encompassing the entire Russian Far Eastern region.

46. The Railway Zone refers to the Chinese Eastern Railway, which crossed Manchuria. Russia built the line, and this area became a Russian sphere of influence. Russian businessmen, civil servants, intelligentsia, railway workers, and others migrated there and turned Harbin, the major commercial and administrative center on the Chinese Eastern Railway, into a Russian city on Chinese territory.

47. Parfenov, Borba, pp. 169–70; Nikiforov, Zapiski, p. 182. Papin
(Krakh Kolchakovshchiny, p. 136) and others argue that this extension of
power and emphasis on Vladivostok as a center was erroneous, but I believe
the Maritime Communists were acting at this point within the limits of Moscow's directives. Later, however, for reasons that will be explained, they
did exceed their orders.

48. Papin, Krakh Kolchakovshchiny, p. 136; Oktiabrskaia revoliutsiia,
pp. 171–72; Nikiforov, Zapiski, p. 181.

49. Nikiforov, Zapiski, pp. 182–83; Golionko, V ogne borby, p. 185;
Iaremenko, "Dnevnik," pp. 277–78; Parfenov, Borba, p. 174.

50. Papin, Krakh Kolchakovshchiny, p. 137.

51. Iaremenko, "Dnevnik," pp. 277–78.

52. Parfenov, Borba, p. 174.

53. See the memoirs listed in the bibliography of Akintievskii, I. Elovskii, G. V. Enborisov, V. M. Moltchanov (Molchanov), P. P. Petrov, F. A.
Puchkov, K. V. Sakharov, S. A. Shchepikhin, Vorotovov, and V. I. Vyrypaev.

54. Gregorii Semenov has written his own account of his role in the
civil war in his O sebe. For other accounts concerning the events above see
White, Siberian Intervention, pp. 195–98; Eudin and North, Soviet Russia and
the East, pp. 122–23; and Varneck and Fisher, Testimony of Kolchak, p. 231.
While Semenov was a Japanese lackey, he also had his own vision—as
leader of a large Mongolian state including Inner and Outer Mongolia and the
Russian Buriat Mongol region. This movement received some Japanese support, but the Japanese were not enthusiastic about any plans unless they
could control them. Ultimately Semenov's Pan-Mongol movement lost its momentum, and his influence among the Mongols dwindled. Baron von Ungern-
Sternberg had a similar vision and tried to lead a Pan-Mongol movement, but
he failed and lost his life in the process (see chap. 3, p. 97).

55. General Akintievskii, "K istorii grazhdanskoi voiny v Sibirii i na
Dalnem Vostoke, 1918–1922," chap. 3, pp. 1 ff.; Sergei A. Shchepikhin,
"Kappelevtsy v Chite v 1920 gody," pp. 17 ff.; Victorin M. Moltchanov, "The
Last White General" (MS, Bancroft Library, University of California, Berke-
ley, 1972), pp. 102–3.

56. Boldyrev, Direktoriia, p. 319; General Kolobov, "Borba s bolshevikami na Dalnem Vostoke," chap. 26, p. 2; Petr S. Parfenov, Na soglashatelskikh frontakh, p. 148.

57. Kolobov, "Borba bolshevikami," chap. 26, p. 2; Boldyrev, Direktoriia, p. 319.

58. Boldyrev, Direktoriia, pp. 319–21.

59. Parfenov, Na soglashatelskikh frontakh, pp. 16–18.

60. General Diterikhs will reappear later in this study, first as a

peripheral figure and then as the last significant White leader in Vladivostok in 1922. For a short biographical sketch, see chap. 7, p. 147. Anatolii Niko-laevich Pepeliaev was a younger brother of Viktor, Kolchak's prime minister who was executed at the same time as Kolchak. General Pepeliaev served in the tsar's army and then in the anti-Bolshevik forces during the civil war. As a military leader he was popular among both officers and enlisted men. This is the same General Pepeliaev who led the foolish, ill-fated raid into Iakutia in 1922 mentioned in chap. 7, p. 161. He was captured and sentenced to death in 1923, but his sentence was commuted to a ten-year prison term in ex-change for issuing an appeal to his former followers to return to Russia (Varneck and Fisher, *Testimony of Kolchak*, p. 241).

61. Ibid.; Parfenov, *Borba*, pp. 169–70; Boldyrev, *Direktoriia*, pp. 325–27. Boldyrev and Parfenov disagreed on important details, but there is substantial agreement on what is presented here.

62. Among the books published on this subject two are especially good: James W. Morley, *The Japanese Thrust into Siberia, 1918*, and John A. White, *The Siberian Intervention*, particularly his excellent fifth chapter, "The New Inland Sea."

63. Bradley, *Allied Intervention*, p. 24.

64. Ibid., pp. 24–31; John W. Young, "The Japanese Military and the China Policy of the Hara Cabinet, 1918–1921" (Ph.D. diss., University of Washington, 1971), pp. 42 ff.

65. Bradley, *Allied Intervention*, p. 36.

66. Ibid., pp. 36–41.

67. Young, "The Japanese Military," pp. 76–79.

68. Ibid., pp. 77–78, 200, and passim; Robert A. Scalapino, *Democracy and the Party Movement in Prewar Japan*, pp. 216–17; and Roger F. Hackett, *Yamagata Aritomo in the Rise of Modern Japan, 1838–1922*, pp. 328–29.

69. *Japan Advertiser*, Feb. 10, 1920.

70. *Dalnevostochnoe obozrenie*, Jan. 11, 1920.

71. *Japan Advertiser*, Jan. 23, 1920.

72. Young, "The Japanese Military," p. 147.

73. The exact date of this decision is in dispute. The State Depart-ment was notified of the February 24 decision of the Japanese cabinet in a February 25, 1920, dispatch of U.S. Ambassador to Japan Morris (U.S., De-partment of State, *Papers Relating to the Foreign Relations of the United States, 1920*, 3 : 504 (hereafter cited as *Foreign Relations 1920*). On February 27, 1920, Morris notified the State Department that the Japanese General Staff had prepared a detailed evacuation plan from the Amur and Transbaikal regions, but not Vladivostok and Nikolsk. Soviet sources give earlier dates. Parfenov (*Borba*, p. 120), using the February 17 issue of *Nichi Nichi*, said

that a special session of the War Ministry was held at which it was decided
to withdraw from the Amur region and strengthen the garrisons in Khabarovsk
and the Transbaikal Province. This decision was based on a report of General Oi, who felt that the Amur region was indefensible because of its location and the strong partisan-Communist base there. A participant, Vladimir
Borodavkin (*Gody grozovye*, p. 182) noted the beginning of Japanese evacuation from the Amur region on February 23 and its completion by March 4, 1920.
John W. Young ("The Japanese Military," pp. 147 and 254, n. 8), using Japanese archival sources, stated that the decision was made in a March 2 cabinet meeting but was not made public until March 31.

74. Morris to Frank L. Polk (acting secretary of state), Feb. 27, 1920,
Foreign Relations, 1920, 3 : 504–5; Hackett, *Yamagata Aritomo*, p. 329.

75. "Japanese Aggression in the Russian Far East," pp. 3244–61.

76. *Japan Chronicle*, Mar. 15, 1920.

77. Information on the Nikolaevsk incident may be found in: Edward H.
Carr, *A History of Soviet Russia*, 1 : 356–57; Varneck and Fisher, *Testimony
of Kolchak*, passim; and White, *Siberian Intervention*, pp. 286–92. The Bolsheviks at first claimed credit for Triapitsyn until his reckless leadership
precipitated the unfortunate May incidents and brought down Japan's wrath.
Triapitsyn and some of his associates were tried and shot and subsequently
treated as anarchists who acted on their own. For a Bolshevik version of
these events see D. S. Buzin-Bich, "Partizansko-povstancheskoe dvizhenie
v nizoviakh reki Amura, 1919–1920 gg.," *Revoliutsiia na Dalnem Vostoke*,
pp. 5–63. White versions are V. Ech, *Ischeznuvshii gorod*, and A. Ia. Gutman-Gan, *Gibel Nikolaevska na Amure*.

78. The threat of bolshevism was a real concern for Japan and was a
reason used for Japan's continued presence in Siberia.

79. Russia (1923–USSR), Ministerstvo inostrannykh del SSSR, *Dokumenty vneshnei politiki SSSR*, 2 : 388–89 (hereafter cited as *Dokumenty*);
Eudin and North, *Soviet Russia and the East*, pp. 308–9.

80. Japanese Publicity Bureau, Mar. 26, 30, and 31, 1920, in *The
News Summary*, Apr. 20, 1920, found in U.S. National Archives, Record Group
45: Naval Records Collection of the Office of Naval Records and Library,
Subject File 1911–1927, Box 613.

The Genro, a group of elder statesmen who had been instrumental in
overturning Tokugawa power in 1867–68, were the most important formula-
tors of policy in the first few decades after 1868 and subsequently were
confidential advisors to the Meiji emperor and his successor and thus were
the most influential statesmen in Japan as late as the early 1920s. Their
importance is indicated by the consultation with the senior Genro, Yamagata
Aritomo, just prior to the Japanese offensive in Siberia, as reported by the

Japanese Publicity Bureau on March 26, 1920 (*News Summary*, Apr. 20, 1920). According to Hackett (*Yamagata Aritomo*, pp. 322 ff.), Hara constantly consulted Yamagata on all important questions. Yamagata approved Japanese occupation of northern Sakhalin and, apparently, the April offensive, but he pressed for a speedy withdrawal from western Siberia to avoid future incidents. Hackett has presented this aged Genro as a very influential moderating force who sought to reach compromises with the cabinet, which wanted to withdraw from Siberia, and Chief of Staff Uehara and his field commanders, who favored an aggressive policy independent of civilians.

81. "Japanese Aggression in the Russian Far East," p. 3246.

82. Ibid., p. 3247.

83. Boldyrev, *Direktoriia*, p. 327; Petr S. Parfenov, "Peregovory s komandovaniem belykh sibirskikh armii v 1920–1922 gg.," *Proletarskaia revoliutsiia* 58 (1926): 152. P. A. Tseitlin had been a Bolshevik since 1905 and was a leader in Vladivostok from 1917 until his death in 1921 (Petrov, *Geroicheskie gody*, p. 379). Professor Higuchi had been a student at Kiev Ecclesiastical Academy and later a teacher at the Orthodox seminary in Tokyo. He and other Orthodox Japanese provided a valuable contact between Japanese expansionists and Russian anti-Communists and performed other services, such as, interpreting and propagandizing. See White, *Siberian Intervention*, pp. 180–81.

84. Boldyrev, *Direktoriia*, pp. 327–29; Moisei Gubelman, "Litso iaponskoi interventsii," *Taezhnye pokhody*, pp. 214–16.

85. "Japanese Aggression in the Russian Far East," p. 3263. See also Boldyrev, *Direktoriia*, p. 331; and Parfenov, "Peregovory," p. 161.

86. Parfenov, "Peregovory," p. 161.

87. Maritime Province, Siberia, "Doklad Vremennomy pravitelstvu Primorskoi oblastnoi zemskoi uprave, Komissii po obsledovaniiu obstoiatelstv sobytii 4–6 aprelia vo Vladivostoke," p. 31 (hereafter cited as "Doklad"). Varneck and Fisher, *Testimony of Kolchak*, pp. 375 ff., contains excerpts from this translation.

88. Japanese Publicity Bureau, Mar. 26–31, 1920 (*News Summary*, Apr. 20, 1920); Nikiforov, *Zapiski*, p. 189. See also Army Intelligence Report of March 2, 1920, in File 2657–H–19, U.S. National Archives, Record Group 165: Records of the War Department General and Special Staffs. This report stated that the Japanese army would like to have driven the SRs and Bolsheviks out of Vladivostok and Nikolsk, but that the Foreign Office prevented this action.

89. Cited in G. Reikhberg, "Sobytiia 4–5 aprelia 1920 g. v Primore," *Istorik-Marksist* 5–6 (1935): 134–35.

90. Rudnev, *Pri vechernikh ogniakh*, pp. 306–7.

91. "Doklad," p. 12.
92. Graves, *America's Siberian Adventure*, p. 328.
93. "Doklad," p. 17.
94. Graves, *America's Siberian Adventure*, p. 328.
95. Allen to Ferrand, April 8, 1920, ARCP File 987.08.
96. Ibid.
97. *Oktiabrskaia revoliutsiia*, pp. 175–78.
98. Nikiforov, *Zapiski*, p. 190.
99. Ibid., pp. 190–92. After the murder of Lazo the Maritime Communists created their most well-known martyr. The hagiography concerning this figure is extensive. See for example, Moisei Gubelman, "Sergei Lazo," *Dalnii Vostok* 1 (Jan.–Feb. 1957):149–59; *Sergei Lazo*; B. L. Beliaev, *Liudi i sobytiia Primoria*, pp. 111–19 and passim; and Vasilii P. Golionko, *V ogne borby*. Lazo is the subject of a poem, a statue, and a major street in Vladivostok, Ulitsa imeni Lazo (formerly called Poltavskaia ulitsa).
100. "Doklad," pp. 151–52.
101. Ibid., pp. 82 ff.; Petrov, *Geroicheskie gody*, p. 180.
102. "Doklad," pp. 21–26, 35–38, and 154.
103. Ibid., pp. 152–54.
104. "Japanese Aggression in the Russian Far East," p. 3263.
105. *Japan Times and Mail*, Apr. 10, 1920.
106. Dr. Girsa's report is given in Morris to Colby, May 10, 1920, 861.00/6965, U.S. National Archives, Record Group 59.
107. "Japanese Aggression in the Russian Far East," pp. 3262–63; *Dokumenty*, 2:441–43.
108. *Golos rodiny, Deistviia Iaponii v Priamurskom krae*, pp. 34–35.
109. "Doklad," pp. 168–69; "Weekly Report," Apr. 22, 1920, ARCP, File 987.08.
110. Boldyrev, *Direktoriia*, pp. 332–34.
111. Ibid., pp. 337, 556, n. 318; also Golionko, *V ogne borby*, p. 219, and "Weekly Report," Apr. 22, ARCP, File 987.08.
112. Boldyrev, *Direktoriia*, p. 326; "Doklad," p. 32.
113. "Doklad," pp. 177–78; Boldyrev, *Direktoriia*, p. 335. Most of the gold stored in Vladivostok had already been sent to safer ground in Blagoveshchensk.
114. The text of these two agreements, taken from "Japanese Aggression in the Russian Far East," pp. 3263–65, is given in Appendix 1. A Russian text of the April 29 agreement is in *Dokumenty*, 2:496–98.
115. "Japanese Aggression in the Russian Far East," p. 3263. This was often referred to as the thirty-verst zone. One verst equals 3,500 feet; one kilometer equals 3,280 feet.

116. Ibid., pp. 3264–65.

117. Boldyrev, *Direktoriia*, pp. 343–44; Vasilii P. Antonenko, "Kratkaia istoriia smeny pravitalstv vo Vladivostoke s 31 ianvaria 1920 g. do evakuatsii oktiabria 1922 g.," p. 7.

118. Boldyrev, *Direktoriia*, p. 341.

119. G. A. Muchnik, *Dvadtsat let partiinoi raboty v Sibiri i na Dalnem Vostoke*, p. 165.

120. Gubelman, "Litso," p. 235; Belikova, *Bolsheviki Primoria*, p. 73.

121. See the Dalkraikom resolution in *Borba za vlast*, pp. 438–39; also Mirovoi, "Partiinia organizatsiia," pp. 316–17, and Melekhin, *Taezhnymi tropami*, pp. 169–80.

122. This will be considered in more detail in the next chapter.

Chapter 3

1. Leonid M. Papin, *Krakh Kolchakovshchiny i obrazovanie Dalnevostochnoi respubliki*, p. 168.

2. *Golos rodiny*, Apr. 28, 1920; *Japan Times and Mail*, May 8, 1920.

3. U.S., Department of State, *Papers Relating to the Foreign Relations of the United States, 1920*, 1 : 513 (hereafter cited as *Foreign Relations, 1920*).

4. *Japan Times and Mail*, May 15, 1920.

5. Ibid.

6. Petr S. Parfenov, *Borba za Dalnii Vostok, 1920–1922 gg.*, pp. 206–8.

7. Ibid., pp. 204–5.

8. Russia (1923–USSR), Ministerstvo inostrannykh del SSSR, *Dokumenty vneshnei politiki SSR*, 2 : 445–46 (hereafter cited as *Dokumenty*).

9. Ibid., p. 514.

10. F. N. Petrov et al., *Geroicheskie gody borby i pobed*, p. 190.

11. Parfenov, *Borba*, p. 240. Khotimskii (1892–1937) had been a Communist only since 1918, but he was a member of the Sibburo and then of the Dalburo from May 23, 1920, until February 1921 (Petrov, *Geroicheskie gody*, p. 378).

12. Papin, *Krakh Kolchakovshchiny*, p. 180.

13. Parfenov, *Borba*, p. 209.

14. Pavel P. Postyshev, *Pervyi partizanskii tungusskii otriad*, p. 46.

15. Parfenov, *Borba*, pp. 209–11. Utkin, while returning from Blagoveshchensk, was murdered by a White officer in Khabarovsk on June 19 (Petr S. Parfenov, *Uroki proshlago*, p. 155).

16. Petr M. Nikiforov, *Zapiski premera DVR*, p. 199; Vasilii G. Boldyrev, *Direktoriia, Kolchak, interventy*, p. 356.

17. In addition to Nikiforov the new coalition government included:

I. G. Kushnarev (Communist)—Communications; V. E. Iakovenko-Khodkevich (Communist)—State Control; Aleksandr Leonov(Communist)—Industry; S. A. Andreev (Internationalist)—Finance; D. I. Solovev (Menshevik)—Production and Supply; A. I. Kabtsan (Menshevik)—Business Manager; A. V. Grozin (Popular Socialist)—Justice; Boldyrev (the only nonsocialist)—Military-Navy; A. N. Kruglikov (Socialist Revolutionary)—Internal Affairs; and A. S. Medvedev (Socialist Revolutionary)—Foreign Affairs. Boldyrev has stated in his memoirs that foreign affairs were actually directed by Vice Minister of Foreign Affairs Boris Skvirskii, a leading Communist, and by A. M. Vyvodtsev. See Boldyrev, *Direktoriia*, p. 358; Nikiforov, *Zapiski*, pp. 199–200.

18. Nikiforov, *Zapiski*, p. 200.

19. The definitive detailed account of this question and, indeed, all aspects of finance in eastern Siberia during the civil war is A. I. Pogrebetskii, *Denezhnoe obrashchenie i denezhnye znaki Dalnego Vostoka za period voiny i revoliutsii, 1914–1924*.

20. See Charles Smith's memo (American Representative on the Inter-Allied Railway Board) to Colby, Sept. 11, 1920, 861.00/7568, U.S. National Archives, Record Group 59: General Records of the Department of State (hereafter cited by file and document number only). Smith's reports must be read with his anti-Japanese and pro-FER views in mind.

21. Pogrebetskii, *Denezhnoe obrashchenie*, p. 15.

22. Ibid., pp. 35–36.

23. Ibid., pp. 33 ff.; *Japan Advertiser*, May 6 and 9, 1920.

24. Counterfeiting was a serious problem in Siberia. For this reason the Maritime leaders wanted to use paper currency of a high quality. The American Banknote Company had produced beautifully engraved notes for the Provisional Government, but it fell before it could use them. The Maritime government obtained these notes and put them into circulation.

25. Pogrebetskii, *Denezhnoe obrashchenie*, pp. 47–53. For the June 5 law and subsequent events, see also John K. Caldwell (consul at Vladivostok) to Colby, June 14, 1920, 861a.51/–.

26. Pogrebetskii, *Denezhnoe obrashchenie*, pp. 54, 57.

27. Ibid., pp. 54–55.

28. Ibid., p. 112.

29. Boldyrev, *Direktoriia*, pp. 360–61; N. A. Andrushkevich, "Posledniaia Rossiia," chap. 2, pp. 25–30; Vladimir P. Anichkov, "Vospominaniia," p. 80.

30. This is the conclusion of many observers, including Pogrebetskii, *Denezhnoe obrashchenie*, pp. 33–34, and Anichkov, "Vospominaniia," p. 87.

31. Dates vary regarding the establishment of this new coalition. Parfenov (*Borba*, pp. 219–20) has given July 2 as the date; Caldwell, in a

July 21, 1920, dispatch (861a.002/–), has given July 10; Papin (*Krakh Kolchakovshchiny*, p. 169), July 7. Nikiforov (*Zapiski*, pp. 211–13) indicated there were two reshuffles, the first on June 28 and the second apparently in early July. *Dalnevostochnoe obozrenie* (July 30, 1920) has said that the bourgeois groups would be allowed four posts, which, with one difference, was what they received. Boldyrev (*Direktoriia*, p. 365) has written what probably is the most accurate account. While giving no specific date, he has stated that early in July a new coalition was formed when four bourgeois members, as well as the Popular Socialist V. I. Dmitrash, entered the cabinet. Soon, M. S. Binasik (Menshevik) became chairman, and on August 10 B. Ia. Gurevich, E. A. Trupp, and I. A. Iakushev (all SRs) joined the cabinet. The most important change was the addition of the bourgeois members. See also General Kolobov, "Borba s bolshevikami na Dalnem Vostoke," chap. 24, pp. 6–7, for a conservative view of the cabinet. He placed more emphasis upon the Jewish make-up than upon their qualifications.

32. Papin, *Krakh Kolchakovshchiny*, p. 169. No date or source is given. Charles Smith in a September 13, 1920, memo to Colby (861.00/7568) stated that the Japanese were behind the formation of the coalition, as did Kolobov, "Borba s bolshevikami," chap. 24, p. 5.

33. Nikiforov, *Zapiski*, p. 208.

34. Petrov, *Geroicheskie gody*, pp. 196–97, stated that this was discussed at the June 18 conference of Party activists. The resolutions of the conference, given in *Borba za vlast Sovetov v Primore, 1917–1922*, pp. 489–93, did not indicate such a discussion, although the general situation in the Far East and the role of the Popular Assembly were subjects of discussion.

35. Nikiforov, *Zapiski*, pp. 208–9. The Maritime Politburo was chaired by Nikiforov and included Kushnarev and probably Gubelman. Moisei Gubelman, who presumably replaced Lazo (murdered by the Japanese) was on the Revshtab, which was created when the Party went underground during the Japanese offensive of April 4–5. He became chairman of the Politburo late in 1920. Undoubtedly Nikiforov and Kushnarev were responsible for deciding upon the more moderate course.

36. Andrushkevich, "Posledniaia Rossiia," chap. 2, p. 23; Kolobov, "Borba s bolshevikami," chap. 24, p. 7.

37. This is indicated in several memoirs, for example, Nikiforov, *Zapiski*, pp. 207 ff.; L. A. Krol, *Za tri goda*, pp. 211–12; Boldyrev, *Direktoriia*, passim.

38. Pogrebetskii, *Denezhnoe obrashchenie*, pp. 74–76.

39. Anichkov, "Vospominaniia," pp. 60–65.

40. The nonsocialists included V. G. Boldyrev (nonpartisan)—Military-Navy; B. Ia. Iakovich (Trade-Industry)—State Control; B. Ia. Briner

(Trade-Industry)—Industry; I.I.Tsimmerman (Trade-Industry)—Finance; and
V. A. Vinogradov (Cadet)—Foreign Affairs. The remaining members were
B. Ia. Gurevich (SR)—Internal Affairs; D. I. Solovev (Menshevik)—Produc-
tion and Supply; V. I.Dmitrash (Popular Socialist)—Business Manager; E.A.
Trupp (SR)—Justice; and I. A. Iakushev (SR)—Agriculture. See Boldyrev,
Direktoriia, p.365; Nikiforov, *Zapiski*, p.211–13; Parfenov, *Borba*, pp. 219–
20; and Caldwell to Colby, July 21, 1920, 861a.002/–.

41. Parfenov, *Borba*, p. 209; Nikiforov, *Zapiski*, pp. 200–220; *Volia*,
May 30, 1920.

42. Andrushkevich, "Posledniaia Rossiia," chap. 2, pp. 20–22.

43. Nikiforov, *Zapiski*, p. 202. Parfenov (*Borba*, p. 215) noted figures
similar to Nikiforov's but differing slightly. See also *Volia*, June 15, 1920,
for election results and its criticism of Communist electoral tactics.

44. Boldyrev, *Direktoriia*, p. 359; Sergei P. Rudnev, *Pri vechernikh
ogniakh*, pp. 351–52.

45. Maritime Province, Siberia. Vremmenoe narodnoe sobranie Dalnego
Vostoka, sessiia 1, *Stenograficheskie otchety*, June 20, 1920, p. 1 (hereafter
cited as *Sten. otchety*).

46. Ibid., June 25, 1920, pp. 10–11.

47. Ibid., pp. 25–26.

48. The text of this treaty is given in U.S. Congress, "Japanese Aggression in the Russian Far East," *Congressional Record*, pp. 3265–66
(hereafter cited as "Japanese Aggression in the Russian Far East"), and
Dokumenty, 3 (1959) : 44–47.

49. *Japan Advertiser*, June 3, 1920; Edward Bell (chargé in Japan) to
Colby, June 4, 1920, in *Foreign Relations, 1920*, 3:551.

50. "Japanese Aggression in the Russian Far East," p. 3265.

51. Ibid., p. 3250. This note also concerned the justification for Japan's recent seizure of Sakhalin Island (until the Nikolaevsk massacre could
be satisfactorily compensated) and Japan's remaining in the Maritime Province (until the menace to Japanese citizens and to Korea could be alleviated).

52. Ibid., pp. 3265–66.

53. Nikiforov, *Zapiski*, p. 220; Boldyrev, *Direktoriia*, p. 365.

54. *Sten. otchety*, July 3, 1920, pp. 2 ff.

55. Ibid., July 17, 1920, p. 11. See also Papin, *Krakh Kolchakovshchiny*, p. 171.

56. *Sten. otchety*, July 17, 1920, pp. 15–16.

57. Ibid., pp. 16–17.

58. Ibid., pp. 20–21.

59. Parfenov, *Borba*, p. 232; P. Karavaev, "DVR sozdana," *V ogne
revoliutsii*, p. 189.

60. Karavaev, "DVR sozdana," p.190; Papin, Krakh Kolchakovshchiny, p. 172.

61. Rudnev, Pri vechernikh ogniakh, p. 315; Russia, July 30, 1920, 861.00/7525, Record Group 59.

62. Boldyrev, Direktoriia, p. 366.

63. Petr S. Parfenov, "Perogovory s komandovaniem belykh sibirskikh armii v 1920–1922 gg.," Proletarskaia revoliutsiia 58 (1926):166; "Iaponskaia interventsiia: sekretnye telegrammy iaponskoi komandovaniia po dalnevostochnym delam," Sbornik materialov po istorii revoliutsionnogo dvizheniia na Dalnem Vostoke, pp. 278–87.

64. Parfenov, "Peregovory," p. 166.

65. Parfenov, Borba, pp. 232–33.

66. John F. Stevens (president, Inter-Allied Technical Board) to Colby, Aug. 11, 1920, 861.77/1657, and Aug. 22, 1920, 861.77/1672.

67. Kolobov, "Borba s bolshevikami," chap. 25, pp. 14 ff.; Nikiforov, Zapiski, p. 222.

68. Rudnev, Pri vechernikh ogniakh, p. 313. Two of the delegates left detailed objective accounts: Rudnev, already cited, and Kushnarev. See I. G. Kushnarev, "Svoi i chuzhie," Sbornik materialov po istorii revoliutsionnogo dvizheniia na Dalnem Vostoke, pp. 262–78. Kushnarev's memoirs are particularly notable because they were published at a time when more diversity of opinion was permitted by the Russian Communists.

69. Kushnarev, "Svoi i chuzhie," pp. 264–67.

70. Vladivo-Nippo, July 27, 1920.

71. Kushnarev, "Svoi i chuzhie," p. 268. See also secret Japanese telegrams, no. 281, General Oi to Colonel Isome, Aug. 3, 1920, 861.77/1769, U.S. National Archives, Record Group 76, and a discussion of these telegrams in Appendix 2, pp. 180–82.

72. Parfenov, Borba, pp. 235–36; Papin, Krakh Kolchakovshchiny, p. 175. Neither Rudnev nor Kushnarev gave details of the terms.

73. Rudnev, Pri vechernikh ogniakh, pp. 324–28; Kushnarev, "Svoi i chuzhie," p. 270.

74. Kushnarev, "Svoi i chuzhie," p. 272.

75. Ibid., pp. 272–74.

76. Rudnev, Pri vechernikh ogniakh, pp. 329–30; Kushnarev, "Svoi i chuzhie," p. 274.

77. Kushnarev, "Svoi i chuzhie," pp. 275–76; Rudnev, Pri vechernikh ogniakh, pp. 339–40; Japan Advertiser, Aug. 31, 1920; Douglas Jenkins (consul at Harbin) to Colby, Aug. 27, 1920, Foreign Relations, 1920, 3:542.

78. Kushnarev, "Svoi i chuzhie," p. 277.

79. Boldyrev, Direktoriia, p. 366; Parfenov, Borba, p. 336.

80. Boldyrev, *Direktoriia*, p. 366. Curiously, Nikiforov, a member of the council, mentioned nothing of this nor of the Kabtsan delegation in his memoirs.

81. Rudnev, *Pri vechernikh ogniakh*, p. 345.

82. The text is given in Papin, *Krakh Kolchakovshchiny*, p. 176.

83. Nikiforov, *Zapiski*, p. 214.

84. Papin, *Krakh Kolchakovshchiny*, p. 172.

85. Ibid., pp. 175–76. See also Nikiforov, *Zapiski*, p. 221.

86. Nikiforov, *Zapiski*, p. 226. Parfenov (*Borba*, p. 245) gave the date as September 10, and Papin (*Krakh Kolchakovshchiny*, p. 178) as September 8. The delegation probably left several days later, as Nikiforov indicated.

87. Rudnev, *Pri vechernikh ogniakh*, p. 345.

88. Nikiforov, *Zapiski*, pp. 225–26.

89. Paul T. Pastall (acting special transportation inspector in Harbin) to B. O. Johnson (an Inter-Allied Railway Commission official), Oct. 12, 1920, U.S. National Archives, Record Group 76: United States Participation in International Conferences, Commissions, and Expositions . . ., Box 9 (hereafter cited as Pastall to Johnson with the date).

90. General Akintievskii, "K istorii grazhdanskoi voiny v Sibiri i na Dalnem Vostoke, 1918–1922," chap. 3, pp. 9 ff.; Kolobov, "Borba s bolshevikami," chap. 26, pp. 11 ff.; Boldyrev, *Direktoriia*, p. 370.

91. Akintievskii, "K istorii grazhdanskoi voiny," chap. 3, pp. 26–27; General Baron Peter N. Wrangel, *Always with Honor*, p. 297.

92. John Bradley, *Allied Intervention in Russia*, pp. 182–83, 210.

93. Nikiforov, *Zapiski*, pp. 226–27; Parfenov, "Peregovory," p. 172; Pastall to Johnson, Oct. 12, 1920.

94. Nikiforov, *Zapiski*, pp. 227–28.

95. Pastall to Johnson, Oct. 12, 1920.

96. Nikiforov, *Zapiski*, p. 227.

97. Ibid., p. 228; *Oktiabrskaia revoliutsiia i grazhdanskaia voina na Dalnem Vostoke*, eds. S. Tsypkin et al., p. 203; Papin, *Krakh Kolchakovshchiny*, pp. 180–81.

98. Papin, *Krakh Kolchakovshchiny*, p. 181.

99. Nikiforov, *Zapiski*, p. 228; Papin, *Krakh Kolchakovshchiny*, p. 181.

100. *Slovo*, Sept. 3, 1920.

101. Pogrebetskii, *Denezhnoe obrashchenie*, pp. 80 ff.; Macgowan to Colby, Oct. 22, 1920, 861.9119/50.

102. "Weekly Report," Aug. 31 and Oct. 12, 1920, American Red Cross Papers, File 987.08.

103. See the statement of Assistant Chief Inspector of the Militia

Nornberg and accompanying comments by Charles Smith in his report of September 21, 1920, to Colby, 861.00/7564.

104. See Boldyrev, *Direktoriia*, pp. 370–72, regarding the several outstanding issues.

105. Rudnev, *Pri vechernikh ogniakh*, pp. 342 ff.; Boldyrev, *Direktoriia*, p. 371; also the statement by Tsimmerman in *Golos rodiny*, Oct. 4, 1920.

106. Nikiforov, *Zapiski*, pp. 223–25.

107. Larisa I. Belikova, *Bolsheviki Primoria v gody grazhdanskoi voiny i inostrannoi interventsii*, p. 83.

108. *Golos rodiny*, Sept. 24, 1920.

109. Rudnev, *Pri vechernikh ogniakh*, pp. 352–53; Boldyrev, *Direktoriia*, p. 372. The best source in English on this subject is Allen S. Whiting, *Soviet Policies in China, 1917–1924*, especially pp. 145 ff. The best Russian account is Moisei A. Persits, *Dalnevostochnaia respublika i Kitai*. Mark Kazanin, a member of the mission, published his memoirs in 1963. See M. I. Kazanin, *Zapiski sekretarii misii*.

110. Kazanin, *Zapiski sekretarii missii*, pp. 98–101; Rudnev, *Pri vechernikh ogniakh*, pp. 52–53.

111. Boldyrev, *Direktoriia*, p. 372.

112. Rudnev, *Pri vechernikh ogniakh*, p. 352; Parfenov, *Borba*, pp. 250–51.

113. See *Japan Advertiser*, Oct. 16, 1920; and the press review in 861.9111/50 and 861.911/105.

114. This problem will be examined in the next chapter.

115. Boldyrev, *Direktoriia*, p. 374; Smith to Colby, Nov. 1, 1920, 861.00/7801.

116. Boldyrev, *Direktoriia*, pp. 378–79.

117. Ibid., p. 379.

118. Ibid., pp. 382–83; *Volia*, Nov. 7, 1920.

119. Parfenov (*Borba*, p. 259) has claimed that Krasnoshchekov questioned Boldyrev, Gurevich (SR), and Berlatskii (Menshevik, added to the council as Boldyrev's assistant at the demand of the Socialist Bloc) regarding their action. Boldyrev (*Direktoriia*, pp. 383–84) has written that Berlatskii, Gurevich, and Kushnarev were thus grilled, omitting his own name. It is interesting to note Kushnarev's lower status among Communists. Formerly one of the most important Communists in the Russian Far East, in November he remained in Vladivostok and subsequently was ignored by Communist leaders and writers—the price for pursuing the wrong line for too long.

120. Parfenov, *Borba*, p. 260; *Vladivostok Daily News*, Nov. 13, 1920.

121. Boldyrev, *Direktoriia*, p. 385; *Vladivostok Daily News*, Nov. 13, 1920.

122. Boldyrev, *Direktoriia*, p. 388.

123. Ibid.

124. The text is in Boldyrev, *Direktoriia*, p. 387; the *Vladivostok Daily News*, Nov. 14, 1920; and "Japanese Aggression in the Russian Far East," p. 3253.

125. Boldyrev, *Direktoriia*, p. 389.

126. Parfenov, *Borba*, p. 259; Nikiforov, *Zapiski*, p. 229.

127. *Vladivostok Daily News*, Nov. 21, 1920. See also Parfenov, *Borba*, pp. 261, 265–67.

128. FER representative Pumpianskii to Paul Pastall in Pastall to Johnson, Nov. 24, 1920.

129. Parfenov, *Borba*, p. 264; Smith to Colby, Nov. 10, 1920, 861.00/ 7820; *Slovo*, Nov. 27, 1920; *Vladivostok Daily News*, Nov. 30, 1920.

130. The resolution of the Trade-Industry Group was given to *Slovo*, Nov. 30, 1920. The resolution of the Progressive Democrats was printed in the *Vladivostok Daily News*, Nov. 23, 1920. See also *Vladivostok Daily News*, Nov. 14, 1920, and *Slovo*, Nov. 11, 1920, for anti-Chita resolutions.

131. "Parties and Governments in the Far East," *The Nation*, Feb. 2, 1921, p. 191.

132. *Vladivostok Daily News*, Nov. 14, 1920.

133. Smith to Colby, Dec. 1, 1920, 861.00/7556; *Volia*, Nov. 28, 1920.

134. For the Menshevik position as stated by Binasik, see the *Vladivostok Daily News*, Dec. 4, 1920. Socialist Revolutionary opinion as expressed by Trupp and Medvedev is given in Smith to Colby, Nov. 29, 1920, 861.00/7956.

135. *Vladivostok Daily News*, Nov. 30, 1920; Parfenov, *Borba*, p. 271.

136. Grigorii M. Semenov, *O sebe*, pp. 154–55.

137. *Golos rodiny, Deistviia Iaponii*, pp. 45–47; also Boldyrev, *Direktoriia*, p. 395.

138. "Japanese Aggression in the Russian Far East," pp. 3266–67.

139. Given in *Volia*, Nov. 28, 1920.

140. A Russian text is given in *Borba za vlast*, p. 742. An English text is in the *Vladivostok Daily News*, Dec. 7, 1920.

141. *Vladivostok Daily News*, Dec. 7, 1920.

142. The text was published in the *Vladivostok Daily News*, Dec. 14, 1920. See also ibid., Dec. 16, 1920.

143. Several sources list the members of this new cabinet, but they all differ. See *Vladivostok Daily News*, Dec. 14, 1920; *Volia*, Dec. 14, 1920;

Nikiforov, *Zapiski*, p. 246; and Boldyrev, *Direktoriia*, p. 398.

144. *Vladivostok Daily News*, Dec. 16, 1920.
145. Boldyrev, *Direktoriia*, p. 398.
146. Smith to Colby, Dec. 12, 1920, 861.00/7954.
147. *Golos rodiny*, Dec. 21, 1920.
148. To this comment the pro-FER *Dalnevostochnoe obozrenie* wryly commented that Krol failed to mention who had died. *Vladivostok Daily News*, Dec. 19, 1920.

Chapter 4

1. See chap. 2, pp. 29–31.
2. See chap. 3, p. 61.
3. See chap. 3, pp. 61–62.
4. Petr S. Parfenov, "Peregovory s komandovaniem belykh sibirskikh armii v 1920–1922 gg.," *Proletarskaia revoliutsiia* 58 (1926) : 187.
5. Savintsev, "Recollections from the period of civil war in China, 1920, by the head of the Information Office of the Ufa Army group," p. 23.
6. Interview of the author with Vladimir B. Rojanski.
7. Vasilii G. Boldyrev, *Direktoriia, Kolchak, interventy*, p. 390.
8. Parfenov, "Peregovory," p. 184. General Takayanagi, however, denied this. He publicly stated that arrangements were made between Semenov and the Chinese and that the Japanese had nothing to do with it. This is highly unlikely. *Vladivostok Daily News*, Dec. 14, 1920.
9. Oi statement in *Japan Chronicle*, Jan. 20, 1921, and in conversation with Charles Smith on November 30, 1921, in Smith to Colby, Jan. 18, 1921, 861.00/8125, U.S. National Archives, Record Group 59: General Records of the Department of State (hereafter cited by file and document number only). According to N. A. Andrushkevich, N. Merkulov was instrumental in persuading the Japanese to allow the Whites to enter the Maritime Province. The Japanese agreed only if the Maritime government approved the transfer. N. A. Andrushkevich, "Posledniaia Rossiia," chap. 3, p. 8.
10. See, for example, Savintsev, "Recollections," p. 30; General Major Akintievskii, "K istorii grazhdanskoi voiny v Sibiri i na Dalnem Vostoke, 1918–1922," chap. 3, p. 28; Boris B. Filimonov, *Belopovstantsy*, 1 : 5; V. Moltchanov ("The Last White General," MS, Bancroft Library, University of California, Berkeley, 1972, pp. 108–9) has stated that all weapons were confiscated by the Chinese.
11. Petr M. Nikiforov, *Zapiski premera DVR*, pp. 229–30; Nikolai K. Iliukhov and I. P. Samusenko, *Partizanskoe dvizhenie v Primore, 1918–1922*, p. 215; Parfenov, "Peregovory," p. 187.

12. Parfenov, "Peregovory," p. 180.

13. Savintsev, "Recollections," p. 23.

14. Boldyrev, *Direktoriia*, p. 390.

15. Ibid.

16. Ibid., p. 391.

17. Grigorii M. Semenov, O *sebe*, p. 154. See also Parfenov, "Peregovory," pp. 176–77.

18. Semenov, O *sebe*, pp. 154–55.

19. Boldyrev, *Direktoriia*, p. 391.

20. There is almost no agreement regarding how many White refugees crossed Manchuria. The figure given is based upon the estimates of Andrushkevich, "Posledniaia Rossiia," chap. 3, p. 8 (30,000); Petr S. Parfenov, *Borba za Dalnii Vostok, 1920–1922 gg.*, pp. 268–71 (35,000); Parfenov, "Peregovory," p. 180 (25,000); *Poslednie novosti*, June 3, 1921 (57,000); Pavel P. Petrov, *Ot Volgi do Tikhago okeana v riadakh belykh, 1918–1922*, p. 181 (29,000).

21. Vladimir B. Rojanski was one of the more fortunate Kappelites who was able to get past a Chinese guard in Harbin. He made connections with friends and earned enough money to emigrate to the United States. Interview with Vladimir B. Rojanski. Also Pastall to Johnson, Dec. 31, 1920, U.S. National Archives, Record Group 76: United States Participation in International Conferences, Commissions, and Expositions . . ., Box 9 (hereafter cited as Pastall to Johnson with the date).

22. Boldyrev, *Direktoriia*, p. 391–93; Parfenov, "Peregovory," pp. 180–81.

23. Boldyrev, *Direktoriia*, pp. 393–94.

24. Parfenov, "Peregovory," p. 182.

25. Ibid.

26. Ibid.

27. Ibid., p. 183.

28. Ibid., p. 187.

29. Ibid.

30. Ibid., p. 177.

31. Parfenov ("Peregovory," p. 178) gave this as published in the Communist newspaper, *Vpered*, on December 9, 1920. He gave December 10 as the date in *Na soglashatelnykh frontakh*, p. 71. Savintsev ("Recollections," pp. 24–25) reported a similar declaration of amnesty in the same organ on November 30.

32. Parfenov, "Peregovory," pp. 188–226; Pastall to Johnson, Dec. 31, 1920, and Jan. 27, 1921; Macgowan to Colby, Dec. 18, 1920, 861.00/7854.

33. Macgowan to Colby, Dec. 21, 1920, 861.00/7857, and Dec. 30, 1920, 861.00/7896.

34. Smith to Colby, Dec. 14, 1920, 861.00/7953.

35. Parfenov, "Peregovory," pp. 226–33.

36. Vasilii P. Golionko, V ogne borby, p. 229.

37. I. K. Artemev, Epizody revoliutsii na Dalnem Vostoke, p. 84. Savelev stated that he could mobilize 10,000 troops if the Ussuri Cossacks were included. Smith to Charles Evans Hughes (secretary of state, March 5, 1921, to 1925), Apr. 12, 1921, 861.00/8650.

38. P. P. Petrov, Ot Volgi, pp. 180–81.

39. This is a complaint found in many Kappelite memoirs and interviews. See, for example, Vladivostok Daily News, Apr. 20, 1921.

40. P. P. Petrov, Ot Volgi, p. 185; Far Eastern Tribune, Mar. 1, 1921; Vladivostok Daily News, Apr. 27, 1921; Smith to Hughes, Apr. 12, 1921, 861.00/8650.

41. Far Eastern Tribune, Feb. 25, 1921; Boldyrev, Direktoriia, p. 409.

42. Smith to Hughes, Apr. 12, 1921, 861.00/8650.

43. Artemev, Epizody, p. 84. This figure approximates the estimates of most other observers, e.g., Bell to Hughes, May 23, 1921, 861a.01/56, (9000); K. Serov, "Stranitsy zhizni," Za vlast Sovetov, p. 75 (17,000 in 3 corps); and Iliukhov and Samusenko, Partizanskoe dvizhenie, p. 222 (3 corps, 15,000).

44. P. P. Petrov, Ot Volgi, p. 180.

45. Japan Advertiser, Apr. 16, 1921; Smith to Hughes, Apr. 12, 1921, 861.00/8650.

46. Japan Advertiser, Apr. 16, 1921; Smith to Hughes, Apr. 12, 1921, 861.00/8650. See also secret Japanese telegrams, no. 652, Feb. 2, 1921, 861.00/8410; nos. 743 and 745, Mar. 22, 1921, 861.00/9412; and others, in U.S. National Archives, Record Group 76 (hereafter, file and date only).

47. On the conditions under which the Kappelites found themselves, see Andrushkevich, "Posledniaia Rossiia," chap. 3, p. 9; Smith to Hughes, Apr. 12, 1921, 861.00/8650; Vladivostok Daily News, Apr. 20, 1921.

48. Smith to Colby, Jan. 11, 1921, 861.00/8113; Vladivostok Daily News, Jan. 21, 1921; Sergei P. Rudnev, Pri vechernikh ogniakh, pp. 362–64.

49. Pastall to Johnson, Mar. 10, 1921; Colonel Vorotovov, "V Zabaikale i na Primorskom fronte v 1920–1921," p. 19.

50. Rudnev, Pri vechernikh ogniakh, p. 355; Boldyrev, Direktoriia, p. 403; V. Ia. Gurevich (SR), Volia Rossii, June 14, 1921.

51. Larisa I. Belikova, Bolsheviki Primoria v gody grazhdanskoi voiny i inostrannoi interventsii, p. 98; Iliukhov and Samusenko, Partizanskoe

dvizhenie, p. 216.

52. Boldyrev, *Direktoriia*, p. 402.

53. Harmon Tupper, *To the Great Ocean*, pp. 322, 324–26, 329.

54. See I. Mamaev, "K voprosy o khunkhuznicheskom dvizheniiam na Dalnem Vostoke," *Revoliutsii na Dalnem Vostoke*, pp. 375–84. The emphasis of this memoir, however, is how many of these khunkhuzes saw the light, became good revolutionaries, and fought on the side of the partisans against the Japanese. Numerous references to Japanese manipulation of khunkhuz bands are found throughout the secret Japanese telegrams referred to in Appendix 2.

55. *Japan Chronicle*, Mar. 7, 1921; *Vladivostok Daily News*, Apr. 20, 1921; Abbott-Davis Report, Bell to Hughes, May 23, 1921, 861a.01/56; Smith to Hughes, Apr. 28, 1921, 861.00/8709; *Far Eastern Tribune*, Feb. 25, 1921.

56. Boldyrev, *Direktoriia*, p. 403. See also A. I. Pogrebetskii, *Denezhnoe obrashchenie i denezhnye znaki Dalnego Vostoka za period voiny i revoliutsii, 1914–1924*, pp. 103–34; Smith to Colby, Jan. 4, 1921, 861.00/8111.

57. Macgowan to Hughes, May 17, 1921, 861.9111/122; *Vladivostok Daily News*, Mar. 17 and Apr. 20, 1921.

58. *Vladivostok Daily News*, Jan. 26, 1921; Artemev, *Epizody*, p. 89.

59. Macgowan to Hughes, May 17, 1921, 861.9111/122; *Slovo*, May 15, 1921; *Golos rodiny*, Apr. 17, 1921.

60. *Slovo*, Mar. 3 and 19, Apr. 13, May 15, 1921; *Far Eastern Tribune*, Mar. 6, 1921.

61. *Vladivostok Daily News*, Mar. 17, 1921; *Far Eastern Tribune*, Mar. 6, 1921.

62. *Vladivostok Daily News*, Apr. 20, 1921; *Far Eastern Tribune*, Mar. 17 and Apr. 20, 1921.

63. Smith and Hughes, Mar. 8, 1921, 861.00/8524.

64. Macgowan to Hughes, Mar. 22, 1921, 861a.5123/–.

65. *Vecher*, Mar. 19, 1921; *Far Eastern Tribune*, Mar. 9 and Apr. 22, 1921.

66. *Golos rodiny*, Mar. 5, 1921.

67. *Far Eastern Tribune*, Mar. 9, 17, and 20, 1921.

68. *Golos rodiny*, Mar. 29, 1921; *Vladivostok Daily News*, Mar. 24, 1921.

69. *Vecher*, Mar. 18 and 21, 1921; *Far Eastern Tribune*, Mar. 22, 1921.

70. *Far Eastern Tribune*, Mar. 22, 23, 1921; *Golos rodiny*, Mar. 21, 1921; *Vladivostok Daily News*, Mar. 31, 1921. The members of the cabinet were listed in the *Vladivostok Daily News*, Apr. 7, 1921.

71. Vladivostok Daily News, Apr. 7 and May 11, 1921; Vecher, Apr. 21, 1921; Far Eastern Tribune, Apr. 22, 1921.

72. Vladivostok Daily News, May 11 and 26, 1921; Far Eastern Tribune, Apr. 20, 22, and 26, 1921.

73. Andrushkevich, "Posledniaia Rossiia," chap. 3, p. 5.

74. Vladimir P. Anichkov, "Vospominaniia," pp. 60–61.

75. Smith and Hughes, Apr. 12, 1921, 861.00/8650.

76. Japan Times and Mail, Apr. 17, 1920.

77. Boldyrev, Direktoriia, p. 349; Japan Advertiser, Apr. 23, 1920.

78. Japan Times and Mail, July 10, 1920. This is the text of the June 24, 1920, protest Medvedev sent to the Japanese Diplomatic Mission in Vladivostok. The text is also given in Golos rodiny, Deistviia Iaponii v Priamurskom krae, pp. 116–18; see also Borba za vlast Sovetov v Primore, 1917–1922, pp. 494–95. For more on Bochkarev, see chap. 6, p. 124.

79. Japan Advertiser, July 27, 1920.

80. Boldyrev, Direktoriia, p. 369.

81. Vladivostok Daily News, Jan. 12, 1921.

82. Ibid., Apr. 13, 1921. Only a few over 380 actually took part in the sessions. Parfenov, Borba, p. 289; Nikiforov, Zapiski, p. 239.

83. Boldyrev, Direktoriia, pp. 415–16; Rudnev, Pri vechernikh ogniakh, pp. 360–62.

84. Rudnev, Pri vechernikh ogniakh, p. 354.

85. Ibid., pp. 354, 383, and 420. See also Boldyrev, Direktoriia, p. 420; Andrushkevich, "Posledniaia Rossiia," chap. 3, passim; Artemev, Epizody, p. 86; and Anichkov, "Vospominaniia," p. 116.

86. Boldyrev, Direktoriia, p. 422.

87. Smith to Colby, Mar. 1, 1921, 861.00/8521.

88. Rudnev, Pri vechernikh ogniakh, p. 348.

89. It is puzzling why Rudnev did not associate with the Democratic Union because of his temperament and education. He was a good friend of Boldyrev and had asked the latter to join him to help balance his party and provide good leadership for the lower classes and Black Hundreds. (Ibid., p. 361.)

90. Ibid., p. 360.

91. For the complete list of Communists, which included Nikiforov, Antonov, and Pshenitsyn, see L. I. Belikova, "Borba Vladivostokskoi partii-noi organizatsii za vossoedinenie oblastei Dalnego Vostoka, ian. 1920-ian. 1921," Materialy po istorii Vladivostoka, bk. 2, 1917–1960, p. 75. Vladivostok's returns are in Oktiabrskaia revoliutsiia i grazhdanskaia voina na Dalnem Vostoke, ed. S. Tsypkin et al., p. 210, and George Montandon, Deux

Ans chez les Bolshevique pour la Croix-rouges de Genève, 1919–1921, p. 228. See also *Japan Chronicle*, Jan. 20, 1921, and *Vladivostok Daily News*, Jan. 12, 1921.

92. Parfenov, *Borba*, p. 287.

93. This is according to *Golos rodiny* editor Kurtev, a Cadet, in Smith to Colby, Mar. 1, 1921, 861.00/8521.

94. Smith to Colby, Jan. 25, 1921, 861.00/8168.

95. Artemev, *Epizody*, pp. 80–81.

96. Semenov, *O sebe*, pp. 156–57; also his "Appeal to All Nations," Feb. 1921, in Perkins to Colby, Feb. 17, 1921, 861.00/8393; secret Japanese telegrams, nos. 693, Feb. 17, 1921, 701, Feb. 27, 1921, 702, Mar. 1, 1921, 861.00/8539; nos. 745, Mar. 22, 1921, 754, Mar. 27, 1921, 776, Apr. 7, 1921, 795, Apr. 15, 1921, 861.00/9413; *Japan Chronicle*, Jan. 27, 1921, and May 26, 1921; Macgowan to Colby, Feb. 12, 1921, 861.00/8182; Charles R. Crane (minister to China) to Colby, Feb. 22, 1921, 861.00/8183; Parfenov, *Borba*, pp. 299–303; Berlin Report 130, June 4, 1921, Dresel to Hughes, June 10, 1921, 861.00/8752.

97. Ivan I. Serebrennikov, *Moi vospominaniia*, 2:300–311.

98. Macgowan to Colby, Nov. 8, 1920, 861.00/7799.

99. Artemev, *Epizody*, p. 81; Andrushkevich, "Posledniaia Rossiia," chap. 3, pp. 2–8, 14–24.

100. Andrushkevich ("Posledniaia Rossiia," chap. 3, pp. 2–8, 14–25) termed it the Committee for the Salvation of the Far East. See also Artemev, *Epizody*, p. 81.

101. Andrushkevich, "Posledniaia Rossiia," chap. 3, pp. 2–8, 14–24.

102. Moltchanov, "The Last White General," p. 115.

103. Rudnev, *Pri vechernikh ogniakh*, p. 362.

104. Smith to Hughes, Mar. 15, 1921, 861.00/8508, and Mar. 29, 1921, 861.00/8570.

105. Artemev, *Epizody*, pp. 82–83; Semenov, *O sebe*, p. 156.

106. Pastall to Johnson, Feb. 12, 1921. See secret Japanese telegrams, no. 652, Feb. 3, 1921, 861.00/8410. Initially the Japanese did approve and support the intent of the congress. See Iu. K. Stark, "Otchet o deiatel-nosti Sibirskoi flotilii v period 1921–1922 gg.," *Morskie zapiski*, 10, 1–2 (1952):7–8.

107. Rudnev, *Pri vechernikh ogniakh*, p. 365.

108. Smith to Hughes, Mar. 8, 1921, 861.00/8524.

109. Smith to Hughes, Mar. 15, 1921, 861.00/8508; Rudnev, *Pri vechernikh ogniakh*, p. 366.

110. Smith to Hughes, Mar. 29, 1921, 861.00/8570.

111. Artemev, *Epizody*, p. 86.

112. The Non-Socialist Council included Nikolai Merkulov, I. I. Eremeev, E. M. Aderson, A. Ia. Makarevich, and V. F. Ivanov as full members, and I. K. Artemev, K. T. Likhoidov, and N. I. Kuzmin as candidate members. See Rudnev, *Pri vechernikh ogniakh*, pp. 366–67, and Artemev, *Epizody*, pp. 86–87.

113. Boldyrev, *Direktoriia*, p. 415; Rudnev, *Pri vechernikh ogniakh*, p. 367.

114. Iliukhov and Samusenko, *Partizanskoe dvizhenie*, pp. 217–20; Boldyrev, *Direktoriia*, p. 417.

115. Boldyrev, *Direktoriia*, p. 417; *Vladivostok Daily News*, Apr. 7 and 13, 1921; Smith to Hughes, Apr. 5, 1921, 861.00/8571.

116. Iliukhov and Samusenko, *Partizanskoe dvizhenie*, p. 219; Smith to Hughes, Apr. 5, 1921, 861.00/8571.

117. Pastall to Johnson, Apr. 6, 1921.

118. Artemev, *Epizody*, p. 87; Rudnev, *Pri vechernikh ogniakh*, p. 367.

119. "Letter from a Kappelite," *Far Eastern Tribune*, Apr. 22, 1921; Boldyrev, *Direktoriia*, p. 417; Smith to Hughes, Apr. 12, 1921, 861.00/9656.

120. P. P. Petrov, *Ot Volgi*, p. 187.

121. *Far Eastern Tribune*, Apr. 7, 1921. According to *Golos rodiny* (Apr. 12, 1921), the orders came from Moscow.

122. *Far Eastern Tribune*, Apr. 10, 1921.

123. Ibid., Apr. 12, 1921.

124. *Golos rodiny*, Apr. 12, 1921; *Far Eastern Tribune*, Apr. 12, 1921; *Vladivostok Daily News*, Apr. 27, 1921.

125. U.S., Congress, "Japanese Aggression in the Russian Far East," *Congressional Record*, p. 3270 (hereafter cited as "Japanese Aggression in the Russian Far East"); Russia (1923–USSR), Ministerstvo inostrannykh del SSSR, *Dokumenty vneshnei politiki SSR*, 4 (1960):78–79 (hereafter cited as *Dokumenty*).

126. "Japanese Aggression in the Russian Far East," pp. 3270–71.

127. U.S., Department of State, *Papers Relating to the Foreign Relations of the United States, 1921*, 2:736–39 (hereafter cited as *Foreign Relations*); Far Eastern Republic, *A Short Outline History of the Far Eastern Republic*, pp. 59–61.

128. Ibid., pp. 61–64.

129. Smith to Hughes, Apr. 12, 1921, 861.00/8650; Bell to Hughes, May 23, 1921, 861a.01/56.

130. The Gludkin affair, for example. See also the report of Nechaev of March 3, 1921, in Smith to Hughes, Mar. 14, 1921, 861.00/8509.

131. General Molchanov stressed the Kappelites shortage of food and money. Moltchanov, "The Last White General," p. 115.

132. Rudnev, Pri vechernikh ogniakh, p. 369; Andrushkevich, "Posledniaia Rossiia," chap. 3, p. 8.

133. See the Boldyrev and Kurtev interviews of Apr. 27 and the Kurtev interview of May 7 in Smith to Hughes, May 10, 1921, 861.00/8723; and the Kurtev interview of May 18 in Smith to Hughes, May 23, 1921, 861.00/8808.

134. Artemev, Epizody, p. 85; Semenov, O sebe, p. 156.

135. P. P. Petrov, Ot Volgi, p. 187; Boldyrev, Direktoriia, p. 419.

136. Stark, "Otchet Siberskoi flotilli," p. 8; Morskie zapiski, 10, 1–2 (1952):8; Rudnev, Pri vechernikh ogniakh, p. 376.

137. Boldyrev, Direktoriia, p. 419.

138. Rudnev, Pri vechernikh ogniakh, pp. 372–74.

139. A. Efimov, "Deistviia otriada Izhevtsev pri zakhvate Vladivostoka v 1921 gody," Vestnik O-va Russkikh Veteranov Velikoi Voiny 59–60 (1931):18–19.

140. Ibid., pp. 20–21; Far Eastern Tribune, May 25, 1921; Japan Chronicle, June 2, 1921; Vladivostok Daily News, May 26, 1921.

141. Far Eastern Tribune, May 26, 1921.

142. Numerous detailed descriptions of the events of May 26 and 27 may be found. Among the best are: Nikiforov, Zapiski, pp. 254–56; V. A. Vrublevskii, "Grazhdanskaia voina v Primore, 1918–1922," V ogne revoliutsii, pp. 180–83; K. Serov, "Stranitsy zhizni," pp. 76–80; Nikolai K. Iliukhov and M. Titov, Partizanskoe dvizhenie v Primore, 1918–1920, pp. 243–44; Boldyrev, Direktoriia, pp. 419–22; Rudnev, Pri vechernikh ogniakh, pp. 374–77; Smith to Hughes, May 29, 1921, 861.00/8811.

143. Efimov, "Deistviia," p. 28.

144. Ibid.; Iliukhov and Titov, Partizanskoe dvizhenie, pp. 243–44; Anichkov, "Vospominaniia," p. 118; Boldyrev, Direktoriia, p. 420; D. Konovalov, "Posledniaia avantiura," Taezhnye pokhody, pp. 247–48.

145. For example, the speech of Foreign Minister Uchida before the Japanese Diet on January 22 reported in the Japan Chronicle, Feb. 3, 1921, and Tachibana's remarks upon arriving in Vladivostok, reported in the Far Eastern Tribune, Feb. 2, 1921.

146. Japan Chronicle, May 19, 1921.

147. Smith to Colby, Jan. 25, 1921, 861.00/8186; Vladivostok Daily News, Jan. 25, 1921; Japan Chronicle, Mar. 10, 1921; Far Eastern Tribune, Mar. 11, 1921.

148. Istoricheskie dokumenty o deistviiakh i zamyslakh mezhdunarodnykh khishchnikov na Dalnem Vostoke, ed. P. M. Nikiforov, pp. 47–52;

Parfenov, *Borba*, pp. 287–88, 299–300. D. C. Poole, head of the Division of Russian Affairs, concluded that the alleged French-Japanese agreement was without foundation. See Poole to Hughes, Jan. 5, 1922, 861a.00/208 and Jan. 7, 1922, 861a.01/210.

149. Semenov (*O sebe*, 148 ff.) has described his role in their larger plan and his relationship with the Chinese, Japanese, and Ungern-Sternberg, who also admitted Chinese and Japanese backing in an interview with K. A. Albertson. Smith to Hughes, Mar. 18, 1921, 861.00/8516, and numerous secret Japanese telegrams indicate this. See also Edward H. Carr, *A History of Soviet Russia*, 3:506–9, and Xenia J. Eudin and Robert C. North, *Soviet Russia and the East, 1920–1927*, pp. 123–25 and 463.

150. *Far Eastern Tribune*, Apr. 13, 1921; Smith to Hughes, May 10, 1921, 861.00/8723.

151. This is indicated by the secret Japanese telegrams, for example, no. 829, May 6, 1921, 861.00/8739, no. 848, May 20, 1921, 861.77/2265, and several others.

Chapter 5

1. Petr M. Nikiforov, *Zapiski premera DVR*, pp. 235–39.

2. The text of the declaration is given in Sergei P. Rudnev, *Pri vechernikh ogniakh*, pp. 377–79.

3. Ibid., p. 397.

4. Smith to Hughes, May 30, 1921, 861.00/8805, U.S. National Archives, Record Group 59: General Records of the Department of State (hereafter cited by file and document number only).

5. Vasilii G. Boldyrev, *Direktoriia, Kolchak, interventy*, p. 431; Smith to Hughes, June 21, 1921, 861.00/8854.

6. Boldyrev, *Direktoriia*, p. 431; Smith to Hughes, June 21, 1921, 861.00/8854.

7. Iu. K. Stark, "Otchet o deiatelnosti Sibirskoi flotilii v period 1921–1922," *Morskie zapiski* 10, 1–2 (1952):13.

8. Pastall to Johnson, May 30, 1921, and June 25, 1921, U.S. National Archives, Record Group 76: United States Participation in International Conferences, Commissions, and Expositions . . ., Box 9 (hereafter cited as Pastall to Johnson with the date); I. K. Artemev, *Epizody revoliutsii na Dalnem Vostoke*, pp. 75 ff; Boldyrev, *Direktoriia*, p. 436.

9. Rudnev, *Pri vechernikh ogniakh*, pp. 377–79.

10. *Slovo*, June 1, 1921.

11. Boldyrev, *Direktoriia*, pp. 437–38.

12. Merkulov interview in Smith to Hughes, May 30, 1921, 861.00/8805.

13. *Dalnevostochnaia zhizn*, June 19, 1921.
14. *Vladivostok Daily News*, June 7, 1921.
15. Temporary Premier V. Kolesnikov's declaration before the Popular Assembly in *Slovo*, July 27 and 28, 1921.
16. *Vladivostok Daily News*, July 1, 1921; Boldyrev, *Direktoriia*, p. 429.
17. Smith to Hughes, June 21, 1921, 861.00/8854.
18. *Vladivostok Daily News*, July 30, 1921.
19. Ibid., July 1, 1921; *Borba za vlast Sovetov v Primore, 1917–1922*, pp. 640–48.
20. *Vladivostok Daily News*, Aug. 20, 1921; Boldyrev, *Direktoriia*, p. 438.
21. Rudnev, *Pri vechernikh ogniakh*, pp. 377–79; *Slovo*, July 27–28, 1921.
22. A. I. Pogrebetskii, *Denezhnoe obrashchenie i denezhnye znaki Dalnego Vostoka za period voiny i revoliutsii, 1914–1922*, p. 134.
23. Ibid.; Macgowan to Hughes, Aug. 16, 1921, 861.9111/149.
24. Pogrebetskii, *Denezhnoe obrashchenie*, p. 135.
25. Artemev, *Epizody*, p. 98; Pogrebetskii, *Denezhnoe obrashchenie*, p. 135.
26. This is according to Kurtev in Smith to Hughes, May 30, 1921, 861.00/8805.
27. Ibid.; *Vladivostok Daily News*, June 7, 1921; Nikiforov, *Zapiski*, pp. 255–56.
28. Nikiforov, *Zapiski*, pp. 255, 259; *Vladivostok Daily News*, June 7, 1921.
29. For example, former militia commander Lepekhin (Smith to Hughes, June 6, 1921, 861.00/8806); V. A. Vrublevskii, "Grazhdanskaia voina v Primore 1918–1922," *V ogne revoliutsii*, p. 181; P. K. Volgin, "Dva etapa," *Sovetskoe Primore* 23 (1957):151; Iliukhov and Vladivostokov (Nikolai K. Iliukhov and I. P. Samusenko, *Partizanskoe dvizhenie v Primore, 1918–1922*, p. 226); and D. Konovalov, "Posledniaia avantiura," *Taezhnye pokhody*, pp. 248–49.
30. Nikiforov, *Zapiski*, p. 256; Smith to Hughes, June 6, 1921, 861.00/8806. V. A. Maslennikov (born 1894), a Bolshevik since 1916, was active in Party work in eastern Siberia since 1918. In 1920 and 1921 he was a secretary of the Maritime Obkom and a member of the Dalburo in 1921 and 1922 (F. N. Petrov et al., *Geroicheskie gody borby i pobed*, p. 368).
31. Nikiforov, *Zapiski*, pp. 255–57.
32. Ibid.

33. Larisa I. Belikova, *Bolsheviki Primoria v gody grazhdanskoi voiny i inostrannoi interventsii*, p. 104.

34. There is no agreement regarding the precise day of the Revkom's creation and its membership. *Geroicheskie gody* (p. 285) and K. Serov ("Stranitsy zhizny," *Za vlast sovetov*, p. 78) have indicated it was formed on May 26. Belikova (*Bolsheviki Primoria*, p. 102) has implied that it was created on May 27. V. Elesh ("Sredi vragov," *Za vlast Sovetov*, p. 174) has stated that the Revkom was formed at a meeting on May 30. Numerous lists of members are given in these same sources. The only real agreement is that Shishkin was elected chairman.

35. Vrublevskii, for example, was sent to Nikolsk to organize a revkom and a short time later was recalled to Vladivostok to help with Party work (Vrublevskii, "Grazhdanskaia," pp. 181–83).

36. *Borba za vlast*, p. 620; Petrov, *Geroicheskie gody*, p. 285; Vrublevskii, "Grazhdanskaia," p. 181.

37. L. I. Belikova, "Sibirskaia voennaia flotiliia v borbe za vlast Sovetov na Dalnem Vostoke, 1917–1922," *Voprosy istorii sovetskogo Dalnego Vostoka*, 1 : 70–72.

38. Iliukhov and Samusenko, *Partizanskoe dvizhenie*, pp. 225–26.

39. Ibid., p. 225; *Geroicheskie gody*, p. 285; Serov, "Stranitsy zhizni," p. 81.

40. *Geroicheskie gody*, p. 286; Vrublevskii, "Grazhdanskaia," p. 183.

41. Many of these are given in *Borba za vlast* for the months of June and July.

42. *Borba za vlast*, pp. 634–36.

43. *Oktiabrskaia revoliutsiia i grazhdanskaia voina na Dalnem Vostoke*, ed. S. Tsypkin et al., p. 226; "Partizanskoe dvizhenie v Primore," *Krasnyi arkhiv*, pp. 40–69; *Borba za vlast*, pp. 656–59.

44. Elesh, "Sredi vragov," p. 181; Volgin, "Dva etapa," p. 151.

45. Iliukhov and Samusenko, *Partizanskoe dvizhenie*, p. 226. V. P. Vladivostokov (1895–1923), a Bolshevik since 1916 and a member of the Vladivostok soviet in 1917 and 1918, was an important partisan leader from 1919 through 1922 (*Geroicheskie gody*, p. 357).

46. *Borba za vlast*, p. 620; M. Gubelman, ed., "Suchanskaia dolina v gody grazhdanskoi voiny," *Krasnyi arkhiv* 91 (1938) : 68–69.

47. Iliukhov and Samusenko, *Partizanskoe dvizhenie*, pp. 226–27.

48. *Borba za vlast*, p. 634–36.

49. Numerous entries are given in *Oktiabrskaia revoliutsiia* for July to September 1921, pp. 226 ff.

50. Serov, "Stranitsy zhizni," p. 83.

51. V. P. Shishkin, "Gody i liudi," *Za vlast Sovetov*, pp. 133–34.

52. *Geroicheskie gody*, p. 288.

53. Ibid.; Nikiforov, *Zapiski*, p. 258; *Vladivostok Daily News*, Sept. 6, 1921; Serov, "Stranitsy zhizni," p. 84.

54. For example, Nikiforov, *Zapiski*, p. 258, and Serov, "Stranitsy zhizni," p. 84.

55. Russia (1923–USSR), Ministerstvo inostrannykh del SSSR, *Dokumenty vneshnei politike SSSR*, 4:153–55 (hereafter cited as *Dokumenty*); Xenia J. Eudin and Robert C. North, *Soviet Russia and the East, 1920–1927*, pp. 210–11; *Soviet Documents on Foreign Policy*, comp. Jane Degras, 1: 246–48.

56. *Dokumenty*, 4:160–65; U.S., Congress, "Japanese Aggression in the Russian Far East," *Congressional Record*, pp. 3272–73 (hereafter cited as "Japanese Aggression in the Russian Far East").

57. Berlin Report 134, June 18, 1921, in Hugh Wilson (U.S. ambassador in Berlin) to Hughes, June 25, 1921, 861.00/8818.

58. Bliukher (1889–1938?), alias Galin, Galen, and Galents, had joined the Party in 1916. He was one of the most effective Soviet military leaders in the civil war and later was sent to China, where he trained Chinese nationalist soldiers at Chiang Kai-shek's Whampoa Military Academy. His distinguished career ended prematurely when he disappeared during Stalin's purges. (Eudin and North, *Soviet Russia and the East*, p. 457.)

59. *Iz istorii grazhdanskoi voiny v SSSR*, 3:751. See chap. 4, p. 133.

60. Orrin Keith, *Japan Advertiser*, July 1, 1921.

61. *Vladivostok Daily News*, June 7, July 1, and Aug. 6, 1921.

62. Grigorii M. Semenov, *O sebe*, pp. 156–57.

63. Both Artemev (*Epizody*, pp. 89–90) and Savelev (Smith to Hughes, June 3, 1921, 861.00/8805) have contended that the Semenovites were most responsible for the coup because they far outnumbered the Kappelites.

64. Rudnev, *Pri vechernikh ogniakh*, p. 390.

65. Bell to Hughes, June 12, 1921, 861.00/8703; Macgowan to Hughes, Sept. 12, 1921, 861a.01/92; Semenov interview with Junius Wood of the *Chicago Daily News* in *Vladivostok Daily News*, June 17, 1921.

66. Rudnev, *Pri vechernikh ogniakh*, p. 389.

67. *Vecher*, June 10, 1921; *Japan Chronicle*, June 23, 1921. See also the anti-Semenov resolutions of other Cossack groups in *Vladivostok Daily News*, June 24, 1921.

68. General Savelev interview in Smith to Hughes, June 11, 1921, 861.00/8806.

69. *Vladivostok Daily News*, June 24, 1921.

70. Rudnev, *Pri vechernikh ogniakh*, pp. 390–91.

71. Kolesnikov (director of foreign affairs) to the Consular Corps, June 23, 1921, 861.9111/136.

72. General Kolobov, "Borba s bolshevikami na Dalnem Vostoke (Horvat. Kolchak. Semenov. Merkulov. Diterikhs)," chap. 28, p. 6; *Vladivostok Daily News*, June 24, 1921; Rudnev, *Pri vechernikh ogniakh*, p. 395; N. A. Andrushkevich, "Posledniaia Rossiia," chap. 4.

73. Details of this interesting episode are given in Semenov, *O sebe*, pp. 163–66; *Golos rodiny*, June 28, 1921; *Vladivostok Daily News*, June 27–28, 1921.

74. *Japan Chronicle*, July 7, 1921; *Vladivostok Daily News*, July 23, 1921.

75. *Slovo*, July 7 and Aug. 12, 1921. The struggle among Cossack leaders is described in Colonel Vorotovov, "V Zabaikale i na Primorskom fronte v 1920–1921," pp. 20 ff. See also Kolobov, "Borba s bolshevikami na Dalnem," chap. 28, p. 3.

76. *Japan Chronicle*, July 7, 1921; Kolobov, "Borba s bolshevikami na Dalnem Vostoke," chap. 28, pp. 9–12. For U.S. attitudes and actions see the following diplomatic dispatches: American Legation, Peking, to Hughes, July 10, 1921, 861a.01/61; Jenkins to Hughes, July 11, 1921, 861.00/8799; Hughes to American Legation, Peking, July 12, 1921, 861.00/8799; Ruddock to Hughes, July 15, 1921, 861.00/8929.

77. *Vladivostok Daily News*, Sept. 3, 1921.

78. *Japan Advertiser*, Sept. 15, 1921.

79. *Vladivostok Daily News*, Sept. 24, 1921; Semenov, *O sebe*, pp. 171–72.

80. Report of Macgowan to Hughes, Sept. 12, 1921, 861a.01/92.

81. Smith to Hughes, June 21, 1921, 861.00/8854; May 30 and June 7, 1921, 861.00/8805; and June 6, 1921, 861.00/8806.

82. Boldyrev, *Direktoriia*, p. 426.

83. Ibid., pp. 426–29.

84. Maritime Province, Siberia. Vremennoe priamurskoe pravitelstvo. Laws, Statutes, etc. "Polozhenie o vyborakh v Priamurskoe narodnoe sobranie."

85. *Vladivostok Daily News*, July 1, 1921. For a Communist account of the meeting and the declaration it issued regarding the elections, see *Borba za vlast*, pp. 640–48.

86. *Vladivostok Daily News*, July 16, 1921.

87. Ibid.

88. Boldyrev, *Direktoriia*, pp. 442, 558; Macgowan to Hughes, Aug. 16,

1921, 861.111/149; *Vladivostok Daily News*, July 16, 1921.

89. *Russkii krai*, July 16, 1921. This newspaper began operations after the May 26, 1921, coup and was the official organ of the government.

90. *Vladivostok Daily News*, July 30, 1921.

91. Ibid.

92. Andrushkevich, "Posledniaia Rossiia," chaps. 4 and 5, pp. 2–4.

93. Rudnev, *Pri vechernikh ogniakh*, p. 405.

94. Boldyrev, *Direktoriia*, p. 436.

95. Rudnev, *Pri vechernikh ogniakh*, p. 399. The new Non-Socialist Council, headed by Andrushkevich, had been elected to replace the old one, which was now the Provisional Priamur Government.

96. Partial lists of the cabinet members may be found in Andrushkevich, "Posledniaia Rossiia," chap. 5, p. 11; *Russkii krai*, Sept. 14, 1921; and Boldyrev, *Direktoriia*, pp. 436–42.

97. See Lenin's report to the Eighth Congress of Soviets in *Dokumenty*, 3 : 405–23.

98. *Dokumenty*, 2 : 444–45, and 514.

99. Boldyrev, *Direktoriia*, pp. 378–79. This was also given in Lenin, *Polnoe sobranie sochinenii* 42 (1963):91 ff.

100. See Edward H. Carr, *A History of Soviet Russia*, 3 : 282–83; and Louis Fischer, *The Soviets in World Affairs*, 1 : 300–301.

101. *Dokumenty*, 3 : 384–85; Far Eastern Republic, *A Short Outline History*, pp. 47–48.

102. Fischer, *Soviets in World Affairs*, 1 : 302–3.

103. *Foreign Relations, 1921*, 2 : 702–5.

104. Fischer, *Soviets in World Affairs*, 1 : 303.

105. *Foreign Relations, 1921*, 2 : 702–5.

106. The instructions given to Abbott and Davis are in *Foreign Relations, 1921*, 2 : 735–36, 741–42. Their full report of July 28, 1921, is in 861a.01/62.

107. *Foreign Relations, 1921*, 2 : 745 ff.

108. Ibid., 746 ff. Boris Z. Skvirskii led the delegation. For more on his background and activities, see Natalie Grant, *Soviet Diplomatic Maneuvers*. Ms. Grant has described how Skvirskii remained in the United States after the Far Eastern Republic was absorbed by Soviet Russia and was, in effect, Soviet representative (or "permanent Moscow agent," as she puts it) during the period that the United States did not recognize the Soviet government. While her study is informative and interesting, Ms. Grant has tended to exaggerate Skvirskii's importance.

109. *Soviet Documents on Foreign Policy*, 1 : 249–51; *Dokumenty*, 4 : 224–76.

110. *Foreign Relations, 1921,* 2:750–52.
111. I have listed only two of the numerous pamphlets in the bibliography.
112. "Japanese Aggression in the Russian Far East," p. 3273.
113. *Dokumenty,* 4:274; George A. Lensen, *Japanese Recognition of the USSR,* p. 15. Lensen's account of Dairen is the best detailed account in English. It is disappointing only because it does not take into consideration events that may have altered Japanese behavior at the talks, such as demands of the military and the winter offensive in the Maritime Province.
114. Moisei A. Persits, *Dalnevostochnaia respublika i Kitai,* p. 236; Lensen, *Japanese Recognition,* p. 16.
115. Lensen, *Japanese Recognition,* p. 24.
116. The text of this draft treaty is given in Lensen, *Japanese Recognition,* pp. 18–25.
117. Lensen, *Japanese Recognition,* p. 30. The entire text is in Lensen, *Japanese Recognition,* pp. 27–30 and Eudin and North, *Soviet Russia and the East,* pp. 212–13.
118. *Vladivostok Daily News,* Oct. 1, 1921.
119. Iliukhov and Samusenko, *Partizanskoė dvizhenie,* pp. 228–29.
120. Serov, "Stranitsy zhizni," p. 85.
121. Iliukhov and Samusenko, *Partizanskoe dvizhenie,* p. 230.
122. Serov, "Stranitsy zhizni," p. 91.
123. Iliukhov and Samusenko, *Partizanskoe dvizhenie,* pp. 229–30.
124. Ibid., 230.
125. Macgowan to Hughes, Dec. 6, 1921, 861a.01/165.
126. *Golos rodiny,* June 21, 1921.
127. Mark Bristol (U.S. high commissioner in Constantinople) to Hughes, July 21, 1921, 861a.01/59.
128. Kolesnikov to the Russian consul in Paris, June 27, 1921, in the Lastours Papers, Hoover Institution.
129. *Dokumenty,* 4:157, 253–54.
130. Macgowan to Hughes, Jan. 6, 1922, 861.00/9214; Poole to Hughes, Jan. 5, 1922, 861a.01/208.
131. Stark, "Otchet Sibirskoi flotilii," 10, 1–2 (1952):18.

Chapter 6

1. John A. White, *The Siberian Intervention,* pp. 389–90; Petr M. Nikiforov, *Zapiski premera DVR,* pp. 283 ff.; S. N. Shishkin, *Grazhdanskaia voina na Dalnem Vostoke, 1918–1922,* pp. 194–95; F. N. Petrov et al., *Geroicheskie gody borby i pobed,* pp. 270 ff.; Nikolai K. Iliukhov and I. P. Samusenko, *Partizanskoe dvizhenie v Primore, 1918–1922,* pp. 231 ff.

2. Sergei P. Rudnev, *Pri vechernikh ogniakh*, p. 413.

3. Vladimir P. Anichkov, "Vospominaniia," p. 124.

4. Rudnev, *Pri vechernikh ogniakh*, p. 411. See the earlier reference to his activities in chap. 4, p. 118.

5. Rudnev, *Pri vechernikh ogniakh*, pp. 411–16; Anichkov, "Vospominaniia," pp. 121–28.

6. Secret Japanese telegrams, no. 1139, Oct. 27, 1921, 861.77/2392, U.S. National Archives, Record Group 76; J. F. Stevens to Hughes, Nov. 8, 1921, 861a.01/109, U.S. National Archives, Record Group 59 (Record Groups 59 and 76 cited hereafter by file and document number only).

7. See the Purington report in 861a.01/17; Rudnev, *Pri vechernikh ogniakh*, p. 414; and Macgowan to Hughes, Dec. 12, 1921, 861a.01/180.

8. Macgowan to Hughes, Dec. 12, 1921, 861a.01/180.

9. Rudnev, *Pri vechernikh ogniakh*, p. 412. For a Communist account see Petrov, *Geroicheskie gody*, pp. 294–305.

10. S. Merkulov interview in *Vladivostok Daily News*, Sept. 17, 1921.

11. *Vladivostok Daily News*, Oct. 3, 1921; A. Efimov, "Ekspeditsiia na Suchan," *Vestnik O-va Russkikh Veteranov Velikoi Voiny*, 64 (1931) : 10–12, 18; 65–66 (1931) : 20–22, 31; 68–69 (1931) : 24–27.

12. Boris B. Filimonov, *Belopovstantsy*, 1 : 80–83; Iliukhov and Samusenko, *Partizanskoe dvizhenie*, pp. 232–34.

13. Iliukhov and Samusenko, *Partizanskoe dvizhenie*, p. 232; Filimonov, *Belopovstantsy*, 1 : 77–80. Lebedev (1898–1937) became a Bolshevik in 1918 and participated in Party political and military activities in the Transbaikal region until he was transferred to the Maritime Province to help lead partisan efforts there. This probably occurred in mid-1921 after the defeat of Ungern-Sternberg in Mongolia (Petrov, *Geroicheskie gody*, p. 366).

14. Filimonov, *Belopovstantsy*, 1 : 83–84.

15. Information on the Siberian Flotilla from a Communist viewpoint may be found in L. I. Belikova, "Sibirskaia voennaia flotiliia v borbe za vlast Sovetov na Dalnem Vostoke, 1917–1922," *Voprosy istorii sovetskogo Dalnego Vostoka*, 1 : 80–89. White viewpoints are given in the memoirs of Admiral Stark in the several issues of *Morskie zapiski* and in the memoirs of Vasilii Antonenko and Boris Filimonov.

16. Filimonov, *Belopovstantsy*, 1 : 84–88; Vasilii P. Antonenko, "Kratkaia istoriia smeny pravitelstv vo Vladivostoke s 31 ianvaria 1920 g. do evakuatsii oktiabria 1922," pp. 37–39; Iu. K. Stark, "Otchet o deiatelnosti Sibirskoi flotilii v period 1921–1922," *Morskie zapiski*, 11, 1–2 (1953) : 5–6; *Vladivostok Daily News*, Nov. 26, 1921; *Golos rodiny*, Nov. 19, 1921.

17. Iliukhov and Samusenko, *Partizanskoe dvizhenie*, pp. 234–35.

18. *Vladivostok Daily News*, Dec. 3, 1921; Filimonov, *Belopovstantsy*, 1:88–97; I. Kochevgin, "Boi za Anuchino," *Za vlast Sovetov*, pp. 304–6.

19. Filimonov, *Belopovstantsy*, 1:95.

20. Ibid., p. 98.

21. Iliukhov and Samusenko, *Partizanskoe dvizhenie*, p. 236.

22. Filimonov, *Belopovstantsy*, 1:98–133. A map of the military situation along the Ussuri Railway in December is given in S. N. Shishkin, *Grazhdanskaia voina na Dalnem Vostoke, 1918–1922*, p. 199.

23. The text is given in Filimonov, *Belopovstantsy*, 1:139–40.

24. Filimonov, *Belopovstantsy*, 2:55–56.

25. *Golos rodiny*, Nov. 21, 1921.

26. Filimonov, *Belopovstantsy*, 1:72.

27. Ibid., 1:72–73; 2:6, 9–12; Ia. Pokus, *Borba za Primore*, pp. 13–15.

28. Pokus, *Borba za Primore*, pp. 20–21; Filimonov, *Belopovstantsy*, 1:239.

29. Nikiforov, *Zapiski*, p. 274; Iliukhov and Samusenko, *Partizanskoe dvizhenie*, p. 239.

30. Rudnev, *Pri vechernikh*, p. 424; Filimonov, *Belopovstantsy*, 1:239.

31. Artemev (*Epizody revoliutsii na Dalnem Vostoke*, p. 113) contended that material support was promised to N. Merkulov by drunken Japanese, but S. Merkulov told Andrushkevich that arms were gained from Vladivostok warehouses by bribing high Japanese officials (N. A. Andrushkevich, "Posledniaia Rossiia," chap. 5, p. 13). Japanese Chief of Staff Isomura told Boldyrev that officially weapons would be given in installments (Vasilii G. Boldyrev, *Direktoriia, Kolchak, interventy*, p. 448). The following winter a certain Major Hara was tried, found guilty, and given a light sentence for distributing arms to the Whites in January 1922. It was felt that the military used Hara as a scapegoat to cover the "crimes" of others. See Vice Consul Nagasaki to Hughes, Oct. 10, 1922, 861a.24/46, and Warren to Hughes, Oct. 27, 1922, 861a.01/167.

32. F. A. Puchkov, "Desiatiletaia godovshchina khabarovskago pokhoda," *Vestnik O-va Russkikh Veteranov Velikoi Voiny*, 65–66 (1931): 14. See also Warren to Hughes, Feb. 10, 1922, 861a.01/109. Merkulov denied to Macgowan that he received military equipment from the Japanese, but so, too, did the Japanese deny giving it (Macgowan to Hughes, Jan. 11, 1922, 861a.01/126).

33. Victorin M. Moltchanov, "The Last White General" (MS, Bancroft Library, University of California, Berkeley, 1972), p. 116.

34. Macgowan to Hughes, Nov. 18, 1921, and Jan. 11, 1922, in

861a.01/126.

35. Filimonov, *Belopovstantsy*, 1:95, 100, 118.

36. Iliukhov and Samusenko, *Partizanskoe dvizhenie*, pp. 236–37.

37. A.K.Flegontov, *Partizanskoi tropoi*, pp.2, 27; Larisa I.Belikova, *Bolsheviki Primoria v gody grazhdanskoi voiny i inostrannoi interventsii*, p. 107; Petrov, *Geroicheskie gody*, pp. 289–90.

38. Pokus, *Borba za Primore*, pp. 16–17, 33–36, 38.

39. Ibid., pp. 19, 36; Vasilii Bliukher, "Volochaevka," *Taezhnye pokhody*, p. 250.

40. Warren to Hughes, Dec. 14,1921, 861a.01/148, and Dec. 17, 1921, 861a.01/151; secret Japanese telegrams, no. 1298, Dec. 19, 1921, and reply, no. 1303, Dec. 26, 1921, 861.77/2471.

41. Moltchanov, "Last White General," p. 120.

42. Pokus, *Borba za Primore*, pp. 41–47; Filimonov, *Belopovstantsy*, 2:24, 29–62.

43. D. I. Boiko-Pavlov, "Po dolinam i po vzgoriam," *Etikh dnei ne smolknet slava*, pp. 446–62.

44. Filimonov, *Belopovstantsy*, 2:45, 62–161; Pokus, *Borba za Primore*, pp. 40–51.

45. Pokus, *Borba za Primore*, pp. 51–81. See also Bliukher, "Volochaevka," pp. 250–54; Boris L. Beliaev, *Dalnevostochnyi perekop*; E. Oboronko, "Volochaevskii boi," *Za vlast Sovetov*, pp. 320–22; A. A. Voloshin, "Volochaevskie dni," *Etikh dnei ne smolknet slava*, pp. 255–65; Petr S. Koltsov, *Volochaevskie dni*; N. I. Riabov and M. G. Shtein, *Volochaevskaia pobeda*; and many others.

46. Pokus, *Borba za Primore*, pp. 81–88.

47. Iakov Davidovich Ianson (1886–1938), a Latvian by birth, had been a Bolshevik since 1905. For his revolutionary activities he was imprisoned and later exiled to Siberia. After the March 1917 revolution Ianson was one of the most important Communist leaders in Irkutsk before becoming in 1921 a Dalburo member and FER foreign minister. After the FER was absorbed by Soviet Russia in 1922, he served in a number of diplomatic capacities in Europe and Asia (Xenia J. Eudin and Robert C. North, *Soviet Russia and the East, 1920–1927*, pp. 459–60; Petrov, *Geroicheskie gody*, p. 381).

48. *Vladivostok Daily News*, Apr. 1, 1922; Iazikov (chairman, FER Special Trade Delegation) to Hughes, Mar. 27, 1922, 861a.01/219.

49. Pokus, *Borba za Primore*, pp. 94–100; U.S., Department of State, *Papers Relating to the Foreign Relations of the United States, 1922*, 2:849 (hereafter cited as *Foreign Relations, 1922*); *Vladivostok Daily News*, Apr.8, 1922.

50. Filimonov, *Belopovstantsy*, 1:72.

51. Moltchanov, "Last White General," p. 117.

52. *Golos rodiny* article, reprinted in *Vladivostok Daily News*, Dec. 10, 1921.

53. F. A. Puchkov, "Desiatiletaia godovshchina," pp. 14–15.

54. Boldyrev, *Direktoriia*, pp. 447, 450; *Vladivostok Daily News*, Dec. 3, 1921.

55. Moltchanov, "Last White General," p. 119.

56. Petrov, *Geroicheskie gody*, pp. 289–92; K. Serov, "Stranitsy zhizni," *Za vlast Sovetov*, p. 90; Iliukhov and Samusenko, *Partizanskoe dvizhenie*, p. 235.

57. Flegontov, *Partizanskoi tropoi*, p. 2.

58. Belikova, *Bolsheviki Primoria*, p.109; Petrov, *Geroicheskie gody*, pp. 291–92.

59. *Borba za vlast Sovetov v Primore, 1917–1922*, pp. 695–97.

60. Ibid., pp. 684–85.

61. Ibid., pp. 689–92; Iliukhov and Samusenko, *Partizanskoe dvizhenie*, p. 245.

62. See the Dalburo letter to all Party committees to this effect, dated March 11, 1922, in *Iz istorii grazhdanskoi voiny SSSR*, 3:763.

63. Andrushkevich, "Posledniaia Rossiia," chap. 5, p. 10.

64. Ibid., chap. 4, p. 4.

65. Ibid., chap. 5, pp. 6–8; Pavel P. Petrov, *Ot Volgi do Tikhago okeana v riadakh belykh, 1918–1922*, p. 190.

66. I. K. Artemev, *Epizody revoliutsii na Dalnem Vostoke*, p. 117; Andrushkevich, "Posledniaia Rossiia," chap. 5, pp. 15–16.

67. Boldyrev, *Direktoriia*, p. 455.

68. Ibid., pp. 452–55; Anichkov, "Vospominaniia," pp. 135–36.

69. Boldyrev, *Direktoriia*, p. 455.

70. Ibid., p. 465.

71. *Golos rodiny*, Jan. 17, 1922; Boldyrev, *Direktoriia*, pp. 451 ff.; Andrushkevich, "Posledniaia Rossiia," chap. 5, p. 17; Rudnev, *Pri vechernikh ogniakh*, pp. 427–28.

72. Boldyrev, *Direktoriia*, pp. 464–65; Rudnev, *Pri vechernikh ogniakh*, pp. 429–30.

73. Boldyrev, *Direktoriia*, p. 452.

74. Rudnev, *Pri vechernikh ogniakh*, pp. 428–29.

75. Antonenko, "Kratkaia istoriia," passim; Boldyrev, *Direktoriia*, pp. 441–42.

76. Stark, "Otchet Sibirskoi flotilii," 10, 1–2 (1953):9–16; also

Andrushkevich, "Posledniaia Rossiia," chap. 5, pp. 24–25.

77. Merkulov told Macgowan he had definite proof of Semenov-Japanese collusion (Macgowan to Hughes, Jan. 11, 1922, 861a.01/167). See also Macgowan to Hughes, Jan. 21, 1922, 861a.01/196. A great deal of courier activity between Semenov and his supporters was reported (Macgowan to Hughes, Jan. 28, 1922, 861.00/9294).

78. Macgowan to Hughes, Mar. 4, 1921, *Foreign Relations, 1922,* 2:847–48.

79. P. P. Petrov, *Ot Volgi,* p. 194. See also Andrushkevich, "Posledniaia Rossiia," chap. 5, pp. 20–28. Andrushkevich noted (pp. 26–27) General Fukuda's lack of interest in a change in government. Fukuda, a Russian specialist who spoke Russian, was also an influential military figure.

80. See nos. 1378–1382, 1395, Mar. 14–18, 1922, 861.77/2702.

81. "Loans" was a euphemism for yen given for concessions or goods in Vladivostok, and, therefore, sale would be a more appropriate term. See Warren to Hughes, Mar. 23, 1922, 861a.01/249, and Apr. 8, 1922, 861a.01/223.

82. *Golos rodiny,* Apr. 3, 1922; Macgowan to Hughes, Apr. 15, 1922, 861.00/9425; Johnson to Hughes, Apr. 10, 1922, 861.77/2499.

83. Macgowan to Hughes, Apr. 1, 1922, 861.00/9408, and Apr. 15, 1922, 861.00/9425.

84. Macgowan to Hughes, Apr. 1, 1922, 861.00/9408; Antonenko, "Kratkaia istoriia," pp. 41–42; Stark, "Otchet Sibirskoi flotilii," 11, 3 (1953):27–43; *Vladivostok Daily News,* Apr. 15, Apr. 22, and May 20, 1922.

85. Macgowan to Hughes, May 12, 1922, 861.00/9561; Kolesnikov to Poole, May 27, 1922, 861a.01/271; G. Grachev, "Iakutskii pokhod gen. Pepeliaeva," *Sibirskii arkhiv* 1 (1929):23–40.

86. Macgowan to Hughes, Mar. 15, 1922, 861.00/9401. An account of Efremov's speech before the Popular Assembly calling for harmony and money was printed in *Golos rodiny,* Mar. 15, 1922. See also *Vladivostok Daily News,* Mar. 4, 1922.

87. Pastall to Johnson, Mar. 20, 1922, U.S. National Archives, Record Group 76: United States Participation in International Conferences, Commissions, and Expositions . . ., Box 9 (hereafter cited as Pastall to Johnson with the date); General Kolobov, "Borba s bolshevikami na Dalnem Vostoke (Horvat. Kolchak. Semenov. Merkulov. Diterikhs)," chap. 28, pp. 19–21.

88. Pacifist, "The Balance Sheet of the 'White' Folly," *Japan Advertiser,* Apr. 7, 1922; P. P. Petrov, *Ot Volgi,* p. 200; Rudnev, *Pri vechernikh ogniakh,* p. 430.

89. *Vladivostok Daily News,* Mar. 18, 1922.

90. See the statement of the Houseowners' Union in *Golos rodiny,*

Jan. 29, 1922. See also *Golos rodiny*, Mar. 26, 1922; Pacifist, "Japanese in Siberia," *Japan Advertiser*, May 4, 1922.

91. *Japan Chronicle*, May 14, 17, and 18, 1922; *Nasha rech*, May 16, 1922.

92. *Vladivostok Daily News* (Mar. 4, 1921) reported a strike of ship-builders who demanded four months' back pay. On May 13 the same newspaper reported that teachers and professors had not been paid for four to six months.

93. Macgowan to Hughes, Feb. 11, 1922, 861.00/9347; *Slovo*, Apr. 25, 1922.

94. Pacifist, "Japanese in Siberia," *Japan Advertiser*, May 4, 1922.

95. *Slovo*, Apr. 25, 1922.

96. Rudnev, *Pri vechernikh ogniakh*, p. 428.

97. P. P. Petrov, *Ot Volgi*, pp. 198–99.

98. Russia (1923–USSR), Ministerstvo inostrannykh del SSSR, *Dokumenty vneshnei politiki SSSR* 4 : 480–82 (hereafter cited as *Dokumenty*).

99. George A. Lensen, *Japanese Recognition of the USSR*, pp. 31–32.

100. F. N. Petrov, *65 let v riadakh Leninskoi partii*, p. 92.

101. Lensen, *Japanese Recognition*, pp. 32–33.

102. Ibid., p. 33.

103. The full text of Shidehara's statement is given in U.S., Senate, *Conference on the Limitation of Armaments*, pp. 1395–1400. A critical and informative commentary by J. P. Jameson (Division of Russian Affairs, State Department, and a member of the United States delegation) on details of the statement is given in 861.00/9239.

104. Ibid., pp. 1400, 1404–12.

105. Lensen, *Japanese Recognition*, pp. 34–40. The full text of the basic agreement is given on pages 34 to 38.

106. Ibid., pp. 40–41.

107. *Vladivostok Daily News*, Mar. 11, 1922; Evgeniia I. Popova, *Politika SShA na Dalnem Vostoke, 1918–1922*, p. 278, n. 49.

108. Lensen, *Japanese Recognition*, pp. 41–42. The secret Japanese telegrams indicated a desire on the part of the military command to destroy the Dairen talks. See, for example, no. 1002, Aug. 19, 1921, 861.77/2268, and no. 1058, Sept. 15, 1921, 861.00/9104.

109. Boldyrev, *Direktoriia*, pp. 467–73; Anichkov, "Vospominaniia," pp. 136–37; P. P. Petrov, *Ot Volgi*, p. 194. Anichkov's son accompanied Boldyrev, as he did on other occasions. Petrov apparently went along, although he did not say so directly, and his presence was not indicated by Boldyrev.

110. Boldyrev, *Direktoriia*, pp. 467–72.
111. Ibid., p. 473.

Chapter 7

1. This title seemed appropriate, especially from the White perspective, and was borrowed from the title that the conservative White leader, N. A. Andrushkevich, gave to his memoirs.

2. Warren to Hughes, June 2, 1922, 861a.01/274, U.S. National Archives, Record Group 59: General Records of the Department of State (hereafter cited by file and document number only).

3. General Kolobov, "Borba s bolshevikami na Dalnem Vostoke (Horvat. Kolchak. Semenov. Merkulov.Diterikhs): vospominaniia uchastnika," chap. 28, p. 21.

4. Pacifist, "Before the Merkulovs' Downfall," *Japan Advertiser*, June 9, 1922.

5. N. A. Andrushkevich, "Posledniaia Rossiia," chap. 6; *Nasha rech*, June 1, 1922.

6. Iu. K. Stark, "Otchet o deiatelnosti Sibirskoi flotilii v period, 1921–1922," *Morskie zapiski* 12, 1 (1954):16.

7. Pavel P. Petrov, *Ot Volgi do Tikhago okeana v riadakh belykh, 1918–1922*, p. 200.

8. *Vladivostok Daily News*, June 17, 1922.

9. Andrushkevich, "Posledniaia Rossiia," chap. 6; P. P. Petrov, *Ot Volgi*, p. 202; Stark, "Otchet Sibirskoi flotilii," 12, 1 (1954):20–21; Sergei P. Rudnev, *Pri vechernikh ogniakh*, p. 440; Boris B. Filimonov, *Konets Belogo Primoria*, pp. 32–45.

10. Stark, "Otchet Sibirskoi flotilii," 12, 1 (1954):16–17.

11. *Nasha rech*, June 1, 1922.

12. *Vladivostok Daily News*, June 17, 1922; P. P. Petrov, *Ot Volgi*, p. 203.

13. *Nasha rech*, June 1, 1922.

14. Andrushkevich, "Posledniaia Rossiia," chap. 6. Vasilii Boldyrev (*Direktoriia, Kolchak, interventy*, pp. 476–77) accused Molchanov of helping N. Merkulov escape to the Japanese headquarters because of the close friendship between the two.

15. Andrushkevich, "Posledniaia Rossiia," chap. 6.

16. Elena Varneck and H. H. Fisher, *The Testimony of Kolchak and Other Siberian Materials*, p. 242, n. 170.

17. Vladimir P. Anichkov, "Vospominaniia," p. 147.

18. G. V. Enborisov, *Ot Urala do Kharbina*, p. 126. For more observa-

tions on Diterikhs see Rudnev, *Pri vechernikh ogniakh*, p. 438, and Andrushkevich, "Posledniaia Rossiia," chap. 6.

19. Andrushkevich, "Posledniaia Rossiia," chap. 6.

20. *Vladivostok Daily News*, June 3, 1922.

21. Boldyrev, *Direktoriia*, p. 476; Andrushkevich, "Posledniaia Rossiia," chap. 6; *Vladivostok Daily News*, June 17, 1922.

22. Stark, "Otchet Sibirskoi flotilii," 12, 1 (1954): 21–23.

23. Rudnev, *Pri vechernikh ogniakh*, p. 442; *Vladivostok Daily News*, June 17, 1922.

24. Andrushkevich, in "Posledniaia Rossiia," chap. 6, claimed that this was confirmed by others. This is supported in Japanese telegram no. 1481, June 8, 1922, 861.77/2764, U.S. National Archives, Record Group 76.

25. *Vladivostok Daily News*, June 17, 1922.

26. Rudnev, *Pri vechernikh ogniakh*, p. 439.

27. P. P. Petrov, *Ot Volgi*, p. 202.

28. Descriptions of the events may be found in Anichkov, "Vospominaniia," pp. 146–47; Boldyrev, *Direktoriia*, pp. 475 ff.; I. K. Artemev, *Epizody revoliutsii na Dalnem Vostoke*, pp. 121–25; and Rudnev, *Pri vechernikh ogniakh*, pp. 432 ff. Macgowan submitted a long report and numerous documents and press reports. See Macgowan to Hughes, June 13, 1922, 861a.01/293.

29. Andrushkevich, "Posledniaia Rossiia," chap. 6; Boldyrev, *Direktoriia*, p. 382.

30. Stark, "Otchet Sibirskoi flotilii," 12, 1 (1954): 24–25.

31. *Vladivostok Daily News*, June 17, 1922; Stark, "Otchet Sibirskoi flotilii," 12, 1 (1954): 25; Andrushkevich, "Posledniaia Rossiia," chap. 6.

32. Andrushkevich, "Posledniaia Rossiia," chap. 6.

33. Rudnev, *Pri vechernikh ogniakh*, p. 440.

34. The text is given in Macgowan to Hughes, June 13, 1922, 861a.01/293.

35. Andrushkevich, "Posledniaia Rossiia," chap. 6.

36. *Japan Advertiser*, June 11, 1922; *Vladivostok Daily News*, July 1, 1922.

37. *Vladivostok Daily News*, June 24, 1922.

38. Saburi (Japanese chargé) to Hughes, June 24, 1922, in U.S. Department of State, *Papers Relating to the Foreign Relations of the United States, 1922*, 2:853 (hereafter cited as *Foreign Relations, 1922*).

39. P. P. Petrov, *Ot Volgi*, pp. 206–7.

40. Dmitrii I. Abrikossow, *Revelations of a Russian Diplomat*, p. 299; Andrushkevich, "Posledniaia Rossiia," chap. 7.

41. P. P. Petrov, *Ot Volgi*, p. 207.

42. Ibid.; Artemev, *Epizody*, p. 138.

43. Stark, "Otchet Sibirskoi flotilii," 12, 2 (1954):25; *Vladivostok Daily News*, July 29, 1922. See also Filimonov, *Konets*, p. 105.

44. Maritime Province, Siberia. Vremennoe priamurskoe pravitelstvo. Laws, Statutes, etc. "Polozhenie o Priamurskom zemskom sobore," this was published in the press, for example, *Slovo*, June 28, 1922. See also Filimonov, *Konets*, p. 52.

45. Andrushkevich, "Posledniaia Rossiia," chap. 7.

46. P. P. Petrov, *Ot Volgi*, p. 209.

47. Artemev, *Epizody*, pp. 132–33; Stark, "Otchet Sibirskoi flotilii," 12, 2 (1954):28.

48. Filimonov, *Konets*, pp. 54–55; Rudnev, *Pri vechernikh ogniakh*, p. 454; *Vladivostok Daily News*, Aug. 12, 1922.

49. Artemev, *Epizody*, pp. 129–30. Rudnev (*Pri vechernikh ogniakh*, pp. 454–55) indicated the same. Artemev considered the recognition of the Romanovs a mistake. He claimed that there were over 30,000 partisans and Socialists who were disgruntled with the Bolsheviks and ready to support the national movement. When they heard about the resolution, they made up with the Bolsheviks. No other evidence exists for such a claim.

50. *Vladivostok Daily News*, Aug. 12, 1922; Kolobov, "Borba s bolshevikami," chap. 28, p. 25; Rudnev, *Pri vechernikh ogniakh*, p. 456.

51. Filimonov, *Konets*, pp. 68–70, 72–75.

52. Rudnev, *Pri vechernikh ogniakh*, p. 457.

53. Filimonov, *Konets*, pp. 71–72, 76.

54. Ibid., pp. 75–79; Rudnev, *Pri vechernikh ogniakh*, pp. 458–59.

55. *Nasha rech*, Aug. 16, 1922; Filimonov, *Konets*, pp. 74–75; Kolobov, "Borba bolshevikami," chap. 28, p. 20. Artemev (*Epizody*, pp. 152–53) has claimed that the parish organization idea was Prince Krapotkin's. At any rate, it was straight out of the pages of history.

56. Filimonov, *Konets*, pp. 102–5.

57. Stark, "Otchet Sibirskoi flotilii," 12, 3 (1954):22; P. P. Petrov, *Ot Volgi*, p. 210; Boldyrev, *Direktoriia*, p. 484; Artemev, *Epizody*, pp. 133–36.

58. Andrushkevich, "Posledniaia Rossiia," chap. 7; Rudnev, *Pri vechernikh ogniakh*, p. 458.

59. A detailed list of White units is given in Filimonov, *Konets*, pp. 122–27.

60. *Borba za vlast Sovetov v Primore, 1917–1922*, pp. 736–37; *Vladivostok Daily News*, Aug. 19, 1922.

61. *Japan Advertiser*, Sept. 6, 1922.
62. Warren to Hughes, Sept. 7, 1922, 861a.01/331. Also Stark, "Otchet Sibirskoi flotilii," 13, 1 (1955): 43, and Abrikossow, *Revelations*, pp. 298–99.
63. George A. Lensen, *Japanese Recognition of the USSR*, p. 49.
64. Ibid., p. 50.
65. A Voensovet (partisan) resolution of mid-June foresaw conflict running as late as January 1923 and therefore a need for winter clothing for the partisan forces. *Borba za vlast*, pp. 711–13.
66. Russia (1923–USSR), Ministerstvo inostrannykh del SSSR, *Dokumenty vneshnei politiki SSSR*, 5 (1961): 535 (hereafter cited as *Dokumenty*); Jacob G. Schurman (ambassador to China) to Hughes, Sept. 18, 1922, 861a.01/342.
67. Xenia J. Eudin and Robert C. North, *Soviet Russia and the East, 1920–1927*, p. 460; Louis Fischer, *The Soviets in World Affairs*, 1, passim.
68. Poole to Hughes, Sept. 26, 1922, *Foreign Relations*, 1922, 2:857–58; Lensen, *Japanese Recognition*, pp. 49–84.
69. *Foreign Relations*, 1922, 2:858–59.
70. *Borba za vlast*, pp. 705–8, 710, 717–20, and 729–30.
71. *Oktiabrskaia revoliutsiia i grazhdanskaia voina na Dalnem Vostoke*, ed. S. Tsypkin et al., p. 251.
72. Narrevkom functions have been well explained in the "Informational Letter," June 18, 1922, *Borba za vlast*, pp. 724–29. See also ibid., pp. 746–47, 766.
73. Edward B. Thomas (vice-consul, Harbin, assigned to Chita) to Hughes, July 12, 1922, 861a.00/22; *Komandarm Uborevich*, p. 243; Thomas to Hughes, Sept. 28, 1922, 861a.00/31.
74. Nikolai K. Iliukhov and I. P. Samusenko, *Partizanskoe dvizhenie v Primore, 1918–1922*, pp. 249–50.
75. *Oktiabrskaia revoliutsiia*, p. 251; Iliukhov and Samusenko, *Partizanskoe dvizhenie*, pp. 250–51; *Borba za vlast*, pp. 711–13.
76. *Borba za vlast*, pp. 711–13, 732–33. The *Vladivostok Daily News* for June through August carried many accounts of partisan terror.
77. *Borba za vlast*, pp. 740–41.
78. The White plans are given in P. P. Petrov, *Ot Volgi*, pp. 211–13; Filimonov, *Konets*, pp. 122–47, 130–31; and Stark, "Otchet Sibirskoi flotilii," 12, 3 (1954): 23–24.
79. Stark, "Otchet Sibirskoi flotilii," 13, 1 (1955): 41.
80. Filimonov, *Konets*, pp. 133 ff.
81. S. N. Shishkin, *Grazhdanskaia voina na Dalnem Vostoke, 1918–1922*, pp. 238 ff., has given one of the best short accounts of the Red offen-

sive from a Communist perspective. The White side has been treated in detail in Filimonov, *Konets*, pp. 179–219.

82. George C. Hanson (consul, Harbin) to Hughes, Sept. 30, 1922, 861a.01/434; Rollin R. Winslow (vice-consul, Vladivostok) to Hughes, Sept. 28, 1922, 861a.01/356; P. P. Petrov, *Ot Volgi*, p. 223; Andrushkevich, "Posledniaia Rossiia," chap. 7.

83. Warren to Hughes, Oct. 11, 1922, 861a.01/380.

84. Artemev, *Epizody*, pp. 172–73.

85. Winslow to Hughes, Oct. 17, 1922, 861a.00/33; Warren to Hughes, Oct. 17, 1922, in *Foreign Relations, 1922*, 2:863–64; *Novosti zhizni*, Nov. 9, 1922, in Hanson to Hughes, Nov. 15, 1922, 861.00/9761.

86. P. P. Petrov, *Ot Volgi*, pp. 225–29; Rudnev, *Pri vechernikh ogniakh*, pp. 460–61; Andrushkevich, "Posledniaia Rossiia," chap. 6.

87. Stark, "Otchet Sibirskoi flotilii," 13, 1 (1955):42.

88. Artemev, *Epizody*, p. 171.

89. Stark, "Otchet Sibirskoi flotilii," 13, 4 (1955):71.

90. Ibid., 13, 1 (1955):42.

91. Warren to Hughes, Oct. 15, 1922, 861a.01/38.

92. Winslow to Hughes, Oct. 17, 1922, 861a.24/44.

93. Japanese chargé d'affaires to Poole, Oct. 16, 1922, 861a.24/21; Warren to Hughes, Oct. 13, 1922, 861a.24/21; Stark, "Otchet Sibirskoi flotilii," 13, 1 (1955):44.

94. Anichkov, "Vospominaniia," p. 150.

95. Stark, "Otchet Sibirskoi flotilii," 13, 2–3 (1955):78–81; Artemev, *Epizody*, pp. 174–77.

96. John and Dorothy Findlay, "Letters from Vladivostok, 1918–1923," *Slavonic and East European Review* 45 (July 1967):522–26; Winslow to Hughes, Oct. 31, 1922, 861a.01/465.

97. P. P. Petrov, *Ot Volgi*, p. 230; Stark, "Otchet Sibirskoi flotilii," 13, 4 (1955):68 ff.

98. Stark, "Otchet Sibirskoi flotilii," 13, 4 (1955):71; Boldyrev, *Direktoriia*, p. 488; Artemev, *Epizody*, p. 183; Andrushkevich, "Posledniaia Rossiia," chap. 8.

99. Boldyrev, *Direktoriia*, p. 488.

100. Rudnev, *Pri vechernikh ogniakh*, p. 462.

101. Findlay, "Letters," pp. 522–26; Winslow to Hughes, Oct. 31, 1922, 861a.01/466.

102. Winslow to Hughes, Oct. 31, 1922, 861a.01/466; Findlay, "Letters," pp. 522–26.

103. Boldyrev, *Direktoriia*, pp. 488–89.

104. *Poslednie novosti*, Jan. 26, 1923.
105. *Borba za vlast*, pp. 795–803.
106. Dalnevostochnyi krai. Ispolnitelnyi komitet. *Biulleten Dalnevo-stochnogo revoliutsionnogo komiteta*, pp. 42–43.
107. *Borba za vlast*, p. 803.

Epilogue

1. H. B. Morse and H. F. MacNair, *Far Eastern International Relations*, p. 665.

Bibliography

When an item is rare, a location is indicated in parentheses at the end of the citation. Library of Congress abbreviations are used, that is, DLC for the Library of Congress; CSt-H—Hoover Institution; NN— New York Public Library; NNC—Columbia University; MH—Harvard University; WaU—University of Washington; CtY—Yale University; and MdBJ—Johns Hopkins University. NA has been used to designate the U.S. National Archives. AN SSSR, Sib. otd. in Russian citations stands for Akademiia nauk, Soiuz sovetskikh sotsialisticheskikh respublik, Sibirskoe otdelenie (Siberian Section of the Academy of Sciences of the USSR).

1. Bibliographies and Research Aids

Annotirovannyi katalog izdanii vypushchennykh izdatelstvom "Sovetskaia Aziia" za 1925–1933 gg. Moscow: Sovetskaia Aziia, 1933. (NN, NNC)

Bibliografiia Vostoka, fasc. 1–9. Leningrad: AN SSSR, Inst. Vostokovedeniia, 1932–1935. (NNC)

Dobranitskii, M. M., ed. *Sistematicheskii ukazatel literatury po istorii russkoi revoliutsii, 1917–1922.* Moscow-Leningrad: Gosizdat, 1926.

Egorov, D. N., ed. *Bibliografiia Vostoka.* Moscow: Nauchnaia assotsiatsiia vostokovedeniia SSSR, 1928. (CtY, MdBJ, NNC)

Foreign Affairs Bibliography: A Selected and Annotated List of Books on International Relations. 4 vols. New York: Harper & Row, 1933–1964.

Hale, Richard W., Jr., ed. *Guide to Photocopied Historical Materials in the U.S. and Canada.* Ithaca: Cornell University Press, 1961.

Hammond, Thomas T., comp. and ed. *Soviet Foreign Relations and World Communism: A Selected Annotated Bibliography of 7000 Books in 30 Languages.* 2d rev. ed. Princeton: Princeton University Press, 1966.
A basic bibliography with useful annotations.

Horecky, Paul L., ed. *Basic Russian Publications: An Annotated Bibliography on Russia and the Soviet Union.* Chicago: University of Chicago Press, 1962.

————. *Russia and the Soviet Union: A Bibliographic Guide to Western-Language Publications.* Chicago: University of Chicago Press, 1965.

Iakovleva, T. I. "Chto chitat o Vladivostoke," *Materialy po istorii Vladivostoka,* Book 2: 1917–1960. Trudy Sib. otd. AN SSSR, ser ist. Vladivostok: Prim. knizh. izd., 1960.

Istoriia sovetskogo obshchestva v vospominaniiakh sovremennikov, 1917–1957: annotirovannyi ukazatel memuarnoi literatury. 2 vols. Moscow: Gos. biblioteka SSSR im. V. I. Lenina, 1958.
A valuable bibliography of memoir literature in books and articles.

Kerner, Robert J., ed. *Northeastern Asia: A Selected Bibliography.* 2 vols. Berkeley: University of California Press, 1939.

Khodak, A. A., comp. *Dokumentalnye publikatsii po istorii grazhdanskoi voiny v SSSR: kratkii obzor.* Moscow, 1961.

Kudriavtsev, F. A., et al., eds. *Borba za vlast Sovetov v vostochnoi Sibiri, 1917–1922: bibliograficheskii ukazatel.* Irkutsk, 1962.

Loewenthal, Rudolf, ed. *Bibliography of Russian Literature on China and Adjacent Countries, 1931–1936.* Cambridge, Mass.: Russian Research Center, 1949.

Maichel, Karol, ed. *Guide to Russian Reference Books.* Vol. 2, History *and Auxiliary Historical Sciences.* Stanford: Stanford University Press, 1964.

————, comp. *Soviet and Russian Newspapers at the Hoover Institution: A Catalog.* Stanford: Hoover Institution, 1966.

A list, including dates of publication, of the valuable newspaper holdings at the Hoover Institution.

———— and Schatoff, M. U., comps. *A List of Russian Newspapers in the Columbia University Library.* New York: Columbia University Press, 1959.

Matveev, Zotik N., ed. *Chto chitat o Dalnevostochnoi oblasti: opyt sistematicheskogo ukazatelia literatury.* Vladivostok: Knizh. delo, 1925.

Proletarskaia revoliutsiia: sistematicheskii i alfavitnyi ukazatel, 1921–1929. Moscow: Gosizdat, 1930. (Cst-H)

Shapiro, A. L., ed. *Bibliografiia istorii SSSR.* Moscow: Vysshaia shkola, 1968.

Very useful.

Slavik, Yan, and Postnikov, S. P., eds. *Bibliografiia russkoi revoliutsii i grazhdanskoi voiny, 1917–1921.* Prague: Russkii zagranichnyi istoricheskii arkhiv v Prage, 1938.

Turunov, A. N., and Vegman, V. D., eds. *Revoliutsiia i grazhdanskaia voina v Sibiri: ukazatel knig i zhurnalnykh statei.* Novosibirsk: Sibkraizdat, 1928. (NN, DLC)

Ukazatel periodicheskikh izdanii emigratsii iz Rossii i SSSR. Munich: Institute for the Study of the History and Culture of the USSR, 1953.

U.S., Library of Congress. *Half a Century of Soviet Serials, 1917–1968: A Bibliography and Union List of Serials Published in the USSR.* Compiled by Rudolf Smits. 2 vols. Washington, 1968.

A basic bibliography, especially useful for locating obscure journals.

————. Slavic and Central European Division. *Newspapers of the Soviet Union in the Library of Congress (Slavic 1954–1960; Non-Slavic 1917–1960).* Washington, 1962.

————. Slavic and Central European Division. *Russian, Ukrainian, and Belorussian Newspapers, 1917–1953: A Union List.* Compiled by Paul L. Horecky. Washington, 1953.
This and the preceding entry are both basic lists.

————. Slavic and Central European Division. *The USSR and Eastern Europe: Periodicals in Western Languages.* Compiled by Paul L. Horecky and Robert G. Carlton. Washington, 1967.

U.S. National Archives. Record Group 84. *List of Foreign Service Post Records in the National Archives.* Compiled by Mark G. Eckhoff and Alexander P. Mavro. Washington, 1967.

————. *List of National Archives Microfilm Publications.* Washington, 1968.

————. Record Group 59. *Preliminary Inventory of the General Records of the Department of State.* Compiled by D. T. Goggin and H. S. Helton. Washington, 1963.

————. Record Group 43. *Preliminary Inventory of the Records of the United States Participation in International Conferences, Commissions, and Expositions.* Compiled by H. S. Helton. Washington, 1955.

Velikaia oktiabrskaia sotsialisticheskaia revoliutsiia: bibliograficheskaia ukazatel dokumentalnykh publikatsii. Moscow: Vsesoiuznoi knizh. palaty, 1961.

Vitkind, Nataliia Y., ed. *Materialy k bibliografii istorii grazhdanskoi voiny na sovetskom Vostoke.* Moscow, 1934. (NN, NNC)

Z. M., comp. "Bibliografiia," *Sbornik materialov po istorii revoliutsionnogo dvizheniia na Dalnem Vostoke.* Chita-Vladivostok: Dalistpart, 1923, pp. 217–28.

————————————2. *Primary Sources*————————————

A. Records and Archives ————————————————————————

American Red Cross •
American Red Cross Records, ARC Headquarters, Washington, D. C.
Siberian Commission.
987.08 Weekly Reports, January–December 1920. Generally the

best information will be found in the "Political and Military Situation" sections.

987.118 Military Relief. Camp Service. Supervisors' Reports, Shkotovo, Siberia.

987.72 Russian Press, Translations from. Siberian Commission.

Red Cross. U.S. American National Red Cross Commission to Siberia. Hoover Institution, Stanford, California. A collection of reports on the situation in Siberia and the operation of the Red Cross there for 1919–1922 gathered by an officer of the Red Cross.

U.S. National Archives, Washington, D.C. •

Consular Files, Chita. Four volumes and two boxes containing records and dispatches to and from the Consulate. Of special interest are numerous volumes of official FER documents that are difficult to locate elsewhere.

————. Vladivostok. Twelve volumes of records, dispatches, and almost a complete press record, in Russian and English, for 1920 to 1922.

Record Group 45. Naval Records Collection of the Office of Naval Records and Library, Subject File 1911–1927.

Record Group 59. General Records of the Department of State, Central Files, 1906–1929.

This valuable material is obtainable for the most part on microfilm. Indispensable for this study were the documents and newspaper material in decimal file numbers 861.00, "Political Conditions in Russia" (861a.00 concerns Siberia) and 861.77, "The Trans-Siberian and Chinese Eastern Railways."

Record Group 76. United States Participation in International Conferences, Commissions, and Expositions. Advisory Commission of Railway Experts to Russia, the Russian Railway Service Corps, and the Interallied Railway Committee, 1917–1922. "Confidential" Records of the President of the Interallied Technical Board, 1919–1922. This group includes the secret Japanese telegrams and consists of twelve boxes of papers, much of which is on the microfilm indicated above. Some of the doc-

uments not on microfilm were very valuable, for example, the
letters of Paul T. Pastall, acting special transportation inspector, to B. O. Johnson, important Interallied Railway Commission
official, in box no. 9 of this collection.

Record Group 80. General Records of the Department of Navy. The
intelligence records in Box 43 were valuable.

Record Group 165. Records of the War Department General and Special
Staffs. The military intelligence records were useful.

B. Unpublished Works and Interviews ─────────────────────────

Interviews •

Cheremshansky, George A. Private interview held in Washington, D.C.,
February 1970. A native of Vladivostok, a conservative, and a
member of several nonsocialist organizations.

Rojanski, Vladimir Borisovich. Private interview held in Seattle,
Washington, August 1970. A former Kappelite who chose to
leave his unit in April 1921.

*New York. Columbia University. Archive of Russian and East Euro-
pean History and Culture.* •

Akintievskii, General Major. "K istorii grazhdanskoi voiny v Sibiri i
na Dalnem Vostoke, 1918–1922." 1960.
A valuable memoir, especially for the military aspects of the
White struggle; very critical of Semenov.

Efimov, A. Collection.
Contains numerous printed sources including books by Khartling
and Filimonov, *Chasovoi, Vestnik O-va Russkikh Veteranov
Velikoi Voiny, Russkaia zhizh,* and others.

Martynov, Aleksandr Nikolaevich. Collection.

Sakharov, General K. Collection.

Vostrotin, Stepan Vasilevich. Collection.

Zolotarev, Mikhail Mikhailovich. Collection.

Stanford, California. Hoover Institution. •

Andrushkevich, N. A. "Posledniaia Rossiia." Translated by E. Varneck. 1931.

One of the most interesting and valuable memoirs on the political situation in Vladivostok from 1920 to 1922. Andrushkevich, a monarchist and newspaperman, was close to political events during the Merkulov government.

Anichkov, Vladimir P. "Vospominaniia."
A valuable memoir by a financial expert who was close to several important White political figures.

Antonenko, Vasilii P. "Kratkaia istoriia smeny pravitelstv vo Vladivostoke s 31 ianvaria 1920 g. do evakuatsii oktiabria 1922." 1922.
Conservative, anti-Semenov point of view. Useful for material on the flotilla and the general political situation.

Bogdanov, A. "Chto ia videl v svoei zhizni."

Harris, Ernest L. Papers. Harris was U.S. consul general at Irkutsk May 8, 1918, to October 13, 1920.

Hitoon, Sergei E. "From the Aral Sea to Western Turkestan." Valuable for information on Ungern von Sternberg.

Kolobov, General. "Borba s bolshevikami na Dalnem Vostoke (Horvat. Kolchak. Semenov. Merkulov. Diterikhs): vospominaniia uchastnika."
A valuable memoir by a competent observer who was close to General Horvath; contains the texts of many documents.

Kriukov, B. A. Collection.
Important documents, intelligence reports, and other materials relating especially to the Merkulov period.

Lastours papers. From the Russian embassy in Paris.

Maritime Province, Siberia. "Doklad Vremennomy pravitelstvu, Primorskoi oblastnoi zemskoi upravy, Komissii po obsledovaniiu obstoiatelstv sobytii 4–6 aprelia vo Vladivostoke." Translated by E. Varneck. 1920.
A basic source for the Japanese offensive in April 1920.

Purlington, C.W. "Statement submitted to the State Department regarding Eastern Siberian Conditions." October 1921.

Railway Service Corps papers.
Reports and memoranda by leading figures in the Corps, such as

John F. Stevens, George Emerson, B. O. Johnson, and William Klemm.

Savintsev. "Recollections from the period of civil war in Chita, 1920, by the head of the Information Office of the Ufa Army group." Valuable for information on Semenov's Chita.

Semenov, Grigorii M. "Istoriia moei borby s bolshevikami," 1937. According to George Guins, this was written by one of Semenov's aides under Semenov's authorization.

Shchepikhin, Sergei A. "Kappelevtsy v Chite v 1920 gody." One of the best and most detailed accounts of Semenov's government in Chita.

Varneck, Elena. Manuscript collection. Five cartons of valuable material written and translated by Mrs. Varneck. These materials were to have been published, but the project was discontinued.

Volkov, Boris. "Pamiati ubiistva ofitserov na mostu reki Khor."

Vorotovov, Colonel. Memoirs. Part 2: "V Zabaikale i na Primorskom fronte v 1920–1921: zapiski uchastnika." Handwritten manuscript by an Orenburg Cossack.

Washington, D.C. National Archives. Decimal File 861.00/9050.●

Harris, Ernest L. "The Allies in Siberia, 1917–1921." 1921. This is a very frank report that is illuminating not only on the political situation in Siberia, but also on various American and Russian officials.

Washington, D.C. Library of Congress.●

Long, Breckinridge. Papers. Third assistant secretary of state, 1917–1920.

Morris, Roland S. Papers. Ambassador to Japan, August 1, 1917, to March 1921.

C. Documents ───

Borba za vlast Sovetov v Primore, 1917–1922: sbornik dokumentov. Vladivostok: Prim. knizh. izd., 1955. An indispensible collection of documents.

Calendar of Soviet Documents on Foreign Policy. Compiled by Jane

Degras. London: Royal Institute of International Affairs, 1941.
*Conference on the Limitation of Armaments, Washington, November 12,
1921–February 6, 1922.* Washington: GPO, 1922.
Dalnevostochnyi krai. Ispolnitelnyi komitet. *Biulleten* Dalnevostoch-
nogo revoliutsionnogo komiteta: ofitsialnoe izdanie.Khabarovsk,
1922–1923. (CSt-H)
"Dogovory, zakliuchennye v Vashingtone," *Vestnik* NKID, 4–5 (Apr.–
May 1922): 137–52.
Eudin, Xenia J., and North, Robert C. *Soviet Russia and the East,
1920–1927: A Documentary Survey.* Stanford: Stanford Univer-
sity Press, 1957.
Far Eastern Republic. *Japanese Intervention in the Russian Far East.*
Washington: The Special Delegation of the FER to the USA,
1922.
The official FER version made public during the Washington
Conference.
————. *A Short Outline History of the Far Eastern Republic.* Wash-
ington: The Special Delegation of the FER to the USA, 1922.
The official history up to the time of the Washington Conference.
————, Laws, Statutes, etc. *Sobranie uzakonenii i rasporiazhenii
pravitelstva Dalnevostochnoi respubliki za 1921–1922 goda.*
Chita, 1921–1922. (CSt-H)
————, Laws, Statutes, etc. *Sobranie uzakonenii i rasporiazhenii
rabochego i krestianskogo pravitelstva izdavaemoe Narodnym
komissariatom iustitsii.* Chita, 1922. (NA)
France, Ministère des Affaires Etrangeres. *Documents diplomatiques:
Conférence de Washington, Juillet 1921–Février 1922.* Paris,
1923.
Golos rodiny. *Deistviia Iaponii v Priamurskom krae: sbornik offitsi-
alnykh dokumentov, otnosiashchikhsia k interventsii derzhav v
predelakh Priamuria.* Vladivostok: Svobodnaia Rossiia, 1921.
(CSt-H)
Great Britain, Foreign Office. *Documents on British Foreign Policy,
1919–1939, First Series. Vol. 14. Far Eastern Affairs April
1920–February 1922.* London, 1966.
Gutman-Gan, Anatolii Ia. *Gibel Nikolaevska na Amure: stranitsy istorii*

grazhdanskoi voiny na Dalnem Vostoke. Berlin: Russkii ekono-
mist, 1924.
   A valuable source on the Nikolaevsk massacre including eye-
   witness accounts.
"Iaponskaia interventsiia: sekretnye telegrammy iaponskoi komandovaniia po dalnevostochnym delam." In *Sbornik materialov po
istorii revoliutsionnogo dvizheniia na Dalnem Vostoke,* pp. 278–
87. Chita-Vladivostok: Dalistpart, 1923.
   See Appendix 2.
Iaponskaia interventsiia 1918–1922 v dokumentakh. Edited by I. I.
Mints. Moscow: Tsentarkhiv, 1934.
   This volume and the next two must be used with caution be-
   cause they contain documents of uncertain validity, such as the
   secret Japanese telegrams and the alleged French-Japanese
   agreement of June 1921.
*Istoricheskie dokumenty o deistviiakh i zamyslakh mezhdunarodnykh
khishchnikov na Dalnem Vostoke.* Edited by P. M. Nikiforov.
Moscow: Moskovskii rabochii, 1923.
*Iz istorii grazhdanskoi voiny v SSSR: sbornik dokumentov i materialov,
1918–1922 gg.* 3 vols. Moscow: Sovetskaia Rossiia, 1960–1961.
   Contains many essential documents.
"Japan in Eastern Siberia." *The Nation,* Oct. 5, 1921, pp. 382–85.
"K istorii grazhdanskoi voiny: Part I: Na Dalnem Vostoke." *Na chu-
zhoi storone* 10 (1925): 224–36.
Kossova, N. "Posledniaia rech S. G. Lazo: k 70-letiiu so dnia rozh-
deniia." *Dalnii Vostok* 2 (1964): 152–53.
Kurdiukov, I. F. "Iz istorii sovetsko-kitaiskikh otnoshenii, 1920–
1921." *Sovetskoe kitaevedenie* 1 (1958): 141–45.
Maritime Province, Siberia. Primorskaia oblastnaia zemskaia uprava.
Vestnik Vremennago pravitelstva Primorskoi oblastnoi zemskoe
upravy. Vladivostok, 1920–21. (CSt-H)
———. Vremennoe narodnoe sobranie Dalnego Vostoka, sessiia 1.
Stenograficheskie otchety (prilozhenie k Vestnik Vremennago
pravitelstva Dalnego Vostoka). Vladivostok, 1920. (CSt-H)
———. Vremennoe priamurskoe pravitelstvo. Narodnoe sobranie.

"Deklaratsiia fraktsii nesotsialisticheskogo sezda, zachutana v zasedanii Narodnago sobraniia 9-go avgusta 1921 goda." Vladivostok, 1921. (CSt-H)

————. Vremennoe priamurskoe pravitelstvo. Laws, Statutes, etc. "Polozhenie o Priamurskom zemskom sobore: ukaz Vremennago priamurskago pravitelstva No. 153, June 27, 1922 g." Vladivostok, 1922. (CSt-H)

————. Vremennoe priamurskoe pravitelstvo. Laws, Statutes, etc. "Polozhenie o vyborakh v Priamurskoe narodnoe sobranie." Vladivostok, 1921. (CSt-H)

————. Vremennoe priamurskoe pravitelstvo. Osvedomitelnyi otdel Sibirskoi flotilii. "Krizis kommunizma." Vladivostok, 1922. (CSt-H)

————. Vremennoe priamurskoe pravitelstvo. *Vestnik* Vremennago priamurskago pravitelstva. Vladivostok, 1921–22. (CSt-H)

————. Vremennoe priamurskoe pravitelstvo. Tsentralnaia izbiratelnaia komissiia. "Instruktsiia po vyboram v Priamurskoe narodnoe sobranie 1921 goda." Vladivostok, 1921. (CSt-H)

Mezhdunarodnaia politika noveishego vremeni v dogovorakh, notakh i deklaratsiiakh, 1920–1927. Edited by Iu. Y. Kliuchnikov and A. Sabanin. 3 vols. Moscow: Litizdat NKID, 1925–29.

Oktiabr na Amure, 1917–1922 gg.: sbornik dokumentov. Blagoveshchensk: Amurskoe knizh. izd., 1961.

Oktiabrskaia revoliutsiia i grazhdanskaia voina na Dalnem Vostoke: khronika sobytii, 1917–1922 gg. Edited by S. Tsypkin et al. Moscow-Khabarovsk: Dalgiz, 1933.

A valuable list of events using newspapers, some of which are not available outside of the Soviet Union, as a source.

"Partizanskoe dvizhenie v Primore." *Krasnyi arkhiv* 82 (1937): 40–69.

Poslednie dni kolchakovshchiny. Edited by M. M. Konstantinov. Moscow-Leningrad: Gosizdat, 1926. (CSt-H)

A valuable documentary collection drawn from both Communist and non-Communist sources.

Revoliutsiia na Dalnem Vostoke. Moscow: Gosizdat, 1923.

A valuable collection of materials—memoirs, documents, etc.

Rossiiskaia missiia v Pekine. "Sobranie dokumentov, otnosiashchikh-

sia do internirovaniia atamana Kalmykova v Girine i ego pobeda
pri poseshchenii konsulstva: fevral-sentiabr 1920 g." Peking,
1920. (NA, 861.00/7665—on microfilm)

Russia (1917–RSFSR), Narodnyi komissariat po inostrannym delam.
Vestnik. Moscow, 1919–22.

Russia (1923–USSR), Ministerstvo inostrannikh del SSSR. *Dokumenty
vneshnei politiki SSSR.* Vols. 2–5. Edited by A. A. Gromyko
et al. Moscow: Gospolitizdat, 1958–61.

*Sbornik dogovorov i drugikh dokumentov po istorii mezhdunarodnykh
otnoshenii na Dalnem Vostoke, 1844–1925.* Edited by E. D.
Grimm. Moscow, 1927.

*Sbornik materialov po istorii revoliutsionnogo dvizheniia na Dalnem
Vostoke.* Edited by M. Preobrazhenskii and M. Malyshev. Chita-
Vladivostok: Dalistpart, 1923. (CSt-H)
Contains memoirs and documents for 1917–1922.

Sergei Lazo: vospominaniia i dokumenty. Edited by G. Reikhberg et al.
Moscow: Gosizdat, 1938.

*Sibirskii revoliutsionnyi komitet (Sibrevkom), avg. 1919–dek. 1925:
sbornik dokumentov i materialov.* Novosibirsk: Novosib. knizh.
izd., 1959.

Soviet Documents on Foreign Policy. Vol. 1. 1917–1924. Compiled by
Jane Degras. London: Oxford, 1953.

*Stenograficheskii otchet peregovorov o sdache vlasti Omskim Pravi-
telstvom Politicheskomu Tsentru v prisutstvii Vysokikh Kom-
missarov i Vysshago komandovaniia Soiuznykh Derzhav, gorod
Irkutsk (stantsiia) ianvar 1920.* Harbin, 1921. (CSt-H, NN)

"Suchanskaia dolina v gody grazhdanskoi voiny." Edited by M. Gubelman. *Krasnyi arkhiv* 91 (1938): 16–88.

U.S., Congress. "Japanese Aggression in the Russian Far East."
Congressional Record, March 2, 1922, pp. 3238–75.
This is identical to FER, *Japanese Intervention in the Russian
Far East,* Washington, 1922.

——, Senate. *Conference on the Limitation of Armament.* Senate
Document no. 126, 67th Congress, 2d sess. Washington, 1922.

——, Senate, Committee on Education and Labor. *Deportation of*

Gregorie Semenoff. Hearings before the Committee on Education and Labor, U.S. Senate, 67th Congress, Second Session. Relative to the Deporting of Undesirable Aliens, April 12, 13, 17, 18, 1922. Washington, 1922.

U.S., Department of State. *Papers Relating to the Foreign Relations of the United States, 1919, Russia.* Washington, 1937.

—————. *Papers Relating to the Foreign Relations of the United States, 1920.* 3 vols. Washington, 1936.

—————. *Papers Relating to the Foreign Relations of the United States, 1921.* 2 vols. Washington, 1936.

—————. *Papers Relating to the Foreign Relations of the United States, 1922.* 2 vols. Washington, 1938.

Varneck, Elena, and Fisher, H. H. *The Testimony of Kolchak and Other Siberian Materials.* Stanford: Stanford University Press, 1935.

Contains documents, memoirs, valuable informational footnotes, and an annotated bibliography of materials on Siberia located at the Hoover Institution.

Vashingtonskaia konferentsiia po organicheniiu vooruzhenii i tikhookeanskim i dalnevostochnym voprosam, 1921–1922 gg. Translated by A. Sabanin. Moscow: NKID, Litizdat, 1924.

A Russian translation of the official documents that were published in English.

"Vrangelevshchina." Edited by I. Mints, *Krasnyi arkhiv* 39 (1930): 3–46, and 40 (1930): 3–40.

D. Books and Articles

"A Chinese Observer in Siberia." *The Living Age,* May 20, 1922, pp. 457–60.

Abrikossow, Dmitrii I. *Revelations of a Russian Diplomat: The Memoirs of Dmitrii I. Abrikossow.* Edited by G, Lensen. Seattle: University of Washington Press, 1964.

Artemev, I. K. *Epizody revoliutsii na Dalnem Vostoke.* Tientsin, 1939. (CSt-H)

A valuable memoir by a participant in the White governments in

1921 and 1922; must be used with care because of inaccuracies in dates and names.

Aussem, O. Kh. "Nikolaevskaia na Amure Kommuna 1920 g." *Proletarskaia revoliutsiia* 28 (1924):36–61.

By an associate of Triapitsyn.

Bessmertnyi, Evgenii D. *Gody zhizni: zapiski starogo moriaka.* Vladivostok: Prim. knizh. izd., 1936. (DLC)

————. "Vstuplenie v zhizn." *Sovetskoe Primore* 24 (1958):111–84.

Bliukher, Vasilii. "Volochaevka." In *Taezhnye pokhody,* pp. 250–54. Moscow: Gosizdat, 1936.

Boiko-Pavlov, D. I. "Kak zarozhalos partizanskoe dvizhenie v Priamure." *Dalnii Vostok* 3 (1957):139–49.

By an important Communist-partisan.

————. 'Partizanskii nalet na Khabarovsk." *Dalnii Vostok* 5 (Sept.–Oct. 1957):158–62.

————. "Po dolinam i po vzgoriam." In *Etikh dnei ne smolknet slava,* pp. 446–62. Moscow: Gospolitizdat, 1958.

Boldyrev, Vasilii G. *Direktoriia, Kolchak, interventy: vospominaniia.* Novonikolaevsk: Sibkraizdat, 1925.

A diary and summary of events by an important, liberal general; indispensible and reliable.

————. "Iz perezhitogo." *Sibirskie ogni* 5–6 (1923):105–26; and 1 (1924): 161–200.

This article and the next are selections from Boldyrev's book-length memoirs.

————. "Perevorot bratev Merkulovykh." *Sibir* 5–6 (1925):23–25.

Borba za Sovety na Dalnem Vostoke. Edited by P. M. Nikiforov et al. Moscow:Gosvoenizdat, 1932.

Useful; memoir-articles from this and other collections are listed under both title of book and author of article.

Borisov, B. *Dalnii Vostok.* Vienna: Izdanie "Novoi Rossii," 1921.

Borodavkin, Vladimir A. *Gody grozovye.* Vladivostok: Dalnevost. knizh. izd., 1964.

Buiko, A. 'Vospominaniia o P. F. Anokhine." *Sbornik materialov po istorii revoliutsionnogo dvizheniia na Dalnem Vostoke.* Chita-Vladivostok: Dalistpart, 1923, pp. 7–11.

Buzin-Bich, D. S. "Partizansko-povstancheskoe dvizhenie v nizoviakh reki Amura, 1919–1920 gg." *Revoliutsiia na Dalnem Vostoke.* Moscow: Gosizdat, 1923, pp. 5–63.
A Communist version of the Nikolaevsk affair.

Chicherin, G. F. *Stati i rechi po voprosam mezhdunarodnoi politiki.* Moscow: Sotsekgiz, 1961.

Daurets, N. P. *Semenovskie zastenki: zapiski ochevidtsa.* Harbin: Maiak, 1921.

Dneprovskii, Stepan P. *Po dolinam i po vzgoriam.* Khabarovsk: Khab. knizh. izd., 1956.

Dvoinykh, Zakhar Ia. *Put krasnoznamentsa-bolshevika: vospominaniia starogo bolshevika.* Moscow: Staryi bolshevik, 1934.

———. *Taezhnye partizany.* Moscow: Molodaia gvardiia, 1936. (DLC, CSt-H)

Ech, V. *Ischeznuvskii gorod: tragediia Nikolaevska n/A.* Vladivostok, 1920. (CSt-H)
A White version of the Nikolaevsk affair. Ech visited the scene a month after the event.

Efimov, A. "Deistviia otriada Izhevtsev pri zakhvate Vladivostoka v 1921 gody." *Vestnik O-va Russkikh Veteranov Velikoi Voiny,* 59–60 (Apr.–May 1931): 18–22.
By a Kappelite commander.

———. "Ekspeditsiia na Suchan." *Vestnik O-va Russkikh Veteranov Velikoi Voiny,* 64 (1931): 10–12, 18; 65–66 (1931): 20–22, 31; 68–69 (1932): 24–27.

Eidus, Khaim T. "Rezultaty Chanchunskoi konferentsii." *Mezhdunarodnaia zhizn* 14 (Oct. 31, 1922): 172–90.

Elesh, V. "Sredi vragov." In *Za vlast Sovetov,* pp. 172–90. Vladivostok: Prim. knizh. izd., 1957.

Elovskii, I. *Golodnyi pokhod Orenburgskoi armii: iz vospominanii uchastnika pokhoda.* Peking, 1921. (CSt-H)

Enborisov, G. V. *Ot Urala do Kharbina: pamiatka o perezhitom.*

Shanghai, 1932.
By an Orenburg Cossack; pro-Semenov.

Etikh dnei ne smolknet slava: sbornik vospominanii uchastnikov grazhdanskoi voiny na Dalnem Vostoke. Khabarovsk: Khab. knizh. izd., 1957.

Etikh dnei ne smolknet slava: vospominaniia uchastnikov grazhdanskoi voiny. Edited by I. Verkhovtsev. Moscow: Gospolitizdat, 1958.

Fay, H. V. V. 'The President of the Far Eastern Republic." *Asia,* Oct. 1921, pp. 876–80, 894.

Filimonov, Boris B. *Belopovstantsy: khabarovskii pokhod zimy, 1921–1922.* 2 vols. Shanghai: Kamkin, 1932. (CSt-H)
A detailed, reliable account of the White winter offensive by a participant; includes documents, maps, and observations on the political situation.

————. *Konets belogo Primoria.* Rockville, Maryland: Kamkin, 1971.
A detailed description of White political and military activities from June to October 1922; published posthumously.

Findlay, John and Dorothy. "Letters from Vladivostok, 1918–1923." Edited by D. Galton and J. Keep. *Slavonic and East European Review* 45 (July 1967): 497–530.
Descriptive, fascinating.

Flegontov, A. *Partizanskoi tropoi.* Khabarovsk: Dalgiz, 1932. (CSt-H)
Memoirs of an important partisan leader.

Gelasimova, Antonina N. *Zapiski podpolshchitsy.* Moscow: Mysl, 1967.

Golionko, Vasilii P. *V ogne borby: iz istorii grazhdanskoi voiny na Dalnem Vostoke, 1918–1922 gg.* Moscow: Gospolitizdat, 1958.

Grachev, G. "Iakutskii pokhod gen. Pepeliaeva." *Sibirskii arkhiv* 1 (1929): 23–40.
A valuable source for the Iakutsk adventure.

Graves, William S. *America's Siberian Adventure, 1918–1920.* New York: Cape and Smith, 1931.
Memoirs of the commander of the American Expeditionary Force; critical of American intervention and of most Russian leaders.

Grebennikov, B. M. "Na bronepoezde no. 3." In *Etikh dnei ne smolknet slava,* pp. 266–71. Khabarovsk: Khab. knizh. izd., 1957.

Gubelman, Moisei, "Litso iaponskoi interventsii: sobytiia 4–5 apr.

1920 goda v Primore." In *Taezhnye pokhody*, pp. 210–44. Moscow: Gosizdat, 1936.

———. "Nash geroicheskii Dalnii Vostok: iz vospominanii." *Tikhii okean* 2 (Mar.–Apr. 1938): 132–50.

———. "Sergei Lazo." *Dalnii Vostok* 1 (Jan.–Feb. 1957): 149–59.

———. "V borbe s iaponskoi interventsiei: iz vospominanii." *Tikhii okean* 3–4 (July–Dec. 1937): 170–84.

Gusev, K. D. "Boi pod Monastyrishchem." In *Etikh dnei ne smolknet slava*, pp. 279–87. Khabarovsk: Khab. knizh. izd., 1957.

Iaremenko, A. N. "Dnevnik Kommunista." In *Revoliutsiia na Dalnem Vostoke*. Moscow: Gosizdat, 1923.

———. "Partizanskoe dvizhenie v Primorskoi oblasti (1918–1920 gg.)," *Proletarskaia revoliutsiia* 7 (1922): 72–96.

Iliukhov, I. K. "Osvobozhdenie." *Sovetskoe Primore* 23(1957): 190–96.

Iliukhov, Nikolai K., and Samusenko, I. P. *Partizanskoe dvizhenie v Primore, 1918–1922*. Moscow: Voenizdat, 1962.
A valuable work that must be used with care because of the exaggerated role attributed to the partisans and to Iliukhov.

———, and Titov, M. *Partizanskoe dvizhenie v Primore, 1918–1920*. Leningrad: Priboi, 1928. (CSt-H)

Irin, T. "Merkulovskii perevorot vo Vladivostoke." In *Revoliutsiia na Dalnem Vostoke*, pp. 395–405. Moscow: Gosizdat, 1923.

Ishii, Viscount Kikujiro. *Diplomatic Commentaries*. Baltimore: Johns Hopkins University Press, 1936.

Janin, Pierre T. C. M. *Ma Mission en Siberie, 1918–1920*. Paris: Payot, 1933.

Kapulin, S. N. "V otriade Shevchuka." In *Etikh dnei ne smolknet slava*, pp. 155–76. Khabarovsk: Khab. knizh. izd., 1957.

Karavaev, P. "DVR sozdana." In *V ogne revoliutsii*, pp. 186–203. Khabarovsk, 1927.

Karpenko, Z. *Grazhdanskaia voina v Dalnevostochnom krae, 1918–1922*. Khabarovsk: Dalpartizdat, 1934.

Karpov, Leonid. "Vosstanie." In *Taezhnye pokhody*, pp. 189–206. Moscow: Gosizdat, 1936.

Kazanin, Mark I. *Zapiski sekretaria missii: stranichka istorii pervykh let sovetskoi diplomatii*. Moscow: Izd. vost. lit., 1963.

Keith, Orrin [pseud.]. Series of articles in the *Japan Advertiser*. July 1, 2, 14, and 18; Aug. 6, 12, and 19; Sept. 1, 9, and 24; and Nov. 5, 1921. Most of these articles concern the FER, but they touch upon conditions in the Russian Far East, Harbin, Japanese policy, and so forth.

————. "The Chita Government at Work." *Asia*, Feb. 1922, pp. 127–33, 156.

————. "Forfeiting Siberian Good-Will." *The Living Age*, Nov. 12, 1921, pp. 417–22.

Kennedy, Captain Malcolm D. *The Estrangement of Great Britain and Japan, 1917–1935*. Berkeley: University of California Press, 1969.

Khartling, K. N. *Na strazhe rodiny: sobytiia vo Vladivostoke konets 1919 g.–nachalo 1920 g.* Shanghai: Izd. T. S. Filimonovoi, 1935. Valuable.

Kochevgin, I. "Boi za Anuchino." *Za vlast Sovetov*. Vladivostok: Prim. knizh. izd., 1957, pp. 304–6.

Komandarm Uborevich: vospominaniia druzei i soratnikov. Moscow: Voenizdat, 1964.

Konovalov, D. "Posledniaia avantiura." In *Taezhnye pokhody*, pp. 245–49. Moscow: Gosizdat, 1936.

Koval, Grigorii F. *Po dolinam i po vzgoriam: iz vospominanii partizana*. Moscow: Sovetskaia Rossiia, 1958.

Krasnogvardeitsyi partizany: sbornik vospominanii uchastnikov grazhdanskoi voiny v Zabaikale. Chita: Chit. knizh. izd., 1957.

Krasnyi ostrov: vospominaniia ocherki dokumenty o borbe za vlast Sovetov na Amure, 1918–1922. Edited by I. I. Mints et al. Khabarovsk: Khabknizhizdat, 1967.

Krichevskii, M. "Razryv russko-iaponskikh peregovorov v Dairene." *Mezhdunarodnaia zhizn* 6 (May 10, 1922): 4–7.

Krol, L. A. *Za tri goda: vospominaniia, vpechatleniia i vstrechi*. Vladivostok: Svobodnaia Rossiia, 1921.

By a leading liberal. Unfortunately for this study, Krol's memoirs end early in 1920. He played a larger political role in 1921 and 1922.

Kushnarev, I. G. "Informatsiia o deiatelnosti dalnevostochnogo pod-
     polnogo komiteta RKP(b) Tsentralnomu komitetu RKP(b) i Sov-
     narkomu, polnomochnym predstaviteliam TsK RKP(b) i SNK
     Sibiri, ianvar 1920 g." In *Borba za vlast Sovetov v Primore,
     1917–1922: sbornik dokumentov*, pp. 298–310. Vladivostok:
     Prim. Knizh. izd., 1955.
     By an important Maritime Communist. This and the next entry
     are reliable and valuable because of their frankness. They were
     both published at times when adherence to the Party line were
     relatively less emphasized.
————. "Svoi i chuzhie: iz doklad I. G. Kushnareva, chlena dele-
     gatsii Vremennago narodnogo sobraniia Primorskoi oblasti v
     Politbiuro kommunistov Dalniago Vostoka." In *Sbornik mate-
     rialov po istorii revoliutsionnogo dvizheniia na Dalnem Vostoke*,
     pp. 262–78. Chita-Vladivostok: Dalistpart, 1923.
Lenin, V. I. *Leninskii sbornik*. 45 vols. Moscow: Gospolitizdat, 1924–45.
————. *Polnoe sobranie sochinenii*. 5th ed. 56 vols. Moscow: Gos-
     politizdat, 1958–1966.
Makeev, A. S. *Bog voiny—baron Ungern: vospominaniia byvshago
     adiutanta nachalnika Aziatskoi konnoi divizii*. Shanghai: Kam-
     kin, 1934.
     Pro-Ungern.
Mamaev, I. "K voprosy o khunkhuznicheskom dvizheniiam na Dalnem
     Vostoke." In *Revoliutsiia na Dalnem Vostoke*, pp. 375–84.
     Moscow: Gosizdat, 1923.
Matveev, N. "Dalnevostochnaia respublika." In *Bolshaia sovetskaia
     entsiklopediia* 20 (1st ed., 1930): 216–21.
Melekhin, I. Ia. *Taezhnymi tropami: vospominaniia uchastnika grazhdan-
     skoi voiny na Dalnem Vostoke*. Kharkov: Prapor, 1968.
Mirovoi. "Partiinaia organizatsiia i rabota na Dalnem Vostoke, 1920–
     1921 gg." In *Revoliutsiia na Dalnem Vostoke*, pp. 303–25. Mos-
     cow: Gosizdat, 1923.
Montandon, George. *Deux ans chez Koltchak et chez les Bolchéviques
     pour la Croix-rouges de Genève, 1919–1921*. 4th ed. Paris:
     Alcan, 1923.

Muchnik, G. A. *Dvadtsat let partiinoi raboty v Sibirii i na Dalnem Vostoke.* Moscow: Izd. Politkratorzhan, 1935.

————. *Za vlast Sovetov.* Moscow: Molodaia gvardiia, 1931. (DLC)

Muchnik (Sibiriak), G. "Borba za Sovety v Primore': po materialam i vospominaniiam uchastnika." In *Sbornik materialov po istorii revoliutsionnogo dvizheniia na. Dalnem Vostoke,* pp. 31–55. Chita-Vladivostok: Dalistpart, 1923.

"Nalet na tyl krasnykh: vospominaniia uchastnika o vestnik deistvii-akh otriada polkovnika Karlova." *Vestnik O-va Russkikh Veteranov Velikoi Voiny,* 65–66 (1931): 15–19; 67 (1931): 20–23; 70 (1932): 9–12, 21; 74 (1932): 10–13.

Nikiforov, Petr M. "Iz istorii iaponskoi interventsii na Dalnem Vostoke: perevorot 4 aprelia 1920 g." *Tikhii okean* 2 (Apr.–June 1935): 144–54.

————. *Zapiski premera DVR: pobeda leninskoi politika v borbe s interventsiei na Dalnem Vostoke, 1917–1922 gg.* Moscow: Gospolitizdat, 1963.

An important memoir with insight into conflicts within the Communist leadership in the Russian Far East. Unfortunately its value is limited by the adherence to the conventional Communist party line and manner of writing.

Noskov, Konstantin. *The Black Year: The White Russians in Mongolia in the Year 1921.* Harbin, 1930. (CSt-H)

Novomeiskii, M. A. *My Siberian Life.* London: Max Parrish, 1956.

Oboronko, E. "Volochaevskii boi." In *Za vlast Sovetov,* pp. 320–22. Vladivostok: Prim. knizh. izd., 1957.

Ossendowski, Ferdinand. "With Baron Ungern in Urga." *Asia,* Aug. 1922, pp. 614–18, 660–62.

Pacifist [pseud.]. "The Balance Sheet of the 'White' Folly: Kappelite Failure Has Cost Vladivostok 11,000,000 Yen." *Japan Advertiser,* Apr. 7, 1922.

————. "Before the Merkulovs' Downfall: A Résumé of the Vladivostok Situation at the End of May." *Japan Advertiser,* June 9, 1922.

————. "Japanese in Siberia: Russia's Suspicions Have Been Increased by Recent Events." *Japan Advertiser*, May 4, 1922.

————. "The Present Phase in Eastern Siberia: Lack of Vision, Failure, and General Breakdown." *Japan Advertiser*, Mar. 8, 1922.

Panov, Vladimir A. *Kak byt dalshe: Dalnevostochnyi vopros.* Vladivostok, 1921. (DLC)

Parfenov, Petr S. *Na soglashatelskikh frontakh.* Moscow-Leningrad: Moskovskii rabochii, 1927.

    Indispensible.

————. "Peregovory s komandovaniem belykh sibirskikh armii v 1920–1921 gg." *Proletarskaia revoliutsiia* 58 (1926): 143–95, and 59 (1926): 208–33.

"Parties and Governments in the Far East." *The Nation*, Feb. 2, 1921, pp. 191–92.

Peffer, Nathaniel. "Behind the Scenes in Siberia." *The Nation*, June 7, 1922, pp. 672–74.

————. "Japan's Absorption of Siberia." *The Nation*, Oct. 5, 1921, pp. 367–69.

Petrov, F. N. "Dairenskaia konferentsiia." In *Bolshaia sovetskaia entsiklopediia* 20 (1930): 181–84.

————. *65 let v riadakh leninskoi partii.* Moscow, 1962.

    This book was translated into English and published as *Past and Present: Reminiscences.* Moscow: Progress Publishers, 1963.

Petrov, Pavel P. *Ot Volgi do Tikhago okeana v riadakh belykh, 1918–1922.* Riga, 1930.

    Indispensible memoir by a Kappelite; one of the best White accounts by a close, competent observer and participant.

Pokus, Ia. E. *Borba za Primore.* Moscow: Gosizdat, 1926. (DLC, CSt-H)

    A second edition of this book was published in Moscow in 1938 and was titled *Shturm Volochaevki i Spasska: narodno-revoliutsionnaia armiia DVR v borbe za osvobozhdenie Dalnego Vostoka, 1921–1922 gg.* This is a valuable account of the military conflict during the winter of 1921–1922 by an important

Communist commander. It is not as long or as detailed as
Filimonov's work on the same subject.

————. "Shturm Spasska." In *Etikh dnei ne smolknet slava*, pp. 288–
94. Khabarovsk: Khab. knizh. izd., 1957.

Postyshev, Pavel P. *Grazhdanskaia voina na vostoke Sibiri, 1917–1922
gg.: vospominaniia*. Moscow: Voenizdat, 1957.

By an important commissar in the Amur region.

————. *Iz proshlego*. Moscow: Molodaia gvardiia, 1958.

————. *Pervyi partizanskii tungusskii otriad: grazhdanskaia voina
v ocherkakh*. Moscow: Molodaia gvardiia, 1933.

Puchkov, F. A. "Desiatiletaia godovshchina khabarovskago pokhoda."
Vestnik O-va Russkikh Veteranov Velikoi Voiny, 65–66 (1931):
13–15.

By a leading Kappelite, chief of staff of General Verzhbitskii.

————. "Vosmaia Kamskaia strelkovaia diviziia v sibirskom Ledia-
nom pokhode." *Vestnik O-va Russkikh Veteranov Velikoi Voiny*,
57–58 (1931).

Reinsch, Paul S. "Japan's Lone Hand." *Asia*, Feb.–Mar. 1920, pp.
164–71.

Riabikov, V. V. *Tsentrosibir*. Novosibirsk, 1949.

Rudnev, Sergei P. *Pri vechernikh ogniakh: vospominaniia*. Harbin:
Zaria, 1928. (CSt-H, MH)

By a conservative and respected jurist; reliable, balanced, and
indispensible. Rudnev was a competent observer before the
White coup of May 26, 1921, and an important participant in
the White government after the coup.

Sakharov, Konstantin V. *Belaia Sibir*. Munich, 1923.

By an important military leader under Kolchak and Kappel.

————. *Cheshskie legiony v Sibiri*. Berlin, 1930.

Semenov, Grigorii M. *O sebe: vospominaniia, mysli i vyvody*. Harbin:
Zaria, 1938.

Valuable, but must be checked against other sources.

Semikorovkin, I. N. "O boevom proshlom." In *Etikh dnei ne smolknet
slava*, pp. 69–88. Khabarovsk: Khab. knizh. izd., 1957.

Serebrennikov, Ivan I. *Moi vospominaniia*. 2 vols. Tientsin, 1937–
1940. (DLC)

Sergeev, Vsevolod L. *Ocherki po istorii belago dvizheniia na Dalnem Vostoke.* Harbin: Izd. Biuro po delam Rossiiskikh Emigrantov v Manzhurskoi Imperii, 1937. (DLC)
Pro-Semenov and pro-Japanese.

Sermiazhnyi, V. *Kak ustanovit poriadok na Rusi.* Harbin: Izd. Organizatsionnyi Komitet D. V. Monarkhicheskago Soiuza, 1921. (NNC)

Serov, I. "Stranitsy zhizni." In *Za vlast Sovetov,* pp. 72–92. Vladivostok: Prim. knizh. izd., 1957.

Seryshev, Stepan. "Vooruzhennaia borba za vlast Sovetov na Dalnem Vostoke." In *Revoliutsiia na Dalnem Vostoke,* pp. 65–129. Moscow: Gosizdat, 1923.

Shevchuk, Ivan P. *Vosmoi Tungusskii: vospominaniia odnogo iz rukovoditelei partizanskogo dvizheniia na Dalnem Vostoke, 1918–1922.* Moscow: Voenizdat, 1958.

Shiriamov, A. "Irkutskoe vosstanie i rasstrel Kolchaka." *Sibirskie ogni* 4 (1924): 122–39.

Shishkin, V. P. "Gody i liudi." In *Za vlast Sovetov,* pp. 126–34. Vladivostok: Prim. knizh. izd., 1957.

Shumiatskii, Boris Z. "Kommunisticheskii internatsional na Dalnem Vostoke." *Narody Dalnego Vostoka* 1 (1921): 19–26.

Sidorov, I. Z., and Samusenko, I. P. "Prikaz vypolnen." *Sovetskoe Primore* 23 (1957): 175–80.

Smith, Charles H. "Four Years of Mistakes in Siberia." *Asia,* June 1922, pp. 479–83.

————. "The Smoke Screen between Siberia and Washington." *Asia,* Aug. 1922, pp. 639–44.

————. "What Happened in Siberia." *Asia,* May 1922, pp. 373–78, 402–3.

Sokolov, B. "Interventsiia iaponskikh imperialistov na sovetskom Dalnem Vostoke." *Tikhii okean* 2 (1937): 125–48.

Stark, Rear-Admiral Iu. K. "Otchet o deiatelnosti Sibirskoi flotilii v period 1921–1922 gg." *Morskie zapiski* 10, nos. 1–2 (1952): 3–27; 11, nos. 1–2 (1953): 2–19; 11, no. 3 (1953): 27–43; 12, no. 1 (1954): 15–33; 12, no. 2 (1954): 19–30; 12, no. 3 (1954): 21–31; 13, no. 1 (1955): 37–47; 13, nos. 2–3 (1955): 68–81; 13, no. 4 (1955): 68–78; 14, no. 1 (1956): 53–70.

A valuable account of political and military events from June
1921 to October 1922 by the head of the White Siberian Flotilla.

Strod, Ivan. "Ungernovshchina i semonovshchina, 1920–1921 gg."
Proletarskaia revoliutsiia 9 (1926): 98–149.

*Taezhnye pokhody: sbornik epizodov iz istorii grazhdanskoi voiny na
Dalnem Vostoke.* Edited by M. Gorkii, P. Postyshev, and I.
Mints. Moscow: Gosizdat, 1936.

"To the Great Civilized Powers." *The Nation,* Jan. 4, 1922, pp. 27–28.

*V ogne revoliutsii: ocherki, stati, i vospominaniia o sobytiiakh, 1918–
v Amurskoi oblasti.* Blagoveshchensk: Amurskoe knizh. izd.,
1958.

*V ogne revoliutsii: sbornik statei i vospominanii o revoliutsionnykh
sobytiiakh na Dalnem Vostoke.* Edited by Ia. Ia. Grunt. Khabarovsk, 1927.

Vershinin, A. A. "V podpole Vladivostoka: vospominaniia starogo
komsomoltsa-podpolshchika." *Dalnii Vostok* 5 (Oct.–Nov. 1959),
167–73; 6 (Nov.–Dec. 1959): 149–55.

Volgin, P. K. "Dva etapa." *Sovetskoe Primore* 23 (1957): 140–66.

Voloshin, A. A. "Sovetskii general Ivan Pavlovich Shevchuk." *Dalnii
Vostok* 1 (Jan.–Feb. 1958): 159–62.

————. "Volochaevskie dni." In *Etikh dnei ne smolknet slava,*
pp. 255–65. Khabarovsk: Knab. knizh. izd., 1957.

Vrublevskii, V. A. "Grazhdanskaia voina v Primore, 1918–1922." In
V ogne revoliutsii, pp. 175–85. Khabarovsk, 1927.

Wood, Junius B. "The Far Eastern Republic." *National Geographic
Magazine,* June 1922, pp. 562–92.

Wrangel, General Baron Peter N. *Always with Honor.* New York:
Speller, 1957.

*Za vlast Sovetov: sbornik vospominanii uchastnikov grazhdanskoi
voiny v Primore v 1917–1922.* Vladivostok: Prim. knizh. izd.,
1957.

Zhuikov-Aleksandrovskii, P. F. "Vospominaniia o podpisanii sogla-
sheniia mezhdu Kitaem i DVR." *Sovetskoe kitaevedenie* 2 (Sept.
1958): 132–35.

Zippin, Max. "The Far East Gets a Respite." *The Nation*, Aug. 21,
     1920, pp. 210–11.

━━━━━━━━━━━━━━━▶ 3. *Secondary Sources* ◀━━━━━━━━━━━

A. General Reference Works ─────────────────────────────

Bolshaia sovetskaia entsiklopediia. 1st ed. 65 vols. Moscow, 1926–
     1949; 2d ed. 51 vols. Moscow, 1950–55.
China Yearbook. Tientsin, 1919–22.
Japan Yearbook. Tokyo, 1919–22.
Kaufman, Isaak M. *Russkie biograficheskie i bibliograficheskie slo-
     vari.* Moscow, 1955.
Diplomaticheskii slovar. Edited by A. Vyshinskii. 2 vols. Moscow,
     1948–50.
Istoriia diplomatii. Edited by V. P. Potemkin. 3 vols. Moscow, 1941.
Lensen, George A., comp. *Japanese Diplomatic and Consular Officials
     in Russia: A Handbook of Japanese Representatives in Russia
     from 1874 to 1968, Compiled on the Basis of Japanese and Rus-
     sian Sources, with a Historical Introduction.* Tokyo: Sophia
     University, 1968.
─────. *Russian Diplomatic and Consular Officials in East Asia: A
     Handbook of the Representatives of Tsarist Russia and the Pro-
     visional Government in China, Japan, and Korea from 1858 to
     1924 and of Soviet Representatives in Japan from 1925 to 1968,
     Compiled on the Basis of Russian, Japanese, and Chinese
     Sources, with a Historical Introduction.* Tokyo: Sophia Univer-
     sity, 1968.
Politicheskii slovar. Edited by B. N. Ponomareva. Moscow, 1958.
Putevoditel po Vladivostoku. Edited by E. A. Laberbis. Vladivostok,
     1920.
Sibirskaia sovetskaia entsiklopediia. 3 vols. Moscow, 1929.
Sovetskaia istoricheskaia entsiklopediia. 12 vols. Moscow, 1961—.

B. Books, Articles, and Unpublished Studies ————————————

Aboltin, N. V. "Kak byl vozvrashchen SSSR severnyi Sakhalin." *Severnaia Aziia* 3 (1927)': 44–54.

Abramov, Zakhov. "Iz istorii iaponskoi interventsii na Dalnem Vostoke." *Borba klassov* 2 (1932)':65–73.

Agalakov, V. T. "Dalnevostochnaia respublika." *Sovetskaia istoricheskaia entsiklopediia* 4 (1963): 959–62.

————. "Organizatsiia revkomov v vostochnoi Sibiri v 1920 gody." *Trudy* Irkutskogo univ. (1958), pp. 82–111.

Aristov, F. F. "Znachenie Sakhalina v strategicheskom otnoshenii." *Novyi Vostok* 2 (1922)': 396–99.

Asada, Sadao. "Japan's 'Special Interests' in the Washington Conference, 1921–1922." *American Historical Review* 67 (Oct. 1961): 62–70.

Avdeeva, Nina A. *Dalnevostochnaia narodnaia respublika, 1920–1922 gg.* Khabarovsk: Khab. knizh. izd., 1957.

————. "Ukreplenie soiuza rabochikh i krestianin v Dalnevostochnoi respublike." In *Iz istorii sovetskogo Dalnego Vostoka*, pp. 54–71. Khabarovsk, 1963.

Babichev, I. "Uchastie kitaikhikh i koreiskikh trudiaschikhsia v borbe protiv interventov i belogvardeitsev na sovetskom Dalnem Vostoke." In *Dalnii Vostok za 40 let sovetskoi vlasti*, pp. 148–71. Komsomolsk-na-Amure: AN SSSR, Sib. otd., 1958.

————. *Uchastie kitaiskikh i koreiskikh trudiashchikhsia v grazhdanskoi voine na Dalnem Vostoke.* Tashkent: Gosizdat uzbek. SSR, 1959.

Beliaev, Boris L. *Dalnevostochnyi perekop.* Moscow: Voenizdat, 1961.

————. *Liudi i sobytiia Primoria: iz istorii borby za vlast Sovetov v Primore v 1917–1922 gg.* Moscow: Voenizdat, 1959.

————. "Semia Sibirtsevykh: iz revoliutsionnogo proshlego Dalnego Vostoka." *Dalnii Vostok* 2 (Mar.–Apr. 1954): 143–52.

Belikova, Larisa I. *Bolsheviki Primoria v gody grazhdanskoi voiny i inostrannoi interventsii.* Vladivostok: Prim. knizh. izd., 1960.

————. "Borba Vladivostokskoi partiinoi organizatsii za vossoedinenie oblastei Dalnego Vostoka, ian. 1920-ian. 1921." In
Materialy po istorii Vladivostoka. Bk. 2: 1917–1960, pp. 57–75.
Trudy Sib. otd. AN SSSR, ser. ist. Vladivostok: Prim. knizh.
izd., 1960.

————. "Istoriografiia Velikoi oktiabrskoi sotsialisticheskoi revoliutsii i grazhdanskoi voiny na Dalnem Vostoke." Dalnii Vostok
3 (1967): 151–58.

————. "Sibirskaia voennaia flotiliia v borbe za vlast Sovetov na
Dalnem Vostoke, 1917–1922." In Voprosy istorii sovetskogo
Dalnego Vostoka, 1:80–89. Vladivostok: AN SSSR, Sib. otd.,
1963.

Belimov, I. T., and Soskin, V. L. "Nekotorye itogi i perspektivy izucheniia istorii Sibiri i Dalnego Vostoka." Voprosy istorii 10
(1959): 35–44.

"Bliukher," Sovetskaia istoricheskaia entsiklopediia 2 (1962): 491.

Borisov, S. Borba za sovetskii Dalnii Vostok. Moscow: Gosvoenizdat,
1940.

Bradley, John. Allied Intervention in Russia. New York: Basic Books,
1968.

Breslav, E. I. Bolshevistskaia pechat Primoria, 1918–1922. Vladivostok: AN SSSR, Sib. otd., 1958.

Buell, Raymond L. The Washington Conference. New York: D. Apple-
ton, 1922.

Burskii, P. D., and Rozenoer, S. M. Ot Urala do velikogo okeana:
putevoditel po Uralu, Sibiri, i Dalnemu Vostoku. Moscow: Izd.
o-va izucheniia Urala, Sibiri, i Dalnego Vostoka, 1928.

Bykovsky, Joseph. "The History of the American National Red Cross."
Vol. 29: "Foreign Relief in the Post-Armistice Period, 1918–
1923." Unpublished monograph available at the American Red
Cross Headquarters, Washington, D.C., 1950.

Carr, Edward H. A History of Soviet Russia. Vols. 1–3: The Bolshevik
Revolution, 1917–1923. London: Macmillan, 1950–53.

Chinese Eastern Railway Company. *North Manchuria and the Chinese Eastern Railway*. Harbin, 1924.

Clyde, Paul H. *International Rivalries in Manchuria 1689–1922*. Columbus: Ohio State University Press, 1926.

Dalnii Vostok za 40 let sovetskoi vlasti. Edited by V. A. Shvarev. Komsomolsk-na-Amure: AN SSSR, Sib. otd., 1958.

Derber, P. "Demografiia i kolonizatsiia sovetskogo Dalnego Vostoka." *Novyi Vostok* 7 (Nov. 7, 1925): 103–14.

Dudchenko, E. M. "Iz istorii komsomola Primoria, 1920–1922." In *Dalnii Vostok za 40 let sovetskoi vlasti*, pp. 281–99. Komsomolsk-na-Amure: AN SSSR, Sib. otd., 1958.

Dushenkin, V. *Ot soldata do Marshala: zhizn i boevoi put marshala Sovetskogo soiuza V. K. Bliukhera*. Moscow: Politizdat, 1964.

Efimov, A. "Pamiati B. B. Filimonov." *Russkaia zhizn*, Aug. 8, 1952.

Emets, V. A. "Dairenskaia konferentsiia." *Sovetskaia istoricheskaia entsiklopediia* 4 (1963): 948.

Fischer, Louis. *The Soviets in World Affairs*. 2 vols. Princeton: Princeton University Press, 1930.

Fleming, Peter. *The Fate of Admiral Kolchak*. London, 1963.

Fletcher, Florence A. "The Far Eastern Republic." Master's thesis, Columbia University, 1923.

Footman, David. "Ataman Semenov." *St. Anthony's Papers on Soviet Affairs* 17 (Feb. 1955).

———. *Civil War in Russia*. London: Faber, 1961.

———. "Siberian Partisans in the Civil War." *St. Anthony's Papers on Far Eastern Affairs* 1 (1957): 24–53.

Foreign Policy Association. *The Far Eastern Republic, Siberia, and Japan*. New York, 1922.

Freeman, A. C. "Japan and the Counter-Revolution in Siberia." *The Nation*, Aug. 10, 1921, pp. 157–60.

Fujisawa, Rikitaro. *The Recent Aims and Political Development of Japan*. New Haven: Yale University Press, 1923.

Glushchenko, I. I. "K voprosy o sovetskoi istoriografii grazhdanskoi voiny i interventsii na Dalnem Vostoke." In *Voprosy istorii* sovetskogo Dalnego Vostoka, pp. 74–79. Vladivostok: AN SSSR, Sib. otd., 1963.

Golionko, V. "Iz istorii iaponskoi interventsii v Primore v 1920 g." Borba klassov 12 (Dec. 1934): 72–81.

Goncharov, G. S. "Sozdanie Narodno-revoliutsionnoi armii Dalnevostochnoi respubliki, 1920-aprel 1921 gg." Vestnik Leningradskogo universiteta, 1 (Jan. 1968): 34–46.

Grant, Natalie. Soviet Diplomatic Maneuvers: An Episode in the History of the Far Eastern Republic. Chestnut Hill, Mass.: Research Institute on Sino-Soviet Bloc, n.d.

Graves, Captain S. G. "Japanese Aggression in Siberia." Current History, May 1921, pp. 239–45.

Grigortsevich, Stanislav S. Amerikanskaia i iaponskaia interventsiia na sovetskom Dalnem Vostoke i ee razgrom, 1918–1922. Moscow: Gospolitizdat, 1957.

————. "Iz istorii amerikanskoi agressii na russkom Dalnem Vostoke, 1920–1922." Voprosy istorii 8 (1951): 59–79.

Gubelman, Moisei I. Borba za sovetskii Dalnii Vostok, 1918–1922. Moscow: Voenizdat, 1958.

————. Kak iaponskikh interventov vygnali s Dalnego Vostoka, 1918–1922. Moscow: Gosvoenizdat, 1937.

————. Lazo. Moscow: Molodaia gvardiia, 1956.

Gudoshnikov, M. A. Ocherki po istorii grazhdanskoi voiny v Sibiri. Irkutsk: Irkutsk. knizh. izd., 1959.

Guins, George C. "Russians in Manchuria." The Russian Review 2 (Spring 1943): 81–87.

Hackett, Roger F. Yamagata Aritomo in the Rise of Modern Japan, 1838–1922. Cambridge: Harvard University Press, 1971.

Hansen, Dr. N. "Japan's Foreign News-Service." The Living Age, Oct. 15, 1921, pp. 163–65.

Iaponiia na russkom Dalnem Vostoke: krovovaia epopeia iaponskoi interventsii. Moscow: Izdatelskoe otd. TsK RCP, 1922.

Ichibashi, Jamato. The Washington Conference and After: An Historical Survey. Stanford: Stanford University Press, 1928.

Igritskii, Iu. I. "Grazhdanskaia voina i interventsiia v SSSR v novei-
    shikh rabotakh zapadnykh istorikov." *Istoriia SSSR* 2 (Mar.–Apr.
    1969):217–37.
Indukaeva, N. S. "Proval amerikanskoi i iaponskoi ekspansii na KVZhD
    1922–1923." *Narody Azii i Afriki* 2 (1962):114–19.
Ioffe, A. "Rossiia i Iaponiia." *Novyi Vostok* 4 (1923):1–11.
————. "SSSR na Dalnyi Vostok." *Mirovoe khoziastvo i mirovaia
    politika* 10–11(1927):26–47.
Istoriia grazhdanskoi voiny v SSSR. 5 vols. Moscow: Gospolitizdat,
    1960.
Istoriia Sibiri s drevneishikh vremen do nashikh dnei. Vol. 4: *Sibir v
    period stroitelstva sotsializma.* Leningrad: Nauka, 1968.
Itin, V. "Iaponskaia politika v Sibiri." *Sibirskie ogni* 3 (1922):146–55.
*Iz istorii sovetskogo Dalnego Vostoka: materialy mezhvusovskoi
    nauchnoi konferentsii, posviashchennoi 40-letiiu osvobozhdeniia
    Dalnego Vostoka ot interventov i belogvardeitsev, sentiabr 1962
    g.* Edited by E. M. Shagin et al. Khabarovsk, 1963.
K desiatiletiiu interventsii: sbornik statei. Moscow-Leningrad: Gosiz-
    dat, 1929.
Kane, Albert E. *China, the Powers, and the Washington Conference.*
    Shanghai, 1937.
Kaplin, L. M. *Bolsheviki na Dalnem Vostoke, 1918–1922.* Moscow:
    Gospolitizdat, 1960.
Kawakami, K. K. *Japan's Pacific Policy: Especially in Relation to
    China, the Far East, and the Washington Conference.* New York:
    Dutton, 1922.
————. "The Far Eastern Republic of Siberia." *Current History,*
    Apr. 1922, pp. 123–27.
Keep, John. "October in the Provinces." In *Revolutionary Russia: A
    Symposium.* Edited by Richard Pipes, pp. 229–75. New York:
    Doubleday, 1969.
Keith, Orrin. "Rebirth of Industry and Commerce in Eastern Siberia."
    The Far Eastern Review 18 (Feb. 1922):127–29.
Khodorov, A. "Rossiia, Amerika, i Iaponiia." *Mezhdunarodnaia zhizn*
    1 (1923):112–19.

Khudiakov, V. Ia. *Vasilii Konstantinovich Bliukher.* Moscow, 1960.

Kolodkin, Milton A. "Russian Interests at the Washington Conference on the Limitation of Armament, 1921–1922, with Special Reference to United States' Policy." Master's thesis, Columbia University, 1955.

Koltsov, Petr S. *Volochaevskie dni.* Moscow: Gospolitizdat, 1962.

Kondratev, Nikolai. *Marshal Bliukher.* Moscow: Voenizdat, 1965.

Krushanov, A. I. "Kommunisticheskaia partiia—organizator razgroma interventov i belogvardeitsev na sovetskom Dalnem Vostoke, 1918–1922." In *Voprosy istorii sovetskogo Dalnego Vostoka,* pp. 41–56. Vladivostok: AN SSSR, Sib. otd., 1963.

————. "Pervye meropriatiia po likvidatsii posledstvii interventsii i grazhdanskoi voiny v Primore: iz istorii partiinogo sovetskogo i khoziastvennogo stroitelstva v oktiabre-noiabre 1922 g." In *Materialy po istorii Vladivostoka.* Bk. 2: 1917–1960, pp. 81–90. Trudy Sib. otd. AN SSSR, ser. ist. Vladivostok: Prim. knizh. izd., 1960.

————. "Zadachi nauchno-issledovatelskoi raboty po istorii sotsialisticheskogo i kommunisticheskogo stroitelstva na Dalnem Vostoke v svete reshenii XXII sezda KPSS." In *Voprosy istorii sovetskogo Dalnego Vostoka,* pp. 5–23. Vladivostok: AN SSSR, Sib. otd., 1963.

————, et al. *Ocherki istorii sovetskogo Primoria ot epokhi pervobytnoobshchinnogo stroia do nostoiashchego vremeni.* Vladivostok: AN SSSR, Prim. knizh. izd., 1963.

Kuno, Yoshi S. *What Japan Wants.* New York: Crowell, 1921.

Kurteev, K. K. *Ekonomicheskaia rol Vladivostoka.* Vladivostok: Svobodnaia Rossiia, 1921.

Kutakov, Leonid N. *Vneshnaia politika i diplomatiia Iaponii.* Moscow: Izd. Mezhdunarodnye otnosheniia, 1964.

Kuznetsov, I. "Polkovodets V. K. Bliukher." *Dalnii Vostok* 1 (Jan.–Feb. 1958): 153–58.

Lappo, D., and Melchin, A. I. *Stranitsy velikoi druzhby: uchastie kitaiskikh dobrovoltsev na frontakh grazhdanskoi voiny v sovetskoi Rossii: 1918–1922.* Moscow: Sotsekizdat, 1959.

Lensen, George A. *Japanese Recognition of the USSR: Soviet-Japanese Relations, 1921–1930.* Tallahassee: The Diplomatic Press, 1970.

Levitskii, V. L. "O nekotorykh nedostatkakh nuzhnoi knigi." *Sovetskoe Primore* 21 (1957)': 318–30.

Maiskii, Ivan M. *Vneshniaia politika RSFSR, 1917–1922 gg.* Moscow: Krasnaia nov, 1923.

Malyshev, Vasilii P. *Borba za vlast Sovetov na Amure.* Blagoveshchensk, 1961.

Manning, Clarence A. *The Siberian Fiasco.* New York: Library Publishers, 1952.

Mansvetov, Fedor. "Dairenskie peregovory Iaponii i Chity." *Volia Rossii* 15 (1922): 3–4.

Martel, Leon C., Jr. "Russian Foreign Policy and the Establishment of the Far Eastern Republic." Master's thesis, Columbia University, 1957.

Materialy po istorii Vladivostoka. Bk. 2: 1917–1960. Trudy Sib. otd. AN SSSR, ser. ist. Vladivostok: Prim. knizh. izd., 1960.

Matveev, Z. "Sovetskaia pechat v Primore." In *Sbornik materialov po istorii revoliutsionnogo dvizheniia na Dalnem Vostoke,* pp. 56–59. Chita-Vladivostok: Dalistpart, 1923.

Melchin, A. I. *Amerikanskaia interventsiia na sovetskom Dalnem Vostoke v 1918–1920 gg.* Moscow: Voenno-morskoe izd., 1951.

———. *Razgrom amerikano-iaponskikh interventov na sovetskom Dalnem Vostoke v 1920–1922 gg.* Moscow: Znanie, 1953.

Mezhdunarodnye otnosheniia na Dalnem Vostoke, 1840–1949. 2d ed. Edited by I. Dinershtein and Iu. Georgiev. Moscow: AN SSSR, Inst. Vostokovedeniia, 1956.

Morinosuke, Kajima. *A Brief Diplomatic History of Modern Japan.* Vermont: Tuttle, 1965.

Morley, James W. *The Japanese Thrust into Siberia, 1918.* New York: Columbia University Press, 1957.

———. "The Russian Revolution in the Amur Basin." *The American Slavic and East European Review* 16 (Dec. 1957): 450–72.

Morse, H. B., and MacNair, H. F. *Far Eastern International Relations*. Boston, 1931.

Naida, S. F., and Naumov, V. P. *Sovetskaia istoriografiia grazhdanskoi voiny i inostrannoi voennoi interventsii v SSSR*. Moscow: Mosk. univ., 1966

Nikolaev, S. N. *Pamiatniki i pamiatnogo mesta v Primore*. Vladivostok: Prim. knizh. izd., 1958.

North Manchuria and the Chinese Eastern Railway. Harbin, 1922.

"Obshchii obzor sobytii na Dalnem Vostoke." *Vestnik NKID*, 6–7 (Aug. 25, 1920): 107–13.

Ogg, Frederick A. "Siberia and the Japanese." *Current History*, June 1921, pp. 464–70.

Osnos, Iu. "Iaponskaia okkupatsiia severnogo Sakhalina." *Borba klassov* 10 (Oct. 1935): 64–75.

———. "Semenov—stavlennik iaponskoi interventsii." *Istoricheskii zhurnal* 7 (1937): 54–63.

———. "Tri mezhdunarodnykh konferentsii DVR." *Istorik-Marksist* 4 (1939): 57–76.

Papin, Leonid M. *Krakh Kolchakovshchiny i obrazovanie Dalnevostochnoi respubliki*. Moscow: Mosk. univ., 1957.
A competent work by a respected Soviet scholar.

———. "Partizanskoe dvizhenie v grazhdanskoi voine, 1918–1922." *Sovetskaia istoricheskaia entsiklopediia* 10 (1967): 879–86.

Parfenov, Petr S. *Borba za Dalnii Vostok, 1920–1922*. 1st ed. Leningrad: Priboi, 1928.
A valuable source, but must be double-checked with other sources because of occasional inaccuracies.

———. *Grazhdanskaia voina v Sibiri, 1918–1920*. Moscow: Gosizdat, 1924.

———. *Uroki proshlago: grazhdanskaia voina v Sibiri 1918, 1919, 1920 gg*. Harbin, 1921.

Parfenov, V. *The Intervention in Siberia, 1918–1922*. New York: Workers Library Publishers, 1941.
While adherence to the Party line and manner of writing detract

from the value of this work, it is useful in corroborating the
dates of events of members of committees and governments, and
for its bibliography and biographical data on important Communist figures.

Parry, Albert. "Washington B. Vanderlip, the 'Khan of Kamchatka.'"
    Pacific Historical Review 17 (Aug. 1948): 311–30.

Pasvolsky, Leo. *Russia in the Far East.* New York: Macmillan, 1922.

———. "Russia Takes Over Vladivostok." *Current History*, Dec.
    1922, pp. 499–501.

Pavlovich, Mikhail. "Iaponskii imperializm na Dalnem Vostoke."
    Novyi Vostok 2 (1922): 2–57.

———. *Sovetskaia Rossiia i imperialisticheskaia Iaponiia.* Moscow,
    1923.

———. "Vashingtonskaia konferentsiia." *Vestnik NKID*, 9–10
    (Dec. 15, 1921): 3–12.

Pelzel, Sophia R. *American Intervention in Siberia, 1918–1920.* Phila-
    delphia, 1946.

Persits, Moisei A. *Dalnevostochnaia respublika i Kitai: rol DVR v
    borbe sovetskoi vlasti za druzhbu s Kitaem v 1920–1922 gg.*
    Moscow: AN SSSR, Inst. narodov Azii, Izd. vost. lit., 1962.

Petrov, F. N., et al. *Geroicheskie gody borby i pobed: Dalnii Vostok
    v ogne grazhdanskoi voiny.* Moscow: Nauka, 1968.

Pew, Robert Maurice. "The Politics of the Far Eastern Republic and
    Soviet-Japanese-American Relations, 1920–1922." Master's
    thesis, Georgetown University, 1963.

Pogrebetskii, A. I. *Denezhnoe obrashchenie i denezhnye znaki Dal-
    nego Vostoka za period voiny i revoliutsii, 1914–1924.* Harbin,
    1924.

"Politicheskie partii DVR." *Volia Rossii* 3 (Oct. 15, 1922): 54–65.

Polkovodtsy grazhdanskoi voiny. Moscow: Molodaia gvardiia, 1960.

Popova, Evgeniia I. "Missiia Stevensa i proval zheleznodorozhnoi
    politiki SShA i Rossii i Kitae v 1918–1922." *Istoricheskie
    zapiski* 60 (1957): 31–85.

———. *Politika SShA na Dalnem Vostoke, 1918–1922.* Moscow:
    AN SSSR, Nauka, 1967.

Postnikov, S. "Separatist Tendencies Among the Russian Emigrés." *Slavonic and East European Review* 17 (1938–39): 356–59.

Pozner, Vladimir. *Bloody Baron: The story of Ungern-Sternberg.* Translated from the French by W. B. Wells. New York: Random House, 1938.

Quigley, Harold S. "Constitution of the Far Eastern Republic." *The American Political Science Review* 16 (Nov. 1922): 665–71.

——. "The Far Eastern Republic: A Product of Intervention." *The American Journal of International Law* 18 (Jan. 1924): 82–87.

Reikhberg, G. E. *Iaponskaia interventsiia na Dalnem Vostoke, 1918–1922: kratkii ocherk.* Moskow: Sotsekgiz, 1935.

——. "Iaponskaia interventsiia na Dalnem Vostoke i borba s nei v 1918–1922 gg." *Istorik-Marksist* 4 (1937): 124–55.

——. "Iaponskai interventsiia na poslednem etape, 1921–1922 gg." *Borba klassov* 6 (June 1935): 60–67.

——. "K istorii interventsii na Dalnem Vostoke: Dalne-vostochnyi proletariat v borbe s iaponskoi interventsiei." *Istoriia proletariata SSSR* 2 (1934): 154–84.

——. *Razgrom iaponskoi interventsii na Dalnem Vostoke, 1918–1922 gg.* Moscow: Sotsekgiz, 1940.

Riabov, N. I., and Shtein, M. G. "Borba rabochikh i krestian Dalnego Vostoka za pobedu Sovetov." *Dalnii Vostok* 1 (Jan.–Feb. 1957): 142–48.

——. "Ognennye gody na sovetskom Dalnem Vostoke." *Dalnii Vostok* 2 (Mar.–Apr. 1959): 179–82.

——. *Volochaevskaia pobeda.* Khabarovsk, 1952.

Rivosh, E. "Nesgibaemyi Bolshevik." *Dalnii Vostok* 6 (Nov.–Dec. 1959): 156–59.

Sbornik statei po istorii Dalnego Vostoka. Edited by M. N. Tikhomirov. Moscow: AN SSSR, otd. ist., Dal. fil., 1958.

Scalapino, Robert A. *Democracy and the Party Movement in Prewar Japan: the Failure of the First Attempt.* Berkeley–Los Angeles: University of California Press, 1953.

Sedov, K. I. "Diskussiia o nekotorykh voprosakh istorii partizanskogo dvizheniia na Dalnem Vostoke v 1918–1922 godakh." *Voprosy istorii* 5 (1964): 156–69.

Sekretareva, Z. I. "Bolshevik." *Dalnii Vostok* 2 (1967): 141–51.

———. "Sergei sderzhalsvoe slovo." *Sovetskoe Primore* 24 (1958): 191–96.

Serebrennikov, I. I. "The Siberian Autonomous Movement and Its Future." *The Pacific Historical Review* 3 (Dec. 1934): 400–15.

Serebrennikov, I. O. *Velikii otkhod: resseianie po Azii belykh russkikh armii, 1919–1923.* Harbin: Azitsev, 1936.

Shapa, Leonid A. *Geroi Dalnevostochnogo perekopa.* Vladivostok, 1959.

Shchebenkov, V. G. "O rabote bolshevikov sredi voisk interventov (k publikatsii bolshevistskoi listovki na iaponskom iazyke)." In *Materialy po istorii Vladivostoka.* Bk. 2: 1917–1960, pp. 77–79. *Trudy* Sib. otd., AN SSSR, ser. ist. Vladivostok: Prim. knizh. izd., 1960.

Shelestov, D. K. "Ob izuchenii istorii grazhdanskoi voiny i voennoi interventsii." In *Sovetskaia istoricheskaia nauka ot XX k XXII sezdu KPSS.* Vol. 1: *Istoriia SSSR: sbornik statei,* pp. 373–94. Moscow: AN SSSR, 1962.

———. "Sovetskaia istoriografiia grazhdanskoi voiny i inostrannoi voennoi interventsii v SSSR." *Voprosy istorii* 2 (1964).

Shereshevskii, Boris M. "Izuchenie istorii borby za vlast Sovetov na Dalnem Vostoke i v Zabaikale." In Izvestiia Sib. otd. AN SSSR, Ser. obshch. nauk., 1 (1965): 97–102.

———. "K voprosy ob istoricheskikh predposylkakh obrazovaniia Dalnevostochnoi respubliki." In *Sbornik statei po istorii Dalnego Vostoka,* pp. 332–42. Moscow: AN SSSR, Sib. otd., 1958.

———. "Plany iaponskikh imperialistov po sozdaniiu anti-sovetskogo bufera na Dalnem Vostoke v 1919–1920 gg. i ikh krakh." In *Voprosy istorii sovetskogo Dalnego Vostoka,* pp. 80–89. Vladivostok: AN SSSR, Sib. otd., 1963.

———. *Razgrom semenovshchiny (aprel-noiabr 1920 g.): o roli Dalnevostochnoi respubliki v borbe za likvidatsiiu "chitinskoi probki" i obedinenie Dalnego Vostoka.* Novosibirsk: AN SSSR, Sib. otd., Nauka, 1966.

————. "Sozdanie Dalnevostochnoi respubliki." *Voprosy istorii* 3 (1966):31–42.

————. *Zabaikale v period Dalnevostochnoi respubliki.* Chita, 1960.

Sherman, I. L. *Sovetskaia istoriografiia grazhdanskoi voiny v SSSR, 1920–1931.* Kharkov, 1964.

Sherower, M. M. "The Nikolaevsk 'Massacre.'" *The Nation,* Aug. 21, 1920, pp. 211–13.

Shishkin, S. N. *Grazhdanskaia voina na Dalnem Vostoke, 1918–1922.* Moscow: Voenizdat, 1957.

Shumiatskii, Boris Z. *Borba za russkii Dalnii Vostok: sbornik materialov dlia politrabotnikov.* Irkutsk, 1922.

Shurygin, A. P. "Borba s inostrannoi voennoi interventsiei i vnutrennei kontrrevoliutsiei v Sibiri i na Dalnem Vostoke." *Voenno-istoricheskii zhurnal* 4 (1960):58–68.

————. "Dalbiuro TsK RKP(b) v gody grazhdanskoi voiny, 1920–1922 gg." *Voprosy istorii KPSS* 8 (Aug. 1966):55–62.

————. "Dalbiuro TsK RKP(b) v period grazhdanskoi voiny i interventsii, 1920–1922 gg." In *Iz istorii sovetskogo Dalnego Vostoka,* pp. 35–53. Khabarovsk, 1963.

————. "Revoliutsionnye volneniia v iaponskikh interventskikh voiskakh, 1918–1922 gg." *Istoricheskii zhurnal* 6 (June 1937): 64–71.

————, and Karpenko, Z. "Borba za sotsialisticheskuiu revoliutsiiu na Dalnem Vostoke." *Istoricheskii zhurnal* 7 (Oct. 1937):109–21.

Smoliakov, A. "Iz istorii komsomola Primoria." *Dalnii Vostok* 6 (Nov.–Dec. 1964): 169–73.

Sokolsky, George E. *The Story of the Chinese Eastern Railway.* Shanghai, 1929.

Sovetskaia istoricheskaia nauka ot XX k XXII sezdu KPSS. Vol. 1: *Istoriia SSSR: sbornik statei.* Moscow: AN SSSR, 1962.

Sovetskii Dalnii Vostok. Edited by S. F. Sukhovii. Chita-Vladivostok, 1923.

Stewart, George. *The White Armies of Russia: A Chronicle of Counterrevolution and Allied Intervention.* New York: Macmillan, 1933.

Svetachev, M. I. "K voprosu o planakh ekonomicheskoi ekspansii SShA i Iaponii na Dalnem Vostoke v 1918–1922 gg." In *Iz istorii sovetskogo Dalnego Vostoka,* pp. 25–35. Khabarovsk, 1963.

Takeuchi, Tatauji. *War and Diplomacy in the Japanese Empire.* Chicago, 1935.

Thiel, Erich. *The Soviet Far East: A Survey of Its Physical and Economic Geography.* New York: Praeger, 1957.

Timofeev, E. D. *Stepan Vostretsov.* Moscow, 1966.

Tinskii, G. *Ataman Semenov, ego zhizn i deiatelnosti.* 1920.

Tompkins, Pauline. *American-Russian Relations in the Far East.* New York: Macmillan, 1949.

Treadgold, Donald W. *The Great Siberian Migration: Government and Peasant in Resettlement from Emancipation to the First World War.* Princeton: Princeton University Press, 1957.

Trukhanovskii, V. G., et al. *Istoriia mezhdunarodnykh otnosheniiakh i vneshnei politika SSSR, 1917–1967 gg.* 3 vols. Moscow: Mezhdunarodnye otnosheniia, 1967.

Tsypkin, S. A. "Uchastie koreiskikh trudiashchikhsia v borbe protiv interventov na sovetskom Dalnem Vostoke, 1918–1922." *Voprosy istorii* 1 (Nov. 1957): 171–85.

Tupper, Harmon. *To the Great Ocean: Siberia and the Trans-Siberian Railway.* Boston: Little, Brown, 1965.

Unterberger, Betty. *America's Siberian Expedition, 1918–1920.* Durham: Duke University Press, 1956.

Ustinzhanin, V. N. "Dairenskoe deistvo." *Volia Rossii* 22 (1922): 11–15.

Vargin, N. F. "K istoriografii bolshevistskogo podpolia v gody inostrannoi interventsii i grazhdanskoi voiny v SSSR." *Voprosy istorii KPSS* 9 (1965): 111–19.

———. "O literature po istorii grazhdanskoi voiny i inostrannoi voennoi interventsii v Sibiri." *Istoriia SSSR* 4 (1964): 140–55.

Vegman, V. "Sibirskii revoliutsionnyi komitet." *Sibirskie ogni* 7 (Nov.–Dec. 1925): 187–88.

Vilenskii, Vladimir D. *Iaponiia*. Moscow, 1923.

――――. *Rossiia na Dalnem Vostoke*. Moscow, 1923.

Vilenskii, V. "Sovetizatsiia Dalne-vostochnoi respubliki." *Kommunisticheskaia revoliutsiia* 1 (1940): 34–45.

――――. *Sovetskaia Rossiia u beregov Tikhogo okeana*. Moscow: Krasnaia nov, 1923.

――――. *Za velikoi kitaiskoi stenoi*. Moscow, 1923.

Voprosy istorii sovetskogo Dalnego Vostoka: materialy Tretei Dalnevostochnoi nauchnoi konferentsii po istorii, arkheologii, etnografii. Vol. 1. Vladivostok: AN SSSR, Sib. otd., 1963.

Vostrotin, S. V. "A Russian View of Manchuria." *Slavonic and East European Review* 11 (1932–33): 20–30.

Weigh, Ken S. *Russo-Chinese Diplomacy*. Shanghai: Commercial, 1928.

White, John A. "The American Role in the Siberian Intervention." *The Russian Review* 10 (Mar. 1951): 26–36.

――――. *The Siberian Intervention*. Princeton: Princeton University Press, 1950.

Whiting, Allen S. *Soviet Policies in China, 1917–1924*. Stanford: Stanford University Press, 1968.

Yakhontoff, Victor A. *Russia and the Soviet Union in the Far East*. London: Allen and Unwin, 1932.

Young, A. M. *Japan in Recent Times*. New York: Morrow, 1929.

Index

Abbott, James, 117

Aboimov, V. P., Peasant, 57

Aderson, E. M., conservative: in Provisional Priamur Government, 100, 136; and Non-Socialist Council, 211n112

Afanasev, General M., Semenovite, 56

Afanasev, Sergei Ivanovich, on Maritime Zemstvo Board, 41

Agarev, A. F., Menshevik, 63

Agitprop, Communist Party, 105, 135

Agreement of April 29, 1920. *See* Japan, foreign relations; Provisional Zemstvo Government

Aigun, Treaty of (1858), 3

Alexei, Tsar, 150

Allies: in Vladivostok, xiv, 5, 12, 13, 187n47; intervention of, ix x, xiv, 7, 9, 26, 32; withdraw from Siberia, 36; Japan claims support of, 47; indebted to Vladivostok government, 50, 82; criticized by Soviet Russia, 107; and Provisional Priamur Government, 143; mentioned, xii, 31, 33, 36, 37, 89, 184

American Banknote Company, 198

American Expeditionary Force. *See* United States

Amur Province: administration in, xn, 185n14; partisan strength in, xiii, 29; and Japanese occupation and withdrawal, xiv, 20, 34, 39, 193–94n73; acquired by Aigun treaty, 3; Communist control of, 20, 25; inclusion in krai government, 26; negotiation with Vladivostok government, 56–57; White agitation in, 131; mentioned, 10, 48, 49, 101

Amur region. *See* Amur Province

Amur River, xn, 3, 7, 35, 87, 131

Amur River Fleet, 126

Amur workers' congress, 27

Anarchist-Communist party, 48

Andreev, S. A., 51, 198n24

Andrushkevich, N. A., White monarchist: prefers Japanese to Communists, 85; and National Democratic Union, 88; and Committee for the Salvation of the Fatherland, 89; and the Merku-

NEP lessens opposition to, 169;
aided by White atrocities, 170;
reasons for Siberian success of,
170–74; mentioned, xii, 7, 23,
37, 56, 73, 74, 83, 84, 101, 102,
116, 125, 139, 155, 156, 181,
188n5, 189n19, 195n83, 196n99,
197n11, 198n17, 203n119, 215n45,
220n13, 222n47, 228n49
Concessions: Japanese, 103, 118;
Vanderlip and Sinclair, 116
Conferences and congresses: Third
Far Eastern Krai Conference of
the Communist Party, 10; First
Congress of Insurgents of the
Maritime Province, 11; First Congress of Workers of the Olga
Uezd, 11, 14; Vladivostok Party
conference, 13; Fourth Far Eastern Krai Conference of the Communist Party, 23, 43; First Congress of Workers of the Maritime
Province, 27–28, 37; Interparty
Conference of Socialists, 48;
Maritime regional Communist
conference, 59; Chita unity conference, 65; Conference of Democratic Parties and Organizations of Vladivostok, 113. *See
also* Changchun; Dairen; Washington Conference on the Limitation of Armaments
Conservatives: in Khabarovsk, xiv–
xv, 51; Japanese approach to
head Maritime government, 39,
46–47; reject coalition cabinet,
52; oppose Iurin mission to
China, 63; oppose FER, 72; relief work for Kappelites, 79; in
Vladivostok, 84–94; mentioned,
42, 54, 61, 84, 116, 199n31, 226-

n1. *See also* Bourgeoisie; Liberals; Moderates; Monarchists; "Old
regimists"; *Tsenzoviki*; Whites
Constituent Assembly: FER, 86–88,
93, 99; Russian, 114; mentioned,
54, 56, 62, 66, 69, 70, 91, 101,
115, 148
Consular Corps: and financial crisis,
51; protests Semenov in Vladivostok, 75, 110; protests property tax, 140; background, 187-
n47; mentioned, 163
Cossacks: traits of, xiii, 124; resented, 7, 166; and Semenov,
27, 57, 78, 85, 110–12, 166–67;
and Zemskii Sobor, 150, 152;
and Kappelites, 168; and Kalmykov, 183n4; mentioned, 46, 61,
78, 113, 131, 207n37, 216n67
Council of Defense, Maritime Provisional Zemstvo Government, 91
Council of Department Heads: established, 50; reformed, 52, 71;
on unity question, 59, 66; and
Kappelites, 74–75; and sale of
Vladivostok goods, 82–83; and
Merkulovs, 138; and Popular
Assembly, 146; replaced, 154;
mentioned, 55, 67, 114
Council of External Zemskii Affairs
of the Priamur Krai, 154
Council of Representatives of Auton-
omous Siberia, 164
Council of Representatives of the
Non-Socialist Population: be-
comes Provisional Priamur Gov-
ernment, 100
Counterfeiting, 198n24
Counterintelligence, 120
Crimea: Wrangel in, ix, 6, 166; evac-
uation of Wrangel from, 61, 122

INSTITUTE FOR COMPARATIVE AND FOREIGN AREA STUDIES PUBLICATIONS ON RUSSIA AND EASTERN EUROPE

1. Sugar, Peter F., and Ivo J. Lederer, eds. *Nationalism in Eastern Europe*. 1969. 478 pp., index.

2. Jackson, W. A. Douglas, ed. *Agrarian Policies and Problems in Communist and Non-Communist Countries*. 1971. 485 pp., maps, figures, tables, index.

3. Muller, Alexander V., trans. and ed. *The Spiritual Regulation of Peter the Great*. 1972. 150 pp., index.

4. Pinchuk, Ben-Cion. *The Octobrists in the Third Duma, 1907–1912*. 1974. 232 pp., bibliog., index.

5. Stokes, Gale. *Legitimacy through Liberalism: Vladimir Jovanović and the Transformation of Serbian Politics*. 1975. 280 pp., maps, bibliog., index.

6. Smith, Canfield F. *Vladivostok under Red and White Rule: Revolution and Counterrevolution in the Russian Far East, 1920–1922*. 1975. 304 pp., maps, illus., bibliog., index.

Institute for Comparative and Foreign Area Studies Publications on Russia and Eastern Europe was formerly Far Eastern and Russian Institute Publications on Russia and Eastern Europe.